AMERICAN HISTORICAL GLASS

THE RIGHT OF THE WORLD
THE LIGHT OF THE WORLD
THE MIGHT OF THE WORLD
. . . LIBERTY . . .

LINCOLN LITHOPHANE

AMERICAN HISTORICAL GLASS

HISTORICAL ASSOCIATION
ADDS DISTINCTION TO GLASSWARE

BY
BESSIE M. LINDSEY

CHARLES E. TUTTLE COMPANY
Rutland, Vermont

Representatives
Continental Europe: BOXERBOOKS, INC., *Zurich*
British Isles: PRENTICE-HALL INTERNATIONAL, INC., *London*
Australasia: PAUL FLESCH & CO., PTY. LTD., *Melbourne*
Canada: M. G. HURTIG LTD., *Edmonton*

Published by the Charles E. Tuttle Company, Inc.
of Rutland, Vermont & Tokyo, Japan
with editorial offices at
Suido 1-chome, 2-6, Bunkyo-ku, Tokyo, Japan

Copyright in Japan, 1967, by Walter Risley

All rights reserved

Library of Congress Catalog Card No. 67-11934

International Standard Book No. 0-8048-0009-X

First printing, 1967
Third printing, 1972

PRINTED IN JAPAN

INTRODUCTORY NOTE

WHILE her husband served in France during the first World War as an A.E.F. (American Expeditionary Forces) surgeon, Bessie Lindsey became an X-ray specialist in one of the larger Chicago hospitals. The skill she developed in taking and "reading" the X-ray pictures was reflected many years later in the superb illustrations of glassware of this book originally entitled *Lore of Our Land Pictured in Glass* and published in two volumes.

Her interest in building a collection of glassware began in the 1920's, stimulated by family pieces of such patterns as Moon & Star, Daisy & Button, and Dahlia. She and her doctor-husband lived in Forsyth, Illinois, a small rural community north of Decatur. Occasionally they found time for glassware-hunting trips into many parts of the Midwest. Mrs. Lindsey began gathering pieces of glassware relating to religion, gardens and flowers, history, political campaigns, etc.

Within 15 years she had acquired a large collection, including 300 pieces of Moon & Star, a complete set of known pieces of the rare Coin glass, and a wide variety of historical items. She did a great deal of painstaking research to establish the identity of her pieces, and to assemble related information. She wrote many articles for newspapers and magazines, and became recognized as an authority.

She was convinced that much of the nation's history is reflected in glass, and in the 1930's she decided to write a book on historical glass. More and more pieces were gathered to fill in the gap. She wanted to limit the book to the items in her own collection. Even then, the work had to be divided into two volumes.

Mrs. Lindsey was a perfectionist. The book was to be fully illustrated, and nothing less than perfect pictures would satisfy her. She photographed each piece, then developed and printed the picture. If it wasn't right, she did it over, after changing the lighting to bring out more detail. Sometimes she spent hours on one item; to her it was just as important to show every detail as it had been in her X-ray work to spot even a hair-line fracture.

The story of each piece of glass was written after all the research material was gathered, and the glass was in front of her. The work was done piece-meal over several years, extending through the World War II period when copper was so scarce that her engraver had to use small pieces of scrap copper to make the cuts for the illustrations.

Mrs. Lindsey was the publisher, and made her own arrangements with the printer. Volume I of the original edition appeared in 1948; Volume II was ready in 1950. This one volume edition under the title *American Historical Glass* contains all of the material in those two volumes, with a revised index.

Walter Risley

FOREWORD

History is a story. A great story, about folks. It is thrilling, because people have done thrilling things. Most tales are daring and noble. Some are wicked and depressing. All are interesting.

What people did yesterday, what people do today, what people will do tomorrow are all chapters in one book. To know just one chapter is not enough for our best interests. It spurs us to learn how the human spirit has risen, through struggle and hardship, from the depths to the peak of spiritual intelligence, as shown by the things people have done.

Honor, patience, faith, and courage have always been important needs. Where can we learn about these so well as through stories of people who had honor, and patience, and faith, and courage; and used them to help make a better world for everyone.

Since 1620, the people of this nation have been engaged in a crusade for better living. History has recorded the experiences of their undertaking. There is no element of surprise in that statement. It is a commonplace. Less well known, but no less true, is the fact that much of the nation's history is reflected in glass. Most items have been made to directly honor some person or place; or commemorate some specific event. Others are indirectly associated with some event or phase of United States history. All are worthy collectibles.

In compiling this book, historical subjects commemorated in glassware, only, are presented. Glassware in the author's possession, only, is used.

In order to present as fully as possible, the spirit of significant scenes commemorated through the medium of glassware, the character of events and a degree of historical unity have been given preference over the iron-clad sequence of events, as well as the time of manufacture of items. The record, so organized, offers a more perfect picture of the birth and building of the nation.

This is not a complete record. Neither have the subjects been fully covered. Emphasis is placed on what was made and why it was made rather than when, or by whom.

It is impossible for one individual to cover all the ground. No one can hope to encounter all the historical items made, or all the facts concerning their production. There is work for those who may become interested in the subject, and the number of historical research workers should increase. Bits of knowledge gleaned by many serious workers, fitted together like the pieces of a jig-saw puzzle, become a report of American progress as told by glassware "talking dishes."

CONTENTS

ILLUSTRATIONS

XIV

CHAPTER I

CHAPTER I

PERIOD OF DISCOVERY AND COLONIZATION

Daring men give a new continent to the
world . . . Christopher Columbus . . . Americus
Vespucius . . . the re-discovery of America . . .
native Indians are encountered . . . treaties are
arranged but colonists eventually are forced to
battle against the red men . . . Tecumseh . . .
Plymouth Colony is established . . . Plymouth
Rock . . . Providence Colony is established . . .
Roger Williams . . . Old Stone Mill at Newport,
Rhode Island . . . Charter Oak . . . Lighthouses
are established . . . Absecon Lighthouse . . .
French and Indian War . . . Ft. Duquesne . . .
Colonists prosper and grow strong . . .

CHRISTOPHER COLUMBUS

We begin some four hundred fifty years ago. Daring men gave a new continent to the world. Christopher Columbus, with his band of eighty-eight adventurers, weighed anchor and put to sea on August 3, 1492, preceding their arrival in the new world. Fifty-two men were with him on board the Santa Maria; eighteen were on the Nina and the remainder were on the Pinta.

After seventy days of many exciting experiences, land was discovered. On the eleventh of October, the Pinta fished up from the sea, a cane, a pole, a stick, and a board. The Nina sighted a branch covered with berries. At 10 p.m., Columbus himself saw and pointed out a light ahead. At 2 o'clock in the morning of October 12, 1492, a sailor aboard the Nina announced the appearance of what proved to be the New World.

No. 1   COLUMBUS MUG

This mug shows the Santa Maria, flagship of Columbus, and also the landing scene. This landing scene seems to illustrate a description which every student of American history has read: "Columbus, dressed in a splendid military suit of scarlet embroidered with gold, and followed by a retinue of his officers and men bearing banners, stepped upon the new world Friday, October 12, 1492. He threw himself upon his knees, kissed the earth, and with tears of joy gave thanks to God. He then formally planted the cross and took possession of the country in the name of Ferdinand and Isabella."

This crystal mug is two and three-fourths inches high, and two and one-half inches in diameter. The reverse shows Columbus' flagship, the Santa Maria. An inscription on the base reads "World's Fair 1893."

No. 2   COLUMBUS MUG

Another mug, crystal also, has profile bust portraits of Columbus and George Washington on obverse and reverse,

3

Top:

No. 1   COLUMBUS MUG

Center:

No. 2   COLUMBUS MUG

Bottom:

No. 3   COLUMBUS MUG

4

No. 4   Columbus Plate

5

No. 5
COLUMBUS PAPERWEIGHT

No. 6
COLUMBUS
STATUETTE

6

respectively. It is the same size as No. 1. An inscription on the base reads "World's Columbian Exposition, 1893."

NOTE: Some Columbian Exposition items are dated 1892 while others are marked 1893. All were produced to celebrate the four hundredth anniversary of the discovery of America by Columbus. The Fair was begun in 1892 but continued during the summer of 1893. Either date is correct.

No. 3 COLUMBUS MUG

A third mug presents a bearded Columbus, full face view. Under the portrait a ribbon bears the inscription "1492—Columbus—1892." The lower third of the mug is fluted. The reverse was left plain by the maker but at the time of purchase was etched with the name of the to-be owner and the words "World's Fair 1893." It is crystal glass, two inches in diameter.

No. 4 COLUMBUS PLATE

A plate, nine inches in diameter, of crystal glass, has profile bust portrait of the Discoverer. It is marked with the dates "1492-1892" above the portrait. Below is the name "Columbus." Pilot wheel border.

No. 5 COLUMBUS PAPERWEIGHT

A paperweight has the bust of Columbus molded in its base. It is one inch deep. The lower half of the edge is fluted. Around the upper half of the edge, an inscription reads "World's Columbian Exposition" "1492-1892." It is of crystal glass with portrait frosted, and is three and one-eighth inches in diameter.

No. 6 COLUMBUS STATUETTE

A portrait bust, or statuette, of Columbus, is sculptured after the portrait by Lotto. It is of crystal glass, frosted finish, and is five and three-fourths inches high.

7

No. 7   Columbus Plate

No. 7   Columbus Plate

A plate, reported in opaque white, in blue glass, and in transparent amber, shows another bust portrait of Columbus. This plate is slightly larger than No. 4, measuring nine and three-fourths inches in diameter. There is an openwork club border. An inscription on the lower part of bust reads "1492 Columbus 1892."

No. 8   World's Fair Game

Columbus' portrait is shown in the crater-like center of an amusing novelty called the World's Fair Game. On this plate, the glass slopes gently upward from the border to a circle in the middle of the plate. The small circle is a depressed area. The game is—to roll a marble from the border position and bring it to rest in the depression by "jiggling" the plate. If you succeed, you visit the World's Fair. Twelve lines leading to the center of the plate, and other lines representing water, suggest that "all roads lead to the World's Fair at Chicago, on Lake Michigan." Inscribed above the portrait is "Columbus 1493," inscribed below the portrait is "Chicago 1893." Inscribed around the border is "The World's Fair Game Patd. July 22, 1890." It is of crystal glass, seven inches in diameter.

No. 9   Columbus Lamps and Lamp Chimney

Portraits of Columbus appear on lamp chimneys and lamps. A chimney seven and one-fourth inches tall shows a medallion portrait combined with floral decoration. It is inscribed "Columbus." For details concerning lamps, see U. S. Coin Pattern Glassware.

No. 10   Columbus-Vespucius Toothpick Holder

Portraits of Christopher Columbus and Americus Vespucius were produced on pattern glassware. For details of this story, see U. S. Coin Pattern Glassware. A toothpick holder in this pattern is decorated with medallions.

9

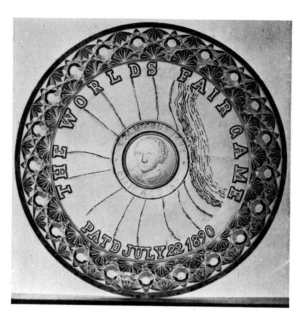

No. 8   The World's Fair Game

No. 9   Lamp Chimney

No. 10
TOOTHPICK HOLDER
OBVERSE

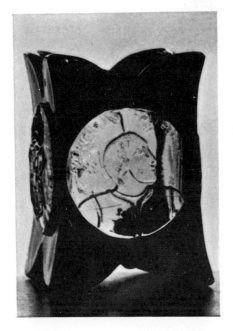

No. 10
TOOTHPICK HOLDER
REVERSE

In one, a bearded Columbus is shown and this name is inscribed below the portrait. Inscribed also "1492-1892." The reverse shows medallion portrait of Americus Vespucius with his name inscribed above it. The right side shows the Coat-of-Arms of Spain, and the left side shows the Coat-of-Arms of the United States. In size, this item is two inches square and three inches high. The medallions are one and five-eighths inches in diameter. This particular item is ruby glass, with medallions and base of crystal. It is found also in crystal glass, with frosted finish on medallions. Also in clear glass with gold decoration on the medallions. The one in color is extremely rare.

The Re-discovery of America

Columbus discovered America. It was later discovered by the Pilgrims and Puritans, Planters and Quakers, Pioneers and other makers of history. All these left an imprint. As years slipped by, many events and circumstances of inspiring import faded into a dimly seen past. Though obscure and half forgotten, they "add up" to something real; a legacy shared by all of us . . . the right to independence.

Things inherited are likely to be taken for granted. Things taken for granted are likely to be neglected. Things neglected are likely to be lost. Re-discovery then, is an adventure much to our advantage, for loss of independence due to the "forgetting" of Americans, is a chapter never to be written as long as re-discovery continues.

The re-discovery of America is possible for anyone, through the medium of the printed page; but just words are sometimes dull. Eye appeal, as furnished through the medium of old glassware, adds much zest and appreciation to the story.

Early settlers encountered native Indians. At Jamestown, Virginia, they used glass beads for barter, a few of which now exist. Some colonists were able to remain on friendly terms with the red-skins. William Penn, Roger Williams, and John Eliot (the Apostle to the Indians) were all considerate of Indian rights. They and their settlements were well treated in return. Mostly, the Indians brooded over the encroachment of white intruders, and here is recorded a major mistake of the American colonists; a disregard of Indian rights. They arranged treaties but eventually were forced to battle against the red men. Indian troubles provide a long and costly chapter in the story of early America.

TECUMSEH

The names of few red men can now be recalled with any degree of pleasure, but the first name on that short list would be that of Tecumseh. He was not bloodthirsty and brutal as was the average Indian but seemed to have more than the usual amount of the finer qualities of his race. Tecumseh was a Shawnee Indian. His tribe had come to Ohio from Florida. He lived at the time when Daniel Boone and other pioneers were forcing their way into the west. The Indians in Ohio considered the country south of the Ohio River as their rightful hunting-grounds, although they did not live there. They resisted the coming of the whites with all the savagery at their command. In turn, the whites crossed from Kentucky into Ohio and were as savage in their revenge as were the Indians.

It was in this atmosphere of butchery and fighting that Tecumseh grew to maturity. When about seventeen years old, he was one of a party that captured some boats on the Ohio River. All the people in them were slaughtered right there except one person who was later burned alive. Such horror was too much for this Indian and he vowed never again to be so cruel. He also persuaded a

13

group of his companions to this same point of view. He kept this resolution and many times protected women and children from the savagery of Indian attack although he, as chief of his tribe, led many attacks on pioneers.

When the War of 1812 began, Tecumseh and many other Indians went into British service. At the Battle of Fort Meigs, a group of Americans had surrendered as prisoners of war to the British and Indians. They were being deliberately tortured and slain by the Indians when Tecumseh arrived on the scene. He stopped the brutality and threatened to slay anyone who would injure another prisoner. Turning to the British General, Proctor, he inquired why such an outrage had been permitted. "Sir," said Proctor, "your Indians cannot be commanded." "Begone," was the angry reply of the outraged Tecumseh, "you are not fit to command. Go, put on petticoats." He served with the British at various points and finally was slain during the Battle of the Thames. It has been said that he was the "greatest Indian in statecraft, diplomacy, devotion to his people, and in dignity of thought and intellectual gifts." His is the most familiar of all Indian names, and he is the only Indian for whom civilized people have named their children. One General of the United States Army, William Tecumseh Sherman, bore his name along with hundreds of boys born in the middle west.

A statue representing the Indian Chief Tecumseh may be seen on the grounds of the Naval Academy at Annapolis. "Between the Lyceum and the Seamanship building stands one of the most picturesque ornaments of the Academy. It is the figure-head from the old United States frigate Delaware, representing the bust of an Indian Chief. The cadets have given the figure the nickname of the 'god of the 2.5,' this being the mark out of a possible 4.0 that each cadet has to receive to be satisfactory in his studies and avoid being dropped or 'bilged.' There is a superstition firmly held by all undergraduates that by making due obeisance, touching the cap in passing the old chieftain, the requisite 2.5 may be assured." Cadets whose

14

No. 11   Tecumseh Mustard Jar

No. 12   Indian Match Holder   No. 13   Indian Cigar Holder

15

No. 14
INDIAN CHIEF PLATE

No. 15
INDIAN CHIEF PLATE

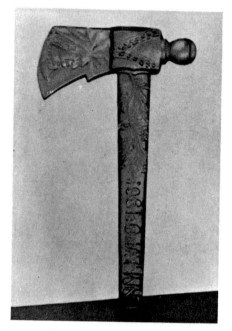

No. 16
INDIAN TOMAHAWK SHOWING
PORTRAIT OF INDIAN CHIEF

16

mark at the end of the year is below 2.5 (or 62.5 per cent) in any branch are deficient, and they are recommended to the Secretary of the Navy for dismissal. When tests are at hand it is customary to toss pennies at the statue base, for help in making the grade; and Tecumseh's aid is sought when the Navy foot-ball team leaves to play against Army.

No. 11   Tecumseh Mustard Jar

A memorial to Tecumseh is found in glassware too. I have no idea when or why it was produced but it is quite similar in general effect to the Log Cabin pattern of glassware so they may have been contemporary. It represents a square block-house such as was used by early settlers in case of Indian attack. A window is seen on each of two opposite sides. The other walls have doors and it is noticeable that the latch-string is not out. The lid extends slightly beyond the log walls on all sides. It represents hand rived shingles. Each of the four sides slopes gently upward to a meeting-place finished by a small square knob. On one side a small opening is provided for the handle of a spoon so it seems to have been intended for use as a mustard jar. The name "Tecumseh" is inscribed just above one door. It is two inches square, and three and three-fourths inches high, to the top of the knob.

No. 12   Indian Match Holder

This hollow sculptured head, of milk-white glass, served as a receptacle for matches. It is two and three-fourths inches high, and two inches in diameter.

No. 13   Indian Cigar Holder

A larger Indian head shows better modeling and more careful attention to details. It is just right, in size, for holding cigars. Of milk-white glass, it is four and one-half inches high, and four and three-fourths inches wide.

17

No. 14   Indian Chief Plate

A plate of milk-white glass, showing the portrait of an Indian Chief is seven and one-half inches in diameter.

No. 15   Indian Chief Plate

Another milk-glass plate, also decorated with an Indian portrait is slightly smaller, its diameter being seven and one-eighth inches.

No. 16   Indian Tomahawk

A tomahawk bears the portrait of an Indian Chief, too. It is of crystal glass, seven and one-eighth inches in length. The handle has an inscription "Pan American." On the reverse of the handle is "Buffalo 1901." This identifies it as a souvenir of the Pan American Exposition held at Buffalo, N. Y., in 1901.

It may be that these various Indian portraits were intended to represent individual persons. Not having authentic knowledge to this effect I shall leave the naming to someone who may have such definite information.

Best known of all Indian items is the crouching, or kneeling, form of an Indian that serves as a knob on the lid of each covered dish in the Westward-Ho pattern of glassware.

There is no event in our country's history more inspiring than the story of the Pilgrim Fathers. It began with unparalleled sacrifice, an exit from home, from friends, from familiar customs and things. Neither was it a temporary absence, with familiar routines to be resumed after a definite interval. It was final. It was permanent. Sacrifice was followed by hardship, by sickness, by danger, discouragements of every sort. Only the highest purpose could enable a people to suffer the hazards known to the Pilgrims and win through to definite and lasting achievement. It was a moral, a spiritual impulse, that motivated them. They were determined to create—somehow and somewhere—what most people today would call HEAVEN ON EARTH. Perhaps that was not quite done. Possibly that never will be completely done. But it was carried through to a richer completion than any other such attempt in the history of man. And it did give a homeland to humanity where anyone, of any class or nationality, could live in a manner worthy of heaven; where any man could, without fear, put his house in order in preparation for that heaven not built with hands.

Such was the foundation, and such is the foundation on which the whole superstructure of today's freedom and liberty is supported and maintained.

No. 17   PLYMOUTH ROCK PAPERWEIGHT

This story of the Pilgrim Fathers is suggested by crystal glass paperweights molded in the shape of the granite boulder on which the Pilgrims stepped from the shallop of the Mayflower. One bears simply the date 1620 as a reminder of that memorable chapter in our country's history.

No. 18   PLYMOUTH ROCK PAPERWEIGHT

Another is similar in form and size, and has added appeal because of an inscription found on the under side: "A

19

rock in the wilderness welcomed our sires from bondage far over the dark rolling sea. On that holy altar they kindled the fires, Jehovah! which glow in our bosoms for Thee." A further inscription, on the beveled edge of the base reads: "Mary Chilton was the first to land upon the Rock Dec. 21, 1620." The words "Pilgrim Rock trade mark" and "Providence Inkstand Co. 1876" are found, too, on this beveled edge.

No. 19   Plymouth Rock Paperweight

A third paperweight is similar to these, but larger. The inscription on the base of this one is the same as on the other. In addition is "Inkstand Co. Prov. R. I." and "Pilgrim Rock trademark 1876." On the beveled edge is inscribed "Mary Chilton was the first to land upon the Rock, Dec. 21, 1620. In attempting to raise up the rock in 1775 it was split asunder. This is a fac-simile of the upper part."

In size, the first named is three and one-fourth inches long, the second is three and three-fourths inches, and the third is four and one-eighth inches in length. The surfaces of all are uneven, and stippled.

No. 20   Symbolical Platter

An oval platter (or bread tray) suggests, by means of symbolism, the essential success of the Pilgrim Fathers' venture, and includes reference to Plymouth Rock. Four symbols: Plymouth Rock 1620, sinking ship 1776, rising sun above the water, and full rigged ship 1876, seem to say that a colony was established in 1620, British rule was scuttled in 1776, and the sun of a new nation appeared on the horizon. In 1876 the new ship of state sailed on, full speed ahead. Possibly the mold maker drew his inspiration from the poem, "The Building of the Ship," by H. W. Longfellow, the concluding lines of which read:

PLYMOUTH ROCK PAPERWEIGHTS

No. 17   *(left)*
No. 18   *(center)*
No. 19   *(right)*

No. 20   SYMBOLICAL PLATTER

"Thou, too, sail on, O Ship of State!
Sail on, O Union, strong and great!
Humanity, with all its fears,
With all the hopes of future years,
Is hanging breathless on thy fate!
We know what Master laid thy keel,
What workman wrought thy ribs of steel,
Who made each mast, and sail, and rope,
What anvils rang, what hammers beat,
In what a forge, and what a heat
Were shaped the anchors of thy hope!
Fear not each sudden sound and shock,
'Tis of the wave, and not the rock;
'Tis but the flapping of the sail,
And not a rent made by the gale!
In spite of rock and tempest's roar,
In spite of false lights on the shore,
Sail on, nor fear to breast the sea!
Our hearts, our hopes, our prayers, our tears,
Our faith triumphant o'er our fears,
Are all with thee,—are all with thee!"

In size, this crystal platter is twelve and one-half inches in length, and nine inches in width. "Give us this day our daily bread" is inscribed on the border. Each end is decorated with a sheaf of wheat.

For our freedom to worship God according to our beliefs, we owe something to a pioneer of religious liberty,
Roger Williams, native of Wales, born in 1604. He was
educated at the University of Oxford, in England. He
studied law, but eventually became a clergyman. The
evils of intolerance and persecution were especially hateful
to him. Sincerity, understanding, and charity, were
among his finest qualities; and he had the courage to live
and do what he believed was right. Because of these things
he left England and came to America. He preached for
several years. He expressed an opinion that the government should have no control over religious matters, that
it was their duty to control crime, but not to control
opinion. He believed that a person was answerable to
God alone for his beliefs. He told people it was wrong
for them to take land from the Indians, who were rightful
owners, without paying them for it.

Of course, enemies were made by this sort of talk. They
wished to be rid of him, and succeeded in having him banished from the colony at Salem, Massachusetts. Williams
found friends among the Indians and "carried on." In
1636, he founded a settlement which he named Providence
because he felt it was God's providence that had given him
guidance and protection and security. The settlement
prospered and became the capital and largest city of the
state of Rhode Island.

A plate, about seven inches in diameter, of milk-glass,
shows a bas relief of the Roger Williams monument in
Roger Williams Park, at Providence, Rhode Island. Plate
border design consists of a flag, eagles, and fleur-de-lis.

No. 21   Roger Williams Plate

No. 22   Old Mill Tumbler

In Touro Park, Newport, Rhode Island, is an old mill, said to be the most widely known object in all that state. It was immortalized in the poem, "The Skeleton in Armor," by H. W. Longfellow. It is the tower referred to in "The Red Rover" by James Fenimore Cooper, written in 1828. Its origin and its age have been subjects of dispute on both sides of the Atlantic, for generations. It seems likely that it was built in the year 1663 by the colonists. The structure is twenty-five feet high, and measures about eleven feet to the underside of the arches. There are eight arches, and eight round piers (or columns) the latter being placed on the cardinal points of the compass. "There is a well-made fireplace over one of the piers, the hearth to which is a slab of slate six inches thick. At each end of the fireplace is a flue, five by eight inches. There is very distinct evidence of there having been two floors above the ground floor; the holes left in the stonework to receive the treads of the staircase may still be seen, between the second and third stories. It is a quite well established fact that the mill was built by order of Benedict Arnold, great-grandfather of the traitor Arnold. His house stood near the mill and was razed soon after the evacuation of the city by the British in 1779. In Leamington, England, there stands a similar mill, erected in 1632. At the time this English mill was building, Arnold lived on a farm about five miles distant from it, and it is not improbable that he used it to some extent as his model on coming to this country."

A crystal commemorative tall tumbler, or beverage glass, is four and one-half inches tall, and two and three-fourths inches in diameter, at the top. Decorations in enamel show a picture of the mill, and an inscription "Old Stone Mill, Newport, R. I." On the reverse is the state seal of Rhode Island, and the state motto "Hope."

The charter given to Connecticut by King Charles, of England, in 1662, became famous in history. When James II came to the English throne he appointed Sir Edmond Andros to be Governor of all New England. Andros ruled harshly, with little regard for the wishes or rights of the colonists. They disliked him. In 1687 he came to Hartford to take away their charter. A band of soldiers came with him. A meeting was held during which the charter was to be surrendered. The General Assembly kept Andros talking until night when candles were lighted. The charter, in a box, was brought and laid on a table. Suddenly the lights were blown out. They were lighted again but the charter was gone. For three years, no one knew where it was, but in 1689, when William III had become King of England and recalled Andros, the charter was taken from the hollow of an oak tree where it had been hidden by Captain Joseph Wadsworth, at the time it disappeared. This tree stood for nearly one hundred and seventy years after, and was always respected as "The Charter Oak." It was blown down in 1856, but the site was marked, at a later time, by a granite monument.

The tree was memorialized also in glassware. At least two flasks were made. One, half-pint size, shows a tall tree in full foliage. Above the tree, the word "Liberty" is inscribed. On the other side is a large American eagle, with head turned left. A large shield is on its breast. An olive branch is held in its talons. A coarse beading on either side frames an oval panel in which the designs are placed. It is reported in a number of colors.

The eagle has always been a favorite motif on American glassware. Many times it forms the only decoration. More often it appears in company with other motifs.

No. 23
CHARTER OAK FLASK

No. 24
LIGHTHOUSE BOTTLE

27

No. 25   ABSECON LIGHTHOUSE PLATE

No. 26
PITTSBURGH LIQUOR GLASS

28

No. 24 Lighthouse Bottle

The lighthouse was an important institution in early times. One was established here as early as 1716.

Crystal bottles in the shape of a lighthouse, were made for use as containers. The one illustrated is seven and one-half inches high, and two and five-eighths inches in diameter at the base.

No. 25 Absecon Lighthouse Plate

A lighthouse in Atlantic City, New Jersey, is memorialized in glass. Erected in 1856, its use was discontinued in 1933. It has been said that this was the most visited lighthouse in our country, during its period of service. It is yet pointed out as an important object, to those who visit this popular playground of the nation.

A crystal plate, seven and one-half inches in diameter, has a likeness of the famous Absecon Lighthouse molded in its base, surrounded by an openwork border.

No. 26 Pittsburgh Liquor Glass

In 1754 the American Colonists became involved in the French and Indian War. During this struggle (in 1758) George Washington led an expedition against Ft. Duquesne. He was victorious. As the English flag floated over the ruins of the Fort, this "Gateway of the West" was re-named Pittsburgh in honor of the English Prime Minister, William Pitt.

A liquor glass refers to this event. It pictures the Arms of the City of Pittsburgh, derived from the Family Arms of William Pitt. It is inscribed "1758—Pittsburgh—1908" "Sesqui-centennial, Sept. 27th to Oct. 3rd 1908." The upper part of this glass is red. The base and lower third are crystal. The medallion decoration is gold. Size: two and one-half inches high, two and three-eighths inches diameter at top, one and seven-eighths inches diameter at base.

CHAPTER II

CHAPTER II

Independence is gained though at great cost, the Revolutionary War . . . Declaration of Independence . . . Independence Hall . . . Carpenter's Hall . . . The Liberty Bell . . . The Constitution of the United States . . . George Washington . . . Benjamin Franklin . . . John Hancock . . . Lafayette . . . Battle of Bunker Hill . . . Louis Kossuth, another famous champion of liberty . . . deaths of John Adams and Thomas Jefferson on July 4, 1826, golden anniversary of the signing of the Declaration of Independence.

Taxes levied, following the French and Indian War, sometimes equalled two-thirds the income of the tax payer. In spite of taxes, Indians, war, and other discouragements, the colonists prospered and grew strong. Eventually, they gained independence though it was purchased at great cost, the Revolutionary War. A worthwhile collection of items relating to persons and events of these years, alone, could be assembled. The place of honor should be awarded to him who was so often called FIRST. Washington had displayed great power on many fields of battle; the colonists had suffered long and endured to the end; but the glory of military power fades away beside the picture of the victorious general, returning his commission to the representatives of a people who would have made him King, and retiring after two terms from the presidency which he could have held for life, and the picture of a war-torn people turning from debt, disorder, almost anarchy; not to division, not to despotism, but to national unity under the ordered liberty of the Federal Constitution.

When death ended his great career it seemed fitting indeed for General Henry (Lighthorse Harry) Lee—Washington's intimate friend—to pronounce before Congress and a crowded assembly, the funeral oration, December 26, 1799. It was in this oration that George Washington was first proclaimed "First in war, first in peace, and first in the hearts of his countrymen."

An oval platter bears Washington's portrait and this inscription. This platter has two companion pieces, the decorative borders and bear-paw handles of all three being identical. All are of crystal glass, but some are found with frosted centers. They are twelve by eight and one-half inches in size. Each companion item also refers to an event in the life of Washington.

No. 27
George Washington
Platter

No. 28
Carpenter's Hall
Platter

34

No. 28   Carpenter's Hall Platter

Carpenter's Hall is pictured on one of these platters. It is accompanied by the inscription "The Continental Congress First Assembled in Carpenter's Hall, Sept. 5, 1774." This building was the meeting place of the First Continental Congress.   Here came George Washington in the "days that tried men's souls," a handsome young colonial officer in military uniform, riding all the way from Virginia on horseback, and destined, for solid information and sound judgment, to win his spurs in the most illustrious body of patriots ever assembled.

No. 29   Independence Hall Platter

On the other platter, Independence Hall is shown, accompanied by the inscription "The Nation's Birthplace, Independence Hall."   The historic building was begun in 1732 as the statehouse of Pennsylvania.   Built between 1732 and 1741 it was used as the statehouse until 1799.

Independence Hall has been the scene of the greatest event in the Nation's history, for here, on July 4th, 1776, was made the American Declaration of Independence. The old Liberty Bell which first proclaimed the nation's freedom hangs here.   It was here that George Washington was made General George Washington.

Benjamin Franklin

Almost the whole life of Benjamin Franklin was bound up with this building, as he pursued the affairs of city, state, or nation.   In this historic place one may yet single out the table on which the Declaration was signed.   It was while standing by this table that Franklin, after signing, said to John Hancock, "We must indeed hang together, or most assuredly we shall all hang separately." Near the table used by Washington as President of the Federal Convention that met in this chamber in 1787 and framed the Constitution of the United States, was the

35

No. 29
INDEPENDENCE HALL
PLATTER

No. 30
BENJAMIN FRANKLIN
FLASK

celebrated high colonial chair with its carved and gilded image of an uncertain sun half in the sea, that led Franklin to say: "Now, at length, I have the happiness to know it is a rising, not a setting sun." Another remark by Benjamin Franklin might well be thought about by each one of us: "I have lived a long time, and the longer I live the more convincing proofs I see of this truth, that God governs in the affairs of men. And, if a sparrow cannot fall to the ground without His notice, is it probable that an empire can rise without His aid?"

No. 30   BENJAMIN FRANKLIN FLASK

Of course, the amazing Benjamin Franklin who played so large a part in so many important objectives, was memorialized in glass.

One of the most popular items is a flask that shows his portrait with the inscription "Benjamin Franklin" just above it. The reverse of this flask shows a portrait of Dr. Thomas W. Dyott, and the inscription "T. W. Dyott, M.D." just above. Inscribed on the edges is "Where liberty dwells there is my country" and "Kensington Glass Works, Philadelphia." This is a pint size flask and may be found in aquamarine or in dark amber.

No. 31   BENJAMIN FRANKLIN STATUETTE

An extremely rare portrait bust, or statuette, is of milk-white glass, with frosted surface. It strongly resembles marble. Close inspection is necessary to realize the object is glass. Workmanship is of the highest quality so that beauty is added to rarity in making it an exceptionally desirable collector's item. Fortunate beyond most, is the collector who comes into possession of a Benjamin Franklin statuette. The weight is notable, being three and one-half pounds. The base is almost square, three by two and one-half inches (narrower at front). It is six and one-half inches in height.

No. 31 Benjamin Franklin Statuette

No. 32   Old Statehouse Tray

Independence Hall, and its many eloquent memories, has been well represented in glassware. A large round tray was made. The center of this tray portrays the building at an early date. Below this is inscribed "Old Statehouse, Philadelphia, Erected 1735." I have found this item in clear glass, in an exquisite blue and in an unusual shade of green. It may have been made in other colors, too.

No. 33   Independence Hall Plate

A small plate, of crystal glass, with scalloped rim, has an alphabet border. In the center, Independence Hall is shown, below which is inscribed "Old Independence Hall." Above the building, the dates 1776-1876 show it to be another centennial item. A flag flies from the steeple. In diameter, it is six and three-fourths inches.

No. 34   Independence Hall Bank

Another memorial is a crystal coin bank, made as a replica of the building. The tall steeple which housed the Liberty Bell gives a lofty and dignified air to the Independence Hall bank. Above the doorway at one end of the building "Bank of Independence Hall 1776-1876" is inscribed. It is five by three and one-half inches in size. The height of the steeple is seven and one-half inches.

No. 35   Liberty Bell Goblet

The Liberty Bell itself was a favorite subject for the mold makers. Its form was made familiar through many glassware items. Liberty Bell salt and pepper shakers, Liberty Bell inkstands, and other novelties were all popular. The Liberty Bell pattern of dishware is too well known for detailed description here, although justice cannot be done without mention of some items. The goblet is a favorite with collectors. The Liberty Bell is pictured on the bowl. Above is "Declaration of Independence."

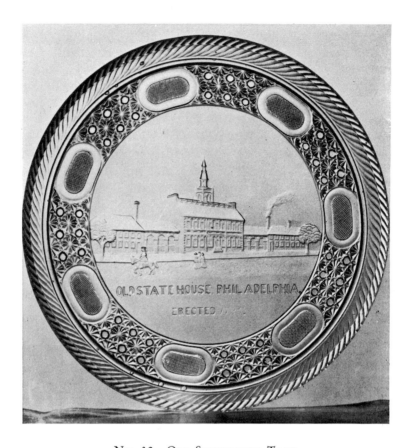

No. 32   Old Statehouse Tray

No. 33   Independence Hall Plate

No. 34   Independence Hall Bank

No. 35
LIBERTY BELL GOBLET

No. 36
LIBERTY BELL SALT

No. 37   LIBERTY BELL PLATE

On pennants at either side, are the dates "1776-1876." On the reverse, in large stippled letters and figures "100 years ago." It is six and one-fourth inches tall, three and one-fourth inches in diameter.

No. 36   Liberty Bell Salt

Small, oval, open, individual salt dishes belong with the pattern. An impression of the Liberty Bell is molded in the base. Above this is inscribed "1776", below it is "1876." It is two and one-fourth inches long, one and one-half inches wide, and one inch deep.

No. 37   Liberty Bell Plate

Plates in all patterns are popular, and the Liberty Bell pattern is no exception. There are small plates, medium sized plates, and large plates. One is eight inches in diameter. An inscription on the bell reads: "Proclaim liberty throughout the land unto all the inhabitants thereof." Inscribed below the bell "Patd. Sept. 28, 1875." Inscribed on the border: "100 years ago", also "Massachusetts, Pennsylvania, New Jersey, New York, Connecticut, New Hampshire, Rhode Island, Delaware, Maryland, North Carolina, South Carolina, Virginia, Georgia" these being the names of the thirteen original states.

No. 38   Liberty Bell Candy Container

This is an appealing novelty because of the metal screw cap, so made that it may be hung up. It is open at the top, only. An inscription "Proclaim Liberty Throughout All the Land" is on the side. On the reverse, an inscription reads "1776-1876 Centennial Exposition." Of crystal glass, it is three and three-fourths inches to the top of the cap, and is two and seven-eighths inches in diameter at the base.

No. 39   Liberty Bell Bank

This replica of the Liberty Bell is a bank for small coins. In the illustration, a slot for dropping coins is visible near

No. 38
LIBERTY BELL
CANDY CONTAINER

No. 39
LIBERTY BELL BANK

44

No. 40 John Hancock Platter

No. 41 Liberty Bell with Shells Platter

45

the top. A threaded metal base may be removed to empty out the coins, when wanted. It is inscribed simply "Patented Sept. 22, 1885." Of crystal glass, it is four and one-eighth inches tall, and four inches in diameter at base.

No. 40   John Hancock Platter

A platter, in opaque white ware (or milk-glass) honors John Hancock. Much of Hancock's fame rests on the fact that he was presiding officer of the Congress that passed the Declaration of Independence, and therefore its first signer; and that he wrote his name in poster size letters. The first thing you see when you look at the historic document is the signature of John Hancock, and you remember his remark, (made when he affixed his signature) "I guess King George can read that without spectacles." The name as it appears on the platter, is identical with the original signature. This event gave origin to a common phrase in business life: "Put your John Hancock here," meaning write your name here.

This platter has a large Liberty Bell in the center, with "Liberty" inscribed thereon. Above and around it are the words and figures: "Declaration Independence 1776-1876." On the border above the bell, "100 years ago" and on the border below the bell the famous autograph "John Hancock." It is quite large, being thirteen and one-half inches long by nine and one-half inches wide.

No. 41   Liberty Bell with Shells Platter

This is much like the item just described. In addition to the bell and inscriptions in the center (as above) the word "of" is added on the upper part of this bell, and "Patd. Sept. 28, 1875" is placed below it. This patent date shows on the back, only, in opaque white ware. The usual "100 years ago" is seen on the upper border. Shells, in high relief, ornament the ends. I have found this platter in both clear and opaque white glass. It is eleven and one-quarter inches by seven and one-eighth inches in size.

No. 42   The Signers Platter

Perhaps the bread tray of the Liberty Bell pattern, is the most popular of all the Liberty Bell series because it bears the names of all the signers of the Declaration of Independence, and the states from which they came. These are inscribed on the lower border. In some, the names are easily read, the impressions being sharp and clear. In others, the names are recognized with considerable difficulty. It comes in clear glass, thirteen by nine and one-half inches.

The Constitution

Each of us owes much of his well-being to an outstanding event that took place in Independence Hall, the drafting of the Constitution; and this event, too, is recorded in glassware. The making of the American Constitution was a stupendous achievement of men who through reading, through reflection, through insight, and through practical experience, had fully grasped the significance of the huge task to which they devoted themselves, and who accomplished that task in a way that has excited the admiration of the civilized world. Those men built a representative republic; they knew what happened in Greece, in Rome, in Venice, and in Florence; they knew what had happened in the making of the modern nations that occupied the continent of Europe. Knowing all this, these men after the most elaborate debate, and discussion both of principles and details, produced the result with which we are familiar.

After reading the Constitution the great Gladstone said: "It is the greatest piece of work ever struck off at a given time by the brain and purpose of man."

Debate and oratory concerning the liberties of man have produced many worthy epigrams such as: "Liberty is the parent of virtue and order." "Liberty will not descend to a people, a people must raise themselves to

No. 42 THE SIGNERS PLATTER

No. 43 THE CONSTITUTION PLATTER

liberty; it is a blessing that must be earned before it can be enjoyed." "Our country cannot well subsist without liberty, nor liberty without virtue." "To have freedom, is only to have that which is absolutely necessary to enable us to be what we ought to be, and to possess what we ought to possess." "The greatest glory of a free born people is to transmit that freedom to their children." "They that can give up essential liberty to obtain a little temporary safety deserve neither liberty nor safety." "The people never give up their liberties but under some delusion." "Eternal vigilance is the price of liberty."

No. 43   THE CONSTITUTION PLATTER

The platter which brings all this to mind, shows a central design of the American eagle holding in its beak a streamer on which is inscribed "Liberty and Freedom 1776." The bird stands on a copy of the "Constitution of the United States," this inscription being placed on a scroll under the feet of the eagle. On the border is the old familiar and well loved motto "Give us this day our daily bread." It is of crystal glass, twelve and one-half by nine inches in size.

Could anyone, at any time, express appreciation of those responsible for our Constitution in a more beautiful manner than did William Cullen Bryant when he wrote:

"Great were the hearts, and strong the minds,
  Of those who framed in high debate,
The immortal league of love that binds
  Our fair broad empire, State to State."

Though the ink with which the Constitution was written is faded, it is re-written in the hearts of each generation. Our form of government, with all its benefits and opportunities and protection it affords does not go on from generation to generation because the founders believed in it and established it and turned it over to us in a completed and indestructible form. It continues because each generation understands in some degree the power and fulfillment of desire insured for them by liberty and freedom and justice. It continues because each generation understands in some degree that liberty and freedom and justice rest on the foundation of Christianity and morality as expressed in the Bible. Each generation must know that the safety of America lies in the excellence of its individuals. If the people lose their standards of right doing, America has no safety, for when the spirit of goodness leaves our citizens, liberty will have gone too.

The wise Dr. Franklin looked into the future and saw all this when he said (in his speech favoring adoption of the Constitution) "I agree to this Constitution with all its faults—if they are such; because I think a general government necessary for us, and there is no *form* of government but what may be a blessing to the people if well administered; and I believe further, that this is likely to be well administered for a course of years and can end only in despotism, as other forms have done before it, when the people shall be so corrupt as to need despotic government, being incapable of any other."

No. 44   Bunker Hill Platter

The Battle of Lexington was fought in April of 1775. In the month of June following, came the Battle of Bunker Hill. The heroes of this occasion were Colonel William Prescott, General John Stark, General Joseph Warren, and Major General Israel Putnam. Colonel Prescott was one of the commanding officers and gave his order to fire when the Red-coats were within a distance of ten rods. General Stark achieved further fame at the Battle of Bennington, in Vermont, when Burgoyne attempted to seize supplies which the American troops had collected there. As Stark saw the British forming for the

No. 44   The Bunker Hill Platter

No. 45
Bunker Hill Cup-Plate

attack he exclaimed, "There are the Red-coats; we must beat them today or Betty Stark is a widow." His bravery so inspired his raw troops that they did defeat the British Regulars. General Warren lost his life at Bunker Hill. As he was trying to rally his troops, a British officer who knew him, seized a musket and shot him. He was buried near the spot where he died. General Gage, the British leader, boasted that the fall of Warren was worth that of five hundred ordinary rebels. Major General Putnam was in command of the American forces. He had charged his men not to fire until they saw the whites of the enemy's eyes and to take good care to pick off the officers by aiming at their waistbands. The troops then delivered a fire so deadly that the British line broke in disorder. A second assault met the same fate, but Gage's troops had spirit for still a third assault which was successful because the ammunition of the Americans had been exhausted. Although our American forces finally lost the Battle of Bunker Hill, the British loss was 1,054 men wounded and killed while the American casualties amounted to but 420. The moral effect of this conflict on American troops and citizens was decidedly tonic. They had proved that hastily assembled volunteers could withstand the assaults of trained British Regulars and that the odds against them in the enterprise in which they had embarked were not so overwhelming as to deny them ultimate success. This is the story it is hoped you will think about when you look at a platter commemorating the Battle of Bunker Hill.

In the center, a picture of the Bunker Hill monument is shown, above which is inscribed "Birthplace of Liberty." Around the border is found: "Prescott 1776 Stark" "Warren 1876 Putnam" "The Heroes of Bunker Hill" "The Spirit of Seventy Six." Handles are shield shaped, showing stars and stripes. It is crystal, thirteen and one-quarter inches long by nine inches wide.

The Bunker Hill monument was begun in 1825, when the cornerstone was formally laid by Lafayette under the direction of the Massachusetts Grand Lodge of Masons, and Daniel Webster delivered the oration. It remained unfinished for a long time. Then, in 1840, largely through the efforts of American women, the required funds for its completion were raised. In July, 1842, the last stone was hoisted to its place. The completed structure was dedicated on the 17th day of June, 1843, when Webster was again the orator.

Because this monument was completed through the efforts of American women, who raised the required funds after the heat of patriotic fervor had cooled, we know something of the character of those ladies of 1840. They were determined not to accept defeat in a good cause, even as their grandmothers were unwilling to accept defeat during the War of the Revolution. At that time an observant British officer told Lord Cornwallis "We may destroy all the men in America and we shall still have all we can do to defeat the women."

A cup-plate commemorates the Battle of Bunker Hill, and the completion of the monument. It is inscribed "Bunker Hill Battle fought June 17, 1775" "Cornerstone laid by Lafayette, June 17, 1825" "Finished by the ladies 1841" "From the fair to the brave." The one pictured is crystal glass, although it was made in several colors. It is three and three-fourths inches in diameter.

It seemed good for Lafayette to assist in commemorating the Battle of Bunker Hill; for the Battle of Bunker Hill—and—the Declaration of Independence so fired his heart that he determined to leave his home in France, and offer his services to the rising republic. His zeal and "love for liberty" were so sincere that he offered to serve in the American Army on two conditions: first, that he should receive no pay, and second, that he should act as a volunteer. He was at once accepted and was appointed Major-General before he had reached the age of twenty. George Washington so heartily approved of this young champion of liberty and freedom that he told him "he should be pleased if he would make the quarters of the Commander-in-Chief his home, establish himself there whenever he thought proper, and consider himself at all times as one of his family." This friendship continued and never for one moment was interrupted. It is written that "if there lived a man whom Washington loved and admired it was Lafayette" and his services through all the varying fortunes of war, endeared him forever to every American, too.

After the fall of Cornwallis, Lafayette returned to France. Several items of glassware were made in commemoration of Lafayette. His portrait appears on a number of flasks, and on mugs and jars.

No. 46   Lafayette Jar

A jar (or container) honoring Lafayette, has a large profile portrait, facing left, on the side. Beneath this is the word "Lafayette." It is seven and one-half inches high, and three and five-eighths inches in diameter at base. Color: aqua.

No. 47   Lafayette Flask

This flask, half-pint in size, presents Lafayette in profile, facing right. His name is inscribed above the portrait.

No. 46   Lafayette Jar

No. 47   Lafayette Flask

Below is "Coventry C—T" (the flask was made at Coventry, Conn.). On the reverse, the French liberty cap on a pole is enclosed in an oval frame. Nine stars are above this frame. Below the frame "S & S" suggests that the flask was made by Stebbins & Stebbins. The edges are ribbed. In color it is olive amber, but was made in other colors, too.

It seems certain that Lafayette memorial items were made to honor him about the time of his visit to the United States in 1824-1825. At this time he visited each state in the Union, and received such honors as have been given to few guests of the nation.

No. 48   John Paul Jones Flask

John Paul Jones, naval hero, was born in Scotland, 1747, the son of a gardener named John Paul. He became an apprentice sailor and when twelve years of age, came to Virginia. When he was twenty-six he inherited an estate from a deceased brother. For some reason he assumed the surname of Jones and was always known from that time on, as John Paul Jones.

When the Revolutionary War began he offered his services to the Colonies and was appointed lieutenant in the American Navy. In 1776 Lieutenant Jones had the honor of displaying from his flagship the first naval American flag. It was of yellow silk, bearing the figure of a pine tree, and a rattlesnake, in a field of thirteen stripes with the legend "Don't tread on me." He sailed to the British coast. His boyhood days had made him familiar with things here and helped him win success in several adventures. His best known exploit was the capture of the English man-of-war Serapis. Jones was in command of the Bonhomme Richard, an old French ship that Benjamin Franklin had secured for him. It was by moonlight on the evening of November 23, 1779, that this battle commenced. During the engagement the vessels were lashed together, and hand to hand fighting ensued. The American vessel became badly damaged so that the British commander expected a surrender. He called out "Has your ship struck her colors?" To this came Jones' surprising reply "I have not yet begun to fight." The Serapis finally struck. But the American ship was so badly damaged that Jones transferred his crew to the Serapis, leaving his own ship to sink.

The bust of John Paul Jones, in uniform, appears on a glass pint flask. Behind him is an expanse of sea. At his right, three men seem engaged in fighting, on ship deck. Two ships, probably intended to represent the Bonhomme Richard and the Serapis, are included in the design on the reverse of the flask. Color: amber.

Louis Kossuth

The story of Louis Kossuth does not belong to the Revolutionary period, in fact. There seems no more fitting place to record it, however, because it is the story of another great champion of liberty.

He was a guest of this nation in 1851 and 1852. Kossuth was known as the Great Hungarian Exile. He and some of his fellow patriots had, for several years, been engaged in a struggle to secure independence for Hungary. Such efforts failed when Russian intervention was added to the resistance of Hungarian tyrants. Kossuth, with many others fled the country. As an exile, he entered Turkey. Since our people also had fought to secure independence for themselves, they felt a great sympathy for the illustrious "Chief of Hungary" and his democratic followers. Congress passed a resolution inviting him to visit the United States. This invitation was accepted and he reached our shores in December, 1851. He remained here until July of the following year.

Everywhere he was received with distinguished honor. He appealed for aid in securing independence for his homeland, and likely would have been granted our help had it not been for the advice of George Washington to

No. 48   JOHN PAUL JONES FLASK

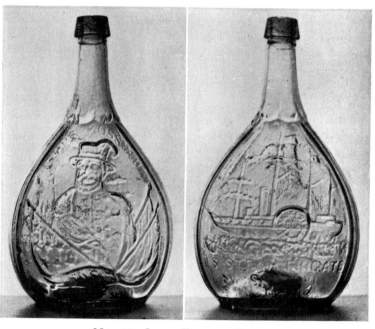

No. 49   LOUIS KOSSUTH BOTTLE

have nothing to do with quarrels on the other side of the Atlantic. They have trouble most of the time, and if we should allow our sympathies and emotions to control our actions, we would be having trouble most of the time too, sharing their quarrels and wars without much benefiting anyone.

Kossuth wore his Hungarian hat, a high crowned head-piece topped with a large feather, and a large velvet embroidered coat. His appearance must have been impressive and it soon became a fad for most of our men and boys to wear the "Kossuth hat."

In the nation's capital, a Congressional dinner (or banquet) was given him. Vice-President W. R. King presided. Kossuth was seated on his right and Daniel Webster (Secretary of State) on his left. All the most important people were there. "Senators, judges, diplomats, military and naval dignitaries, and cabinet ministers, were there to do him honor." After the health of the President, and of the judiciary of the United States had been given, Judge Wayne of the Supreme Court proposed: "CONSTITU-TIONAL LIBERTY TO ALL THE NATIONS OF THE EARTH, SUPPORTED BY CHRISTIAN FAITH AND THE MORALITY OF THE BIBLE," a toast which was enthusiastically received.

Some mention of the ship which brought Kossuth to our shores should be made. The "fine American steam-frigate Mississippi" was chosen for this honor. Many other memories cluster around the Mississippi, and it is written that "no ship ever performed more faithful service or came to a more glorious end." The Mississippi was the flagship of Commodore Perry on his expedition to Japan in 1853 when President Fillmore sent him to negotiate our first treaty with Japan.

Admiral George Dewey saw naval service on the Mississippi, too. Eight days after the firing on Fort Sumter (1861) he was transferred to this ship, with the rank of lieutenant. In 1863, Union forces were working to get control of the Mississippi River. Admiral Farragut, with seven vessels, attempted to run past Confederate batteries about 135 miles above New Orleans. As the Mississippi was passing the assault to which she was subjected, she grounded. Efforts to remove her were futile so it was necessary to abandon and destroy her. Officers and crew were saved. "It is the story of the ship that Dewey was the last man to leave her, and it is officially corroborated." After being abandoned, the vessel was soon blazing. She floated off the bank that wrecked her, and drifted down the river some distance before an explosion sent her to the bottom. And so the great ship named Mississippi found rest under the waters of the great river named Mississippi.

No. 49   Louis Kossuth Bottle

A calabash shaped bottle was produced in honor of Louis Kossuth. The obverse shows a full face bust of the "Great Exile." Two furled flags are on either side. Above is the name "Louis Kossuth." On the reverse, the Mississippi and lines representing water are shown. Beneath this is inscribed "U. S. Steam Frigate Mississippi S. Huffsey." (This is the name of the glass works that produced the bottle.) The name of the mold maker is inscribed on the base.

No. 50   George Washington Flask

Another event that took place at a much later time, is so closely related to affairs of the Revolutionary period that it seems to belong here.

In 1826, the nation had planned a great and brilliant celebration of the 4th of July, because it was the 50th (or golden) anniversary of the Declaration of Independence. The two men who had been most influential in bringing the document into being, were still living, although both were old and feeble.

Thomas Jefferson was 83 and John Adams was 90 years of age at this time. It was hoped they might be brought

No. 50
GEORGE WASHINGTON FLASK
HONORING JOHN ADAMS AND
THOMAS JEFFERSON

No. 50
"ADAMS & JEFFERSON" INSCRIBED ON FLASK

61

together at some chosen place, as honored guests for the day. As the time came near, it was learned that neither could attend. Someone was sent to Mr. Adams, with instructions to secure from him a toast to be presented at the celebration, which was to be in Quincy, Massachusetts. "I give you," said he, "INDEPENDENCE FOREVER."

On the morning of the 4th there was much ringing of bells, music of bands, and the roar of guns, as people welcomed the birthday of the nation. There was no joy in the homes of Adams and Jefferson, for it was apparent they would not survive the day. Mr. Adams was asked: "Do you know what day it is?" "Oh, yes!" he replied, "it is the glorious 4th of July. God bless it! God bless you all! It is a great and glorious day." "Thomas Jefferson" he whispered, a little later, "still survives." These were his last words, but they were not true for Thomas Jefferson had passed away an hour or two before.

Could one day be more eventful in the life of a nation? It has been said this was "the most remarkable coincidence that has ever taken place in the history of nations."

A flask honoring George Washington was used to commemorate the dramatic occurrence. A portrait of Washington decorates the obverse. Above the portrait, "General Washington" is inscribed. On the reverse, is an American eagle, above which is inscribed "E Pluribus Unum." An inscription was added and suggests the story just related: "Adams and Jefferson July 4th, A.D. 1776 (three stars are placed after this date) Kensington Glass Works, Philadelphia." The flask is reported in several colors.

CHAPTER III

CHAPTER III

PERIOD OF ORGANIZATION

The American flag is created and unfurled
. . . Betsy Ross makes the first flag . . . William
Driver gives the flag a nickname, Old Glory . . .
the flag inspires song writers; George F. Root
and "rally round the flag" . . . The Great Seal
is adopted . . . the Patent Office is created . . .
the United States Mint is established.

The birth of this nation was a great occasion. It was the very first time in history that any country had championed religious freedom and personal liberty. There must be a banner to signal, or announce, this glad event to the rest of the world. On June 14, 1777, the Flag of the United States was adopted by Congress as the emblem of the Union; and it is June 14th of each year we now set aside for special observance as the birthday of our flag.

The resolution of adoption was worded as follows: "Resolved, that the flag of the United States be thirteen stripes, alternate red and white; that the union be thirteen stars, white in a blue field representing a new constellation." Since the resolution did not say just how the stars should be arranged, in the beginning they were placed in different ways, including a circle. Two ideas about placing them in a circle have been offered. One, to indicate the equality of the states. Another, that it symbolized a hope the Union would be without end.

Many times in the past, as well as today, our citizens have thrilled to the sound of marching feet and martial music; and to the sight of valiant men and of no less brave women.

The very life of every patriotic event centers around the red, white, and blue banner THE AMERICAN FLAG. "A song for our banner, This watchword recall, Which gave the Republic her station; United we stand—divided we fall, It made and preserves us a nation."

An interesting glass platter, rectangular in shape, notched border, shows the stars and stripes, with the stars arranged in a circular manner. Since there are thirty-eight stars in the group, the platter likely was produced in the year 1876. There were thirty-eight states in the Union at that time. The flag is found on many other items of glassware too, most often used as one unit of a design.

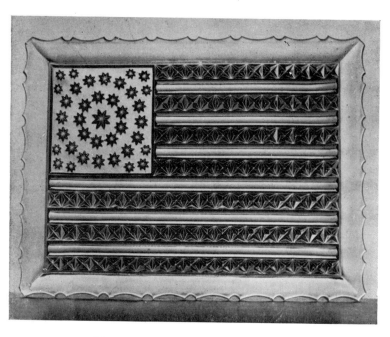

No. 51   AMERICAN FLAG PLATTER

The American Flag platter shows thirteen stripes, thirty-eight stars, is of crystal glass, and is eleven by eight inches in size.

No. 52   Old Glory Plate

Credit for having made the very first American flag is given to Betsy Ross, a Quaker lady, who lived in Philadelphia. It is said that a committee of three men, George Washington, George Ross, and Robert Morris, called on Mrs. Ross and told her of a plan they had for making an American flag. They asked her if she would make one for them, and she agreed to try. When the completed flag was submitted to Congress for approval, it was unanimously adopted thus giving to Betsy Ross the enviable distinction of having made the first flag, in June, 1776.

Since the records of Congress do not say who made the first flag, this story must be called tradition, although there is nothing recorded to disprove its accuracy either. There is no recorded fact concerning the subject, and the Betsy Ross story is the only answer to the question of who made the first American flag.

At a much later time, the nick-name "Old Glory" was given to the flag. On March 17, 1824, in Salem, Massachusetts, William Driver celebrated his twenty-first birthday. His mother and a group of Salem girls made the day memorable by presenting him with a lovely American flag. Said he: "I name her 'Old Glory' " and the American flag has been known as Old Glory ever since.

William Driver was a sailor, and now, whenever he sailed the seas, Old Glory sailed with him in all parts of the world. When he quit the sea, in 1837, and retired to a home in Nashville, Tennessee, Old Glory went with him there, too.

A short time before his death, the old Captain gave his daughter, Mary Jane, a bundle. He told her it contained his flag Old Glory and asked her to keep it always, to

No. 52   Old Glory Plate

No. 53   Rally Round the Flag Plate

68

love it and cherish it as he had done. As requested, OLD GLORY was kept and treasured as a priceless heirloom in the Driver family, for many years.

In 1922, it was placed in the Smithsonian Institution in Washington, D. C. It is carefully preserved under glass, and is eagerly viewed by the multitudes who visit the nation's capital every year.

In glassware, we find a most attractive plate illustrating the story of Betsy Ross making the first flag. She is shown in the costume of a Quakeress. The nick-name of the flag "OLD GLORY" is inscribed above her head. It is a small plate, five and one-half inches in diameter. Clear (or crystal) glass.

No. 53   RALLY ROUND THE FLAG PLATE

The flag has been an inspiration to composers of patriotic music. The BATTLE CRY OF FREEDOM was one of the greatest war songs of the nineteenth century. Written by George F. Root in 1862, it is estimated that sales reached a total of 700,000 copies. Because recruiting for the Union forces was so encouraged by this song-hit it was said that the composer "accomplished more for his country than many generals." The first stanza is the one best known:

> "Yes, we'll rally round the flag,
>   boys, we'll rally once again,
>   Shouting the battle cry of freedom;
>   We will rally from the hillside,
>   We'll gather from the plain,
>   Shouting the battle cry of freedom."

This is a song that may as well be sung now, as in 1862. The glassware item commemorating this inspiring "flag" song, is a concave disc of milk-white glass, with frosted surface. It probably was used on a small table easel, or could have been hung on a wall. The only decoration is a rather crudely fashioned flag, with the inscription: "RALLY ROUND THE FLAG." In size it is eight and three-eighths inches in diameter.

SEAL OF THE UNITED STATES

After the Declaration of Independence, a committee of three men were appointed to prepare a device for the great seal of the United States. They were Benjamin Franklin, John Adams, and Thomas Jefferson. This responsibility was taken seriously, for their study and planning lasted for several years. On June 20, 1782, a seal was adopted. This seal has never been changed and is in charge of the Secretary of State. Without its use on official papers, an order would not be executive.

A red, white, and blue shield is borne on the breast of an American eagle, holding in his right talon an olive branch, and in his left a bundle of thirteen arrows. In his beak is a scroll with the motto "E Pluribus Unum" which means "out of many, one." Above the eagle is shown a constel-lation of thirteen stars on a blue field, breaking through a cloud. An explanation accompanied the report when it was offered to Congress, and—much simplified—is as follows: Thirteen red and white vertical bars represent the several states all joined in one unit. A blue horizontal band above these, unites the whole and represents Congress. The bars are kept closely united by this band and this has a two-fold meaning. One, the preservation of the union of states through the function of Congress. Two, that Congress depends on the close union of the states and strength resulting from it for its support. The colors, red, white, and blue, are those used in the flag. White sig-nifies purity and innocence. Red, hardiness and valor. Blue, vigilant perseverance and justice. The olive branch and arrows denote the power of peace and war, which is exclusively vested in Congress. The constellation denotes a new State taking its place among the Nations. The shield is borne on the breast of an American eagle without any other supporters, to denote that the United States of America ought to rely on their own virtue.

The reverse side of the seal shows an unfinished pyramid, symbolizing the hoped-for strength, growth, and duration of the Nation. Over this is an eye in a triangle accompanied by the words, "Annuit Coeptis" (God has favored the undertaking). These allude to the many interpositions of Providence in favor of the American cause. Under the pyramid is "MDCCLXXVI" (1776) and the words, "Novus Ordo Saeclorum (a new order of things). The date is that of the Declaration of Independence, and the words under it signify the beginning of the new American era which commenced from that date. (This information is taken from "Messages and Papers of the Presidents," published by authority of Congress).

No. 54   Columbia Tray

The great seal does not appear in glassware in exact detail; but many items suggest that this device was the source of inspiration for design.

A large tray is shield-shaped. In the center, within an oval frame, the profile head of Columbia is superimposed against thirteen vertical bars and the uniting band above them. The tray may be found in several fine colors, the most sought-for being a deep amethyst. One should be very well satisfied, however, to own this item in crystal, in blue, or in amber. It is eleven and one-half inches long, by nine and one-half inches wide.

No. 55   Emblem Tall Eagle

A small, milk-white, covered container shows that it is emblematic of the Great Seal. It is in the form of a tall

71

No. 54 Columbia Tray

eagle, bearing a shield, above which is a ribbon inscribed "E Pluribus Unum." It is six and three-fourths inches high.

No. 56 Emblem Mug

"E Pluribus Unum" meets the eye again, on a crystal mug. Additional decoration consists of the shield, arrows, and thirteen stars. It is five inches high, and two and one-half inches in diameter.

No. 57 Emblem ABC Plate

An alphabet border small plate has a central emblematic design, consisting of the eagle, arrows, olive branches, and shield. It is inscribed, above the eagle "Centennial—1776 —Exhibition." Below the eagle is the date 1876. Inscribed on a ribbon held in the eagle's beak "Union and Liberty." The plate is crystal, six and three-fourths inches in diameter.

No. 58 Emblem Pickle-Dish

This dish offers the motto "E Pluribus Unum." It also has the eagle, the shield, arrows, and olive branches, which are distinguishing features of the Seal. These all appear on the border. A vine bearing two cucumbers ornaments the center, and suggests the use for which the dish was intended. It is crystal, ten inches by five and three-fourth inches in size.

No. 59 Emblem Cream-Pitcher

The body of an interesting cream-pitcher has the contour of a shield. It shows the vertical bars and union. The union is thickly studded with stars. Two curving legs unite this shield-shaped body with a flat, circular base. It comes in a very clear crystal, five and three-fourths inches high. One item of a four-piece table set.

No. 55
EMBLEM TALL EAGLE

No. 56
EMBLEM MUG

No. 57   Emblem ABC Plate

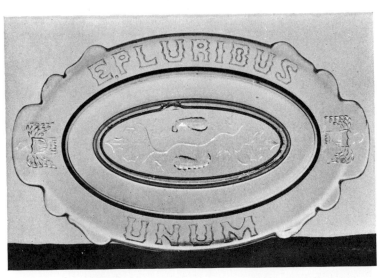

No. 58   Emblem Pickle-Dish

No. 59   Emblem Cream-Pitcher

No. 60   Three Shields Covered Dish

No. 60   THREE SHIELDS COVERED DISH

This dish is distinguished by a shield motif, three times repeated. The base of the dish is shield-shaped, the lid of the dish is in the form of a smaller shield, and the finial shows the shape of a quite small shield. These forms are emblematic of the design shown on the Seal (or Coat-of-Arms) of the United States. It is crystal glass, seven and one-half inches long, and five and one-half inches wide.

No. 61   EMBLEM CENTENNIAL GOBLET

This goblet shows two identical shield designs (one on either side) derived from the great Seal of the United States. Thirteen stars are on each shield, the central star placed within a keystone. On each side of the goblet, between the shield designs, are large keystones, each inscribed: "1776 July 4th 1876." Since the 1876 Centennial was held in the State of Pennsylvania, and since Pennsylvania is called the Keystone State, because it was the middle in geographical position of the original thirteen states (according to Funk & Wagnalls Dictionary) it seems probable the mold maker had this in mind when he placed the central star on the shield within a keystone to suggest: This star stands for the State of Pennsylvania. The larger keystones with their inscriptions might suggest that within the Keystone State, liberty was born on July 4th, 1776, and the event celebrated there in 1876. An inscription, "Centennial" is on the foot of this goblet. It is of crystal glass, five and one-half inches high, by three and one-eighth inches in diameter.

No. 62   EMBLEM LAMP

A lamp is decorated with shields of medium size. There are nine around the bowl, which is four and one-eighth inches in diameter.

No. 61
EMBLEM
CENTENNIAL GOBLET

No. 62
EMBLEM LAMP

No. 63   Emblem Lamp

No. 64   Emblem Sugar-Bowl

No. 63   Emblem Lamp

Another lamp is small and flat, and has an applied handle. A shield motif is repeated six times around the bowl. It is inscribed on the metal collar, "Pat'd. Apr. 19, 1875. M'ch 21, 1876." Crystal glass, four inches in diameter and three and one-half inches high.

Many other lamps, and lamp chimneys too, carry emblematic designs.

No. 64   Emblem Sugar-Bowl

This is one item of a four-piece table set, consisting of covered sugar-bowl, covered butter-dish, cream-pitcher, and spoon-holder. It is the most spectacular of all emblem glassware. No olive branch appears in this design. It is all warlike. The form of an alert American eagle, with shield, alternates with ordnance. This design is repeated three times around the bowl. Ammunition, resting on a shield, forms the finial. It appears to be of the Spanish-American War period. The sugar-bowl is six inches high, and four and one-half inches in diameter.

Patents

Article 1, Sec. 8, of the Constitution of the United States authorizes Congress to issue letters patent for useful inventions. The first patent law was approved April 10, 1790. It placed the granting of patents in the hands of the Secretary of State, the Secretary of War, and the Attorney General. George Washington was then President. Thomas Jefferson was Secretary of State, so personally examined many petitions for patents. Only three patents were granted the first year, thirty-three the second, and eleven the third. The number of patent rights issued has increased so that many thousands of patents are now granted each year, and the total number is considerably more than two million.

Of the glassware items mentioned so far, a patent notice is found on seven of them.

In glassware patents, the design of the piece is protected as well as the form.

A great many items of glassware show some sort of inscription to say that patent rights are held. The dates tell us that much historical glassware was made for sale at World's Fairs, and other expositions, although production of novelties and containers with reference to timely contemporary events is also much in evidence.

The new nation now had political liberty, religious freedom, a constitution, a flag, a seal (or coat-of-arms), and a patent system that encouraged initiative and development. Another highly important matter must have attention at once: something definite must be done about money. By an Act of Congress passed in April, 1792, the first United States Mint was established at Philadelphia. Machinery and metals were imported, coinage laws were passed, and a number of coins were authorized to be made.

Six different silver United States coins are recorded in glassware: dollars, half-dollars, quarter-dollars, twenty-cent pieces, dimes, and half-dimes were used as decorative medallion motifs on a full line of tableware. All are dated 1892, half-dimes excepted.

The story cannot be completed without reference to personal experience. In 1892 my parents observed their fifteenth, or crystal, wedding anniversary. A butter-dish in the U. S. Coin pattern was given to them at this time. It was purchased in November, in a local store, and was the subject of much conversation. As I remember the story, the clerk who sold the dish told the buyer the pattern was produced because 1892 was the centennial year of the founding of the United States Mint and was intended to honor that event. I do not know of any authentic record to this effect so cannot offer conclusive evidence; but 1892 *was* the centennial year. The six coin motifs *did* represent all the silver coinage authorized and produced in our own mints, with one exception, the three-cent piece. Also, all of the items of table glassware in general use at that time were made in this pattern with one exception, the individual salt. I have always hoped that a "salt-dip" decorated with a three-cent piece would some day be found to complete the silver coinage record and also complete the list of forms usually offered.

Although coin motifs were not identical with silver coins, in making this pattern, a federal law was violated so production was stopped. Forms in the Coin pattern are identical with those showing portraits of Christopher Columbus and Americus Vespucius. It has been said that this portrait series superseded the Coin pattern, but it seems more likely that the patterns were contemporary in 1892, the Coin design featuring the Centennial of the United States Mint while the portrait items commemorated the discovery of America; and that production of the Coin ware was stopped while the production of the portrait pieces continued.

Because of an early interest in my mother's butter-dish, I began buying this pattern as soon as it became collectible. A balanced six-piece table setting was secured consisting of a great variety of forms.

UNITED STATES COIN PATTERN

FORM	COIN
Bowl, flat, 4 sizes	dollar, half-dollar, or quarter-dollar.
Bowl, flat, scalloped top	dollar, half-dollar, or quarter-dollar.
Bread-tray, rectangular	dollar and half-dollar.
Butter-dish	dollar and half-dollar, stacked coins finial.
Cake-plate, on standard	dollar and quarter-dollar.
Celery holder	quarter-dollar.
Compote, covered, on high standard, 4 sizes	dollar, half-dollar, or quarter-dollar, stacked coins finial.
Compote, covered, on low standard	quarter-dollar and twenty-cent piece, stacked coins finial.
Compote, open, on high standard, fruit, several sizes	dollar, half-dollar, or quarter-dollar.
Cream-pitcher	quarter-dollar.
Cruet	quarter-dollar; stopper, dime.
Epergne	dollar and quarter-dollar.
Goblet (a)	dime.
Goblet (b)	half-dollar.
Mug	dollar.
Pickle-dish	half-dollar and quarter-dollar.
Pitcher, water	dollar.
Pitcher, milk	half-dollar.
Preserve-dish	dollar and half-dollar.

FORM	COIN
Salt and pepper shakers	quarter-dollar.
Sauce-dish, flat, 2 sizes	quarter-dollar.
Sauce-dish, footed	quarter-dollar.
Sauce-dish, footed, scalloped top	quarter-dollar.
Spoon-holder	quarter-dollar.
Sugar-bowl	half-dollar and quarter-dollar, stacked coins finial.
Syrup-jug	quarter-dollar.
Toothpick holder	dollar.
Tumbler	dime.
Water-set tray	dollar.
Waste bowl for water-set (also called finger-bowl)	quarter-dollar.
Wine glass, champagne	half-dime.
Wine glass, claret	half-dime.

Lamps:

    (a) square bowl, coins on bowl and on standard, 4 sizes; dollar or half-dollar.

    (b) round bowl, panelled, coins on standard, 4 sizes; dollar, half-dollar, or quarter-dollar.

    (c) round bowl, panelled, on low foot, handle, coins on foot; twenty-cent piece.

    (d) opaque white, in two parts; round bowl, panelled, similar to (b).

    (e) flaring bowl, plain, coins on standard.

Rarities:

    (a) berry-bowl having scalloped top.

    (b) sauce-dish having scalloped top.

    (c) berry-bowl having red band at rim.

    (d) toothpick holder, red glass, with medallions and base clear, or with medallions frosted, or with portrait medallions.

    (e) toothpick holder, clear glass, with red medallions.

Candlesticks were not factory made, but may be provided by any collector having a degree of ingenuity. The standards of milk-glass lamps may be unscrewed from the bowls and provided with candle-cups; or the bowls may be removed from six-inch clear glass compotes, and the standards ground to fit candle-cups.

Two water tumblers having designs resembling American silver dollars pressed in the base may be found by persevering collectors. One is dated 1878, and the other 1879. The 1879 item has a plain body, but the other shows a panelled design. They are not U. S. Coin pattern forms, but do harmonize well with it. Tumblers in the U. S. Coin pattern are ornamented with the obverse and reverse sides of a dime.

Most U. S. Coin pattern forms show both obverse and reverse sides of the coin represented. Half-dimes show the reverse only, and so have no date.

The U. S. Coin pattern is found most often in clear glass. Coin medallion motifs in general, are either frosted, or clear. A few exceptions are noted. A toothpick holder is stained red, but coin medallions and the base are clear, or coins may be frosted. Red staining is found on a berry-bowl too; a broad band of red, near the rim, on outside surface. A lamp shows ten coin motifs stained amber. The lamp-bowl is square in form, with one amber motif on each side. Six amber motifs form a decorative band that encircles the standard.

The portrait forms may be all clear, clear and frosted, clear and red, clear and amber, clear with medallions decorated with gold (gilded); and one type of lamp comes in milk-white glass. I have seen the toothpick holder only, in clear and red (as in the U. S. Coin); and the lamp only, in clear and amber (as in the U. S. Coin). Most commonly found are the items in all clear, clear with motifs frosted, or clear with motifs gilded.

The phrase "foreign coin" is often used to designate the portrait series. This is probably due to one of the medallions which is derived from the Coat-of-Arms of Spain, and has some resemblance to a coin. There are four decorative medallion motifs on each item in the portrait series. One, portrait of Christopher Columbus; two, portrait of Americus Vespucius; three, medallion derived from the Coat-of-Arms of the United States; four, medallion derived from the Coat-of-Arms of Spain. This

85

fourth medallion commemorates the aid received by Columbus from Isabella, Queen of Spain, without which the voyage of discovery could not have been made.

Special mention should be made of one flat sauce-dish in my collection. It has four frosted and two clear quarter-dollars, someone's error.

No. 65 U. S. Coin Pattern Water-Set Tray

This is an important piece of glassware, a rare form within a rare pattern. It is fittingly impressive, for it displays ten medallion decorations, resembling "the almighty dollar," a coin which (it has been humorously said) Americans love to chase.

Medallions are the size of an actual dollar. Five of them show the "heads" side of the coin, while the remaining five present the eagle side, or "tails" as the reverse side of a coin is often called. The glass is of brilliant crystal and provides a pleasing background for the frosted coins. Diameter: ten inches. Height of rim: one inch.

No. 66 U. S. Coin Pattern Sauce-Dish

This is one of the pattern rarities. It is so classified because of its scalloped rim. In other respects it is the same as the footed sauce-dish more often found. Six medallions, frosted, are the actual size of, and closely resemble, quarter-dollars. Diameter: three and three-fourths inches. Height: two and one-half inches.

No. 67 U. S. Coin Pattern Celery Holder

This item, too, displays six frosted medallions resembling quarter-dollars. Above these designs the glass is deeply panelled. This adds to the brilliancy and effectiveness of the crystal ware. Height: six and one-fourth inches. Diameter: three inches.

No. 68 U. S. Coin Pattern Sugar-Bowl

The sugar-bowl has many coins. Six medallions resembling half-dollars in both size and design, are on the

No. 65   U. S. Coin Pattern Water-Set Tray

87

No. 66   U. S. Coin Pattern Sauce-Dish

No. 67   U. S. Coin Pattern
Celery Holder

No. 68   U. S. Coin Pattern Sugar-Bowl

No. 69   U. S. Coin Pattern
Toothpick Holder

base. Six more, resembling quarters, are placed around the lid. The finial represents stacked coins; two dollars, two half-dollars, and two quarters. All coins are frosted. Height: seven inches. Diameter: four inches.

No. 69   U. S. Coin Pattern Toothpick Holder

The toothpick holder here illustrated is another of several rarities encountered. It is so because of its color. The body of the piece is stained wine red, while the coins and base are crystal. Two medallions show the obverse design of a silver dollar. Two more show the reverse (or eagle) design. This form is the same as No. 10 in Chapter I. It is more readily found in all clear glass, clear and frosted, or clear and gilded; but in any combination is a popular item with collectors. Height: three inches. Base is two inches square.

No. 70   U. S. Coin Pattern Salt and Pepper Shakers

The upper half shows panelling. The lower half is ornamented with four medallions resembling quarter-dollars. Two are obverse and two are reverse. They are three inches high, and the diameter of the base is one and one-half inches. Pewter tops.

No. 71   U. S. Coin Pattern Tumbler

The lower portion only, of the tumbler, is decorated. Six medallions, resembling dimes, encircle the base. Three are obverse and three reverse. Height: three and three-fourths inches. Diameter of top: two and three-fourths inches.

No. 72   U. S. Coin Pattern Goblet

The goblet appears as a tumbler set upon a pedestal. Its decoration is identical with that of the tumbler. Two stacked coins showing milled edges form a knob in the stem, and the base is slightly broader than the top. Height:

No. 70   U. S. Coin Pattern Salt and Pepper Shakers
No. 71   U. S. Coin Pattern Tumbler

No. 72   U. S. Coin Pattern Goblet (dime) *(right)*
No. 73   U. S. Coin Pattern Goblet (half-dollar)
No. 74   U. S. Coin Pattern Champagne
No. 75   U. S. Coin Pattern Claret

91

six and one-fourth inches. Diameter of top: two and three-fourths inches.

No. 73   U. S. Coin Pattern Goblet

This probably was designed as an ale glass. The medallions resemble half-dollars. Six in number, three are obverse and three reverse. Its capacity is greater than that of the "dimes" goblet. Its base is the same in diameter, but the knob has a smaller diameter than No. 72. Height: six and three-fourths inches. Diameter of flared top: three and one-eighth inches.

No. 74   U. S. Coin Pattern Champagne

Medallions on the champagne glass represent half-dimes. They differ from other coins in one respect. Only one side, the "wreath" side, is shown. This accounts for the fact that half-dimes are not dated 1892 since the date is not on this side of the coin. As in other "drinking" forms, medallions are six in number. Height: four and three-fourths inches. Diameter of flaring top: two and one-fourth inches. Diameter of base: two and one-half inches.

No. 75   U. S. Coin Pattern Claret Wine

Medallions are the same as those on the champagne, six half-dimes. They are smaller in size, however. Height: four and one-fourth inches. Diameter at top: one and five-eighths inches. Diameter at base: two and one-eighth inches.

No. 76   U. S. Coin Pattern Scalloped Top Bowl

Medallions represent quarter-dollars, nine in number. Five are obverse (Liberty seated) and four are reverse (eagle). The scalloped top of this bowl makes it a rare form within the pattern. It is seven inches in diameter, and two and one-eighth inches high. Another bowl in my possession is identical except for size. It is six inches in diameter, and one and three-fourths inches high.

No. 76 U. S. Coin Pattern Scalloped Top Bowl

No. 77 U. S. Coin Pattern Syrup Jug
No. 78 U. S. Coin Pattern Mug
No. 79 U. S. Coin Pattern Cruet

93

No. 77   U. S. Coin Pattern Syrup Jug

Medallions represent quarter-dollars, six in number; three obverse and three reverse. Height to top of metal cover, seven inches. Inside the top of this cover is the following: "O. K. Pat. Jan. 29, 84."

No. 78   U. S. Coin Pattern Mug

This probably was designed as a beer mug. Six dollar medallions encircle the base, three obverse and three reverse. Height: four and three-fourths inches. Diameter of top: two and three-fourths inches.

No. 79   U. S. Coin Pattern Cruet

The cruet shows ten coins. Six quarter-dollar medallions encircle the base, three obverse and three reverse. The stopper shows four dimes, two obverse and two reverse. Extreme height: five and one-half inches.

No. 80   U. S. Coin Pattern Flat Sauce-Dish

Medallions represent quarter-dollars, six in number. Three are obverse and three reverse. Diameter: three and seven-eighths inches. Height: one and one-half inches.

A larger sauce-dish is identical with this one, except for size. It is four and one-fourth inches in diameter, and one and three-fourths inches in height.

No. 81   U. S. Coin Pattern Finger-Bowl

This scarce item was no doubt intended to do double duty, as a finger-bowl and as a waste-bowl with the water-tray. There are six quarter-dollar medallions. Above these is a broad band of plain glass. Diameter: four inches. Height: two and three-eighths inches.

No. 82   U. S. Coin Pattern Spoon-Holder

Once more, we have six quarter-dollar medallions for decorative feature. Above this is a fluted band of plain glass. Height: four and three-fourths inches. Diameter at top: two and seven-eighths inches.

No. 80   U. S. Coin Pattern Flat Sauce-Dish
No. 81   U. S. Coin Pattern Finger-Bowl

No. 82   U. S. Coin Pattern Spoon-Holder
No. 83   U. S. Coin Pattern Cream-Pitcher *(right)*
No. 84   U. S. Coin Pattern Lamp

95

No. 83   U. S. Coin Pattern Cream-Pitcher

The creamer is identical with the spoon-holder, to which has been added a handle and a pouring spout. Extreme height: five and one-eighth inches. Diameter of base: three inches.

No. 84   U. S. Coin Pattern Lamp

A small hand lamp has four medallions representing the twenty-cent piece, on its base. They are molded on the under side and do not show well. The upper surface of the handle is corrugated, supposedly for the striking of matches. Height: five inches. Diameter of base: three and three-eighths inches.

No. 85   U. S. Coin Pattern Bowl

Nine handsome dollar medallions ornament this flat berry-bowl; five obverse, and four reverse. Top diameter is nine inches. Height: three inches.

No. 86   U. S. Coin Pattern Water Pitcher

The water pitcher, too, displays dollar medallions. They encircle the base. Three are obverse and three reverse. Above this decorative feature the glass is panelled. Extreme height: nine and five-eighths inches. Diameter of base: four and three-fourths inches.

No. 87   U. S. Coin Pattern Milk Pitcher

The milk pitcher presents the same appearance as the water pitcher, with two exceptions. Coins represent half-dollars, and the size is smaller. Extreme height: eight and three-eighths inches. Diameter of base: four and one-eighth inches.

No. 88   U. S. Coin Pattern Low Compote

This dish is a favorite because it displays the twenty-cent piece medallion. It is the only tableware I have found that is so ornamented. Nine of these encircle the dish,

No. 85   U. S. Coin Pattern Bowl

No. 86   U. S. Coin Pattern Water Pitcher
No. 87   U. S. Coin Pattern Milk Pitcher

No. 88
U. S. COIN PATTERN
LOW COMPOTE

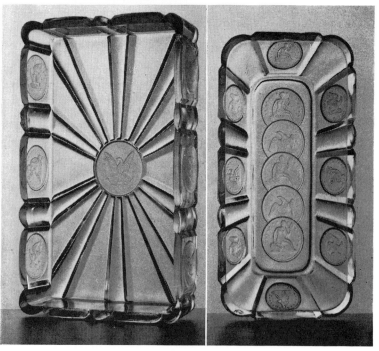

No. 89   U. S. COIN PATTERN PRESERVE-DISH
No. 90   U. S. COIN PATTERN PICKLE-DISH

five obverse and four reverse. The same number of quarter-dollar medallions encircle the lid. This is surprising, and suggests the lid and base are not properly matched. In many years of searching I have never seen a lid with twenty-cent piece medallions. I have seen a number of dishes like the one pictured, base showing twenty-cent pieces and lid the quarter-dollars. There seems to be no reason to doubt that it was so sold. It could be that the dish was intended to be sold without cover, but buyers preferred covered dishes, so purchased six-inch compote lids extra.

The design of the two coins is similar. Obverse is Liberty seated. Reverse is the eagle. The quarter, of course, is larger. Another difference is in the inscription below the eagle. On one it reads: "Quar Dol," on the other: "Twenty Cents." A slight difference on the obverse is noticeable: the quarter has arrow points at the sides of the date while the twenty-cent piece has no arrow points. On the quarter, the eagle holds three arrows in its left talon. There are but two arrows on the twenty-cent piece.

Stacked coins furnish a knob for the lid, and the top coin displays the liberty head. This dish is often referred to as a honey-dish. Diameter of bowl: five and seven-eighths inches. Extreme height: seven and one-fourth inches.

No. 89   U. S. Coin Pattern Preserve-Dish

Eleven medallions ornament the preserve-dish. Ten half-dollar forms, and one dollar, reverse side. It is rectangular in shape, eight by five inches in size. Depth is one and three-fourths inches.

No. 90   U. S. Coin Pattern Pickle-Dish

Thirteen coin medallions may be counted on the pickle-dish. Five overlapping half-dollar forms, three obverse and two reverse, feature the base. Sloping sides display

No. 91 U. S. Coin Pattern Cake-Plate

eight quarter-dollar designs, four obverse and four reverse. Length: seven and three-eighths inches. Width: three and three-fourths inches.

No. 91   U. S. Coin Pattern Cake-Plate on Standard

Fifteen medallions are used here. Nine dollar forms, five obverse and four reverse, ornament the surface. Six quarter-dollar forms, three obverse and three reverse, encircle the standard. Height: six and one-half inches. Diameter of top: ten inches.

No. 92   U. S. Coin Pattern Epergne

The Coin pattern is highly original in design, but in this form it reaches the peak of originality. It is so different that its purpose is questioned. It is most often called an epergne, although it does not seem suited to such usage. Some call it a money-changer, intended for use by cashiers, for holding small change, and toothpicks. Others think it is a spice-dish. In the latter part of the nineteenth century at which time the Coin pattern was produced, it was common practice to chew stick cinnamon, whole cloves, cubeb berries, dried orange peel, etc., to suppress halitosis. Users of tobacco, liquor, and onions, as well as persons in less than perfect health, used this means to prevent giving offense. Some dishes were made for holding whole spices, and usually had four compartments. This strange-looking form in the Coin pattern may have been intended for such a purpose. It does have four compartments in the base, although the divisions are shallow. Six medallions ornament the base. The dish illustrated is portrait type. The portrait of Columbus appears twice and the likeness of Americus Vespucius once. Two medallions show U. S. Arms, and the other displays Spanish Arms. A cup which forms the top of the dish, has four medallions. One portrait of Columbus, one of Vespucius, one U. S. Arms, and one Spanish Arms. In the U. S. Coin series, dollar medallions ornament the base and quarter-dollar forms dec-

101

No. 92
U. S. Coin
Pattern
Epergne
Portrait
Type

No. 93   U. S. Coin Pattern
Tall Covered Compote

orate the cup. Length: eight and three-fourths inches. Width: seven and one-fourth inches. Extreme height: five and one-eighth inches. Depth of cup: two inches.

No. 93   U. S. Coin Pattern Tall Compote

Twenty-four medallions are used on the covered compote. Nine quarter-dollar forms are on the body of the dish and nine on the lid. Five are obverse and four reverse on each. Six dime medallions encircle the standard, three obverse and three reverse. The dish appears as a covered bowl set upon a standard. The lid of this compote is identical with No. 88. Diameter: five and seven-eighths inches. Height: nine and one-fourth inches.

No. 94   U. S. Coin Pattern Sauce-Dish

This form is the same as No. 66, with one exception. The rim is plain. This is the sauce-dish most readily found.

No. 95   U. S. Coin Pattern Bread-Tray

Fifteen coins feature the bread-tray. Five overlapping dollar medallions are on the base; two obverse and three reverse. Dollars also are used at the four corners of the rim. Six half-dollar medallions alternate with these. Length: ten inches. Width: seven inches.

No. 96   U. S. Coin Pattern Butter-Dish

Five dollar-forms are on the base of the butter-dish. One at each corner of the square flange, and one (reverse) in the center of the round base. Six half-dollar forms encircle the lid, and the knob is composed of three stacked dollars. Extreme width: six and one-half inches. Extreme height: four and one-half inches. Diameter of lid: five inches.

No. 97   U. S. Coin Pattern Lamp

The bowl of this lamp is square in shape, with slightly rounded corners. Several diagonal lines appear on these

No. 94   U. S. Coin Pattern Sauce-Dish

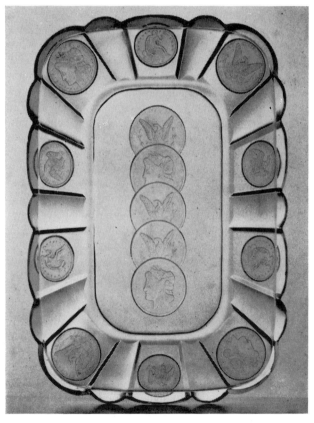

No. 95   U. S. Coin Pattern Bread-Tray

No. 96 U. S. Coin Pattern Butter-Dish

No. 97 U. S. Coin Pattern Lamp *(left)*
No. 98 U. S. Coin Pattern Lamp Portrait Type *(right)*

105

No. 99
U. S. Coin
Pattern
Fruit Compote

No. 100
U. S. Coin Pattern
Milk-Glass Lamp
Portrait Type

corners. Dollar medallions, two obverse and two reverse, decorate each of the four sides. Six half-dollar forms encircle the standard. Height: ten inches.

No. 98   U. S. Coin Pattern Lamp

This lamp has a round bowl of plain glass, panelled. It is the portrait type, showing six medallions encircling the standard. Two portraits are of Columbus, one of Vespucius, two U. S. Arms, and one Spanish Arms. Height: nine and one-half inches.

No. 99   U. S. Coin Pattern Fruit Compote

Medallions on this item are quarter-dollars. Nine of them, five obverse and four reverse, alternate around the bowl. The dish illustrated has a flaring bowl which is slightly curved. Not all show this same curve. There is some variation in these flaring rims. Six dime forms encircle the standard. Diameter of bowl is seven inches. Height: five and three-fourths inches.

No. 100   U. S. Coin Pattern Lamp

This lamp has a round, panelled bowl. Six medallions are on the standard. Two of these show portraits of Columbus, two others show the Coat-of-Arms of the United States, one shows portrait of Vespucius, and one the Coat-of-Arms of Spain. Three of the six panels on the bowl are ornamented with a flower (resembling an orchid) and a few leaves, tied with a ribbon bow. If this interpretation is correct, the designer intended to express this thought: "An orchid (special honor) to Columbus, Vespucius, Spain, and the United States of America; on the four hundredth anniversary of the great discovery." The remaining panels are plain. The lamp is unusual, too, because it is made in two pieces, the bowl and base being separate. Unions are threaded and the parts screwed together as is done in some metal connections. Height: nine and three-fourths inches. Color: opaque white. A smaller size is eight inches in height.

107

One Pattern

The money forms, and portrait forms of this pattern are presented as one unit. Because forms in both types are parallel, this seems to be a logical procedure. There is no more dramatic story in the realm of glassware, than is found here; and the story is incomplete without mention of both types. It follows, then, that collections which include specimens of both types, are more comprehensive, more complete, and more satisfying.

Addenda

The following item was secured after printing had begun. Since a consecutive number could not then be assigned, the symbol (a) is placed after the last number which makes the identification number 100(a).

The lamp is all clear glass, eight and one-half inches in height.

No. 100(a)
U. S. Coin Pattern Lamp

CHAPTER IV

CHAPTER IV

The Volunteer State, Tennessee

The Constitution of the United States did not go into effect at once, after having been adopted by the convention. Each state must vote on its adoption, and it was not to go into force until nine states had accepted it. Rhode Island was the last of the thirteen to accept, which it did in 1790. Soon, new states began to seek admission. Vermont was admitted the very next year, and was closely followed by Kentucky in 1792. In 1796, Tennessee became the sixteenth state admitted to the Union, and this event is recorded in glassware.

The Tennessee Centennial Exposition was held in Centennial Park, Nashville, Tennessee, in 1897; so it seems probable that commemorative items date to that time.

No. 101   Volunteer Plate

The popular name "Volunteer State" was given Tennessee because 30,000 men volunteered for service during the Mexican War when only three regiments had been called for. The glassware industry produced a Volunteer Plate to commemorate the Volunteer State. A scene in the center of this plate represents an army camp. In the foreground a lone volunteer stands guard, musket in hands, beside a flagpole from which floats a flag whose field shows sixteen stars. Ten tents are in the background. On the border of the plate, left side, crossed muskets with bayonets fixed, are shown. A mounted cannon is on the right side of the center. At the top, the word "Volunteer" is inscribed. At the bottom, the word "Plate" appears. All letters are stippled, and the remarkable feature of the plate is shown in this stippling. Each dot of stippling is a perfect star. In the letter O (which is but three-fourths of an inch in height are counted seventy-two stars. There must be almost (or quite) one thousand, in all. The plate is ten inches in diameter. Colors: crystal, green.

111

No. 101   Volunteer Plate

No. 102   Tennessee Mug

No. 102   Tennessee Mug

A very attractive mug also commemorates Tennessee statehood. It is of so-called camphor glass. On the obverse, a design is composed of a Cherokee rose, and clematis blossoms, within a shield, above sprays of laurel. The reverse shows an American flag having sixteen stars which identifies it with the sixteenth state. I have been told the blossoms used were the official flowers of the exposition, chosen because Tennessee was originally a part of the Cherokee Territory. The mug is three inches in diameter, and three and one-half inches high.

California

California became a state September 9, 1850. It has been called El Dorado (the gilded) because of gold discoveries, the Gold State, and the Grape State. It is also known as the Eureka State because of the state motto "Eureka" which means "I have found it."

The bear symbol is connected with California, too. This may be traced to the bear flag war which was an insurrection against the Mexican Government in 1846. A republic, known as the Bear Flag Republic was proclaimed, and a flag showing the figure of a bear was raised.

No. 103   Eureka Platter

Two glassware items refer to the State of California. One, a bread tray (or platter) in the clear diagonal band pattern, has the state motto "Eureka" inscribed diagonally across its surface. This reference is, no doubt, to the gold rush history. It is eleven and one-half inches in length, and nine inches wide. Color: crystal, clear and stippled.

113

No. 103   Eureka Platter

No. 104   California Bear Plate

No. 104 California Bear Plate

The second item is a club border milk-glass plate. It shows a central design composed of bruin within a wreath of flowers, fruits, and grain. Above is the inscription "California." Below is "Mid-Winter Fair."

The California Mid-Winter International Exposition was held in San Francisco, in 1894. The buildings were colored in Oriental fashion. Surrounded by orange trees, magnolias, and palms, they presented a tropical effect of splendor and luxury.

An outstanding feature of the Fair was a reproduction of a pioneer mining camp. A number of actual cabins in which some of the "Bonanza Kings" began their adventures, were included. Many relics of the gold rush days were exhibited and viewed with "rapt attention" by visitors from all parts of the world.

Other Statehood Items

The centennial year has been celebrated by other states, too; and no doubt glassware commemorating such events was made. These celebrations did not distribute souvenirs over such a large area as did national expositions, so that items concerning statehood come to light more slowly and are more difficult to locate and secure.

The Louisiana Purchase

The transaction known in American History as the Louisiana Purchase gave to the United States an area of nearly a million square miles, embracing all the territory between the Mississippi River and the crest of the Rocky Mountains. This territory was first explored by Frenchmen; then the province was held by Spain for forty years. Spain and the United States had considerable trouble about the navigation of the Mississippi River. In 1800 Napoleon Bonaparte procured its cession back to France. In 1803

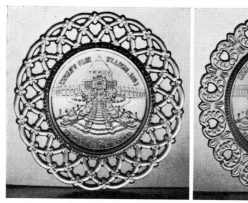

No. 105   LOUISIANA PURCHASE EXPOSITION PLATE *(left)*
No. 106   LOUISIANA PURCHASE EXPOSITION PLATE *(right)*

No. 107   LOUISIANA PURCHASE
EXPOSITION TUMBLER

116

President Jefferson sent our Secretary of State James Monroe (the future president) and Robert R. Livingston to France to purchase, if possible, a part of this territory including New Orleans and the mouths of the river. Napoleon surprised these commissioners by offering to sell the whole territory. This offer was accepted, the purchase price being fifteen million dollars. This sum, plus interest payments and incidentals made the price to us, about four cents per acre. This more than doubled the size of the United States and made possible the prospect of its becoming one of the greatest nations on the earth.

No. 105   Louisiana Purchase Exposition Plate

The World's Fair held in St. Louis, Missouri, 1904, commemorated the centennial of the Louisiana Purchase. Festival Hall and Cascade Gardens (built at a cost of one million dollars) was called "the beautiful centerpiece of the exposition."

Two plates are found to recall this loveliness, although the intricate detail responsible for its popularity could not be captured in so small a presentation as a plate. The central design on these plates represents a "great picture created by architect, engineer, and landscape gardener." "Three leaping cascades spring from the Terrace of States, which is crowned by Festival Hall, and that capped in turn by a golden dome larger even than the famed covering of St. Paul's Cathedral, and the dancing water flows into the Grand Basin which extends past four of the main exhibit palaces, then branches into lagoons that thread the remainder of the main picture as the canals thread the City of Venice." "When night comes nature gives place to art and the picture glows as if touched by a magician's wand, for electricity has become Aladdin's lamp and changes the cascades to an emerald green, yet again to a dull phosphorescent glow, and at times liquid fire seems

117

to be spreading down the incline, while flames follow and creep over the lagoon."

An inscription, "World's Fair St. Louis 1904" is placed above the design. Another, "Festival Hall & Cascade Gardens" is below it. The familiar forget-me-not and open-work design, was used as a border. Size: seven and one-fourth inches in diameter. Color: crystal.

No. 106   Louisiana Purchase Exposition Plate

This plate has the same central design, the same inscriptions, and is the same size as No. 105. The border is altogether different. Color: crystal glass, with frosted center.

No. 107   Louisiana Purchase Exposition Tumbler

Another much favored souvenir was an ice tea, or beverage, glass. On its surface, four features that were popular with exposition visitors are shown. Festival Hall and Cascade Gardens, the Louisiana Purchase Monument, the Palace of Machinery, and the famous Union Railway Station in St. Louis are shown molded in the glass. Each is accompanied by its correct inscription: "Louisiana Purchase Monument," "Cascade Gardens," "Palace of Machinery," "St. Louis Union Station." The inscription letters are quite small. Size: five inches high, three and three-fourths inches in diameter. Colors: milk-glass, crystal.

No. 108   Napoleon Bottle

Napoleon Bonaparte, the "Little Corporal" who ruled France, and who sold us the Louisiana Territory, was memorialized in glass. A Toby bottle shows him in all the splendor of his military uniform. It probably was produced at an earlier time (there is nothing on the bottle to indicate when it was made) but it could have fittingly been distributed at this time. In size, this bottle is seven inches high. Color: crystal.

No. 108   Napoleon Bottle

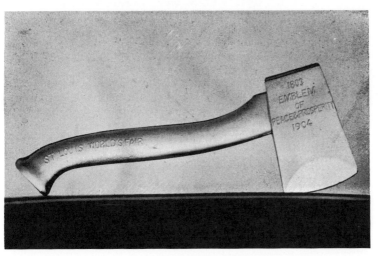

No. 109   Louisiana Purchase Exposition Axe

119

A chopping axe, inscribed "Emblem of Peace and Prosperity" "St. Louis World's Fair" calls attention to the part played in advancing civilization by this important tool, when wielded by the muscled arms of our sturdy pioneers. Size: ten inches long. Color: crystal.

Uncle Sam

"Uncle Sam" is a personification of the United States Government. Several explanations are said to have been given as to the origin of this expression, but the one generally accepted is the following, taken from "Messages and Papers of the Presidents" published by authority of Congress.

During the War of 1812, Elbert Anderson (an army contractor) bought large quantities of provisions for the army and had them shipped to himself at Troy, New York. The shipping mark was "E. A." above a line, and "U. S." below it. One of the inspectors at Troy, was Samuel Wilson, popularly known as Uncle Sam Wilson. At that time the letters U. S. were so rarely used that few people understood the association. One day someone asked a workman the meaning of the initials "E. A." and "U. S." The prompt reply was "Elbert Anderson" and "Uncle Sam" referring to Sam Wilson.

This interpretation became accepted among the workmen and they, in turn, communicated the explanation to their comrades from all parts of the country, since the mystic "E. A." and "U. S." elicited inquiry in general. The story went the rounds of the press and so "Uncle Sam" became the popular name for the United States Government.

Uncle Sam has been portrayed in many ways. He is shown most often in cartoons of the day. He has grown to be the most used of all cartoonists' figures. He may be seen, most any time, on some editorial page, or front cover, as a figure with long chin whiskers, sharply pointed nose, wearing a high-topped hat, a long-tailed coat and striped trousers. His clothing often is sprinkled with stars and the whole effect is that of an overgrown, awkward, and gawky individual. He usually is associated (directly or indirectly) with the Democratic donkey, the Republican elephant, the Tammany tiger, the seedy and sneaking representative of Prohibition, the apoplectic and greedy fellow of the Trusts, the Laborer with cap and dinner-pail, or the meek, insignificant little dwarf who represents "The People." His cartoon utterances have become threadbare from long usage but they have become so established in the public mind that any attempt at change would be quickly challenged and resented. He is the Federal Voice, and his influence in forming and molding public opinion is of considerable importance; for the message of a simply drawn picture is quickly recorded on the mind, where a column or page of written opinion or fact might be skipped or sketchily read.

No. 110   Uncle Sam Bottle

In glassware, a rather tall bottle shows Uncle Sam to be wearing long hair matching the usual long whiskers and long nose. He is correctly garbed in the customary striped trousers and long-tailed coat, which is studded all over with five-pointed stars. The neck of the bottle conveniently provides his high-crowned hat. His left hand grasps the barrel of a musket which rests beside him. Size: nine and one-half inches high. Color: crystal.

No. 111   Uncle Sam Hat

Uncle Sam's hat is represented in glassware, too. Made of white milk-glass, it is fittingly decorated in red, white, and blue. It is reported as having been used as a salt-dish,

No. 110   Uncle Sam Bottle

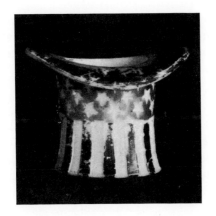

No. 111   UNCLE SAM HAT

No. 112   UNCLE SAM COVERED DISH

a toothpick holder, a match holder, and as a coin bank. Size: two and one-half inches high. Crown is two and one-half inches in diameter. Rim, at largest part, three and five-eighths inches across.

No. 112   Uncle Sam Covered Dish

Another "Uncle Sam" item is a white milk-glass covered dish which represents a battleship. Uncle Sam is shown sitting on the lid. The boat is six and one-half inches long, three inches wide, and four and one-half inches high.

Columbia

"Columbia" is a female personification of the United States Government, and an older representation than "Uncle Sam." The word is often used interchangeably with "Goddess of Liberty" although the latter phrase should more correctly be used as a personification of liberty.

A profile portrait representing Columbia is shown in the Columbia tray No. 54.

No. 113   Terrestrial Globe Covered Dish

A covered dish, in the form of a terrestrial globe, with Columbia's head forming the finial, offers some degree of uncertainty at this time. The mold maker who executed this piece was an expert and experienced workman, for topographical features (mountains, rivers, lakes, etc.) are clearly and accurately, though minutely shown.

Perhaps it is a symbolical piece and the maker intended to express the thought that "all the world supports liberty" or in more modern phrasing "liberty is tops." If so, production might logically be placed about 1876 when all the world helped Columbia celebrate the one hundredth anniversary of her time of liberation.

The following inscriptions are placed in their correct positions on the globe: "North America—South America

No. 113   Terrestrial Globe Covered Dish

125

— Europe — Asia — Africa — Atlantic Ocean — Pacific Ocean."

The dish is of crystal glass, with land areas finely stippled. Size: extreme diameter is eight inches. Diameter of the bowl is five and one-half inches. Height of dish is ten inches.

No. 114 JOHN BULL

"John Bull" is a nickname applied to the typical Englishman. It is used also as a personification of the British Government, much as "Uncle Sam" is used as a personification of the United States Government. John Bull (it should be remembered) was the personification of OUR government for more than 150 years, until we won our independence from Britain.

A glassware statuette shows John Bull seated on a bale of cotton. A bulldog sits beside him, holding a newspaper. An inscription "John Bull" is on the base. Another inscription "The Times" is on the newspaper. Size: seven inches high. Base is three and three-fourths inches in diameter. Color: clear glass, frosted finish. Possibly the item is of English origin.

No. 115 BRITANNIA STATUETTE

Britannia is the British equivalent of the United States personification, Columbia. She is represented as a seated figure, clothed in long flowing draperies. Her right hand rests on an oval shield at her side. On this shield the Union Jack is shown.

The Union Jack was the flag under which the United States was colonized. It flew from the "Mayflower" when the Pilgrims came to Plymouth in 1620, and it flew from the "Constant" which brought English settlers to Jamestown in 1607. It was known as the King's Colors and was derived from earlier flags. One of these, the "Cross of St. Andrew," Scotland's patron Saint, had been the national

126

No. 114
JOHN BULL STATUETTE

No. 115
BRITANNIA STATUETTE

standard of that country. It was a white diagonal cross on a field of blue. The other was the "Cross of St. George" . . . a red cross on a field of white. In the latter part of the thirteenth century, Edward I of England, became so interested in the story of St. George and the dragon that he adopted the "Cross of St. George" as the flag of England. In 1606, James VI became King of Scotland. Three years before this he had become King of England, as James I. He decreed that the Cross of St. Andrew and the Cross of St. George be combined on one field, to suggest the linking of destinies of the two countries. After awhile, this new flag of King James became known as Union Jack, the word "Jack" being derived from "Jacques" the French word for James.

In her left arm Britannia holds a spray of laurel. On her head rests a helmet. The figure is well executed, in every respect. It is of English origin, as shown by the English registry mark. It also carries a maker's mark. This is an anchor combined with the letters J and D. The figure is eight inches high, and the diameter of the fluted base is four and one-half inches. Color: clear glass, with all frosted finish.

From the surrender of Cornwallis in 1781, until the year 1812, the nation knew no fighting. Her energies and abilities were freely and fully used in creative enterprises. Then, clouds of war gathered once more. England and France were fighting. England needed sea-men for her navy. In supplying the necessity, she treated this nation with indignities no self-respecting people would endure. Thousands of native Americans were taken from their own ships, placed on the gun-decks of British vessels, and forced to fight the battles of England. Other wrongs were inflicted, too. In June 1812, the United States declared war against England; a war that lasted more than two years. The treaty of peace was signed December 24, 1814. By the terms of this treaty, neither Great Britain nor the United States gained anything. The right of searching American vessels was not mentioned in the treaty, but Great Britain had seen that such a practice could not continue against a spirited nation. American ships never have been searched since that time.

No. 116   Frigate Constitution Oval Dish

The frigate Constitution became renowned for her many victories in the War of 1812. The bill which permitted construction of this historic old ship passed both houses of Congress and was signed by President Washington March 27, 1794, only four years after the Constitution of the United States had been ratified by the last of the thirteen states. Her dimensions were: length, 175 feet; beam, 43 feet 6 inches; hold, 14 feet 3 inches. She was classed as a 44-gun frigate of 1,576 tons.

The Constitution is best remembered for her defeat of the powerful English Guerriere. This success meant much to the American people because defeat of an English man-of-war was an almost unheard-of thing at that time.

Old Ironsides, as the ship was popularly known, gradually went the way of all material things, and fell into decay. In 1828 she was condemned as unseaworthy and ordered scrapped. There was a great clamor for "the eagle of the sea" to be preserved. Oliver Wendell Holmes' poem "Old Ironsides" was a factor in creating this force of public opinion. In 1833 she was reconditioned. Again, the years took their toll and it looked as though the end was near, for Old Ironsides. Once more, a nation-wide appeal was made to save her. A fund was raised by numerous small contributions and the project was completed in 1931. Only fifteen per cent of the original materials were found strong enough to be retained.

In early days it was the custom for ships to carry on their bows, the carved image of a hero, either of mythological origin, or of their time. A carved image of Hercules ornamented her bow when she first sailed the high seas, but since that day six or seven different figures and scrolls were successors of the mighty Hercules. It is said that she carried the figure of Neptune with his trident during her battle with the Guerriere. The figure of Hercules was restored to Old Ironsides, since she received her baptism of fire under his guidance.

On July 22, 1798, manned by 400 men, the Constitution sailed from Boston on her maiden cruise. On July 1, 1931, manned by a crew of 83, she again sailed from Boston— not to wrench supremacy from a sea of enemies, but to enable people to see the most famous of all our early ships. Secretary of the Navy, Charles Francis Adams, said: "We hope that the children and patriotic citizens, whose contributions made possible the restoration of the famous old ship, will accept the invitation to board her. 'Old Ironsides' is more than an inspiration, she is an American tradition."

No. 116   Frigate Constitution Oval Dish

No. 116   Frigate Constitution Oval Dish

An oval dish, of the Sandwich "lacy" type, is believed to commemorate the frigate Constitution. Eight round medallions are featured in the highly decorative design. A ship which strongly resembles pictures of the Constitution is shown in four of these medallions. In the other four a design derived from the Coat-of-Arms of the United States is used. It shows the eagle with shield, olive branch, and arrows. Since the Constitution was sometimes called "the eagle of the sea," the mold maker may have intended to present a twofold idea: that the dish honors the Frigate Constitution, the (American) eagle of the sea. Size: the dish pictured is six and one-eighth inches long, three and three-fourths inches wide, and one and seven-sixteenths inches high. Color: crystal, with lacy, stippled background.

No. 117   The Frigate Franklin Flask

Another early American vessel, pictured in glass, is the frigate Franklin. She was launched in Philadelphia in 1818 and was the largest and finest warship in our navy for some time. She carried 74 guns but history does not record any glowing engagements in which she was involved. She was the squadron flagship for some time. After serving for more than one hundred years, she was junked.

A pint flask commemorates the Franklin. The obverse shows Masonic symbols. The reverse pictures a frigate under full sail, flying an American flag from the stern. Wavy lines represent water and under them is inscribed "Franklin." The edges carry inscription, too: "Free Trade and Sailors Rights," "Kensington Glass Works, Philadelphia." Colors: aqua, and some other colors.

The inscription "Free Trade and Sailors Rights" was a slogan coined during the War of 1812, when England interfered with our commerce, searched our vessels for deserting British seamen, and seized our citizens for

No. 117
THE FRIGATE FRANKLIN FLASK

No. 117
THE FRIGATE FRANKLIN FLASK

forced British service. The association of this slogan with the finest warship afloat at the time reflects a fervent patriotic spirit; that American citizens were determined to continue defending their rights as free men, with modern and powerful ships and guns and any other necessary resources. Although the flask was made some time after the war was over, and some time after the Franklin was placed in service, an idea of "In peace, prepare for war" seems to have taken hold. Perhaps this was an early step in the conception of national preparedness.

CHAPTER V

CHAPTER V

136

The people found many new needs. They had to learn how to do things that had never been done before. Their success in doing things in new ways was so amazing they eventually became the most ingenious and inventive people in the world.

On land, they moved from the day of buffalo and Indian trails, ox-cart travel, covered wagon, stagecoach, and pony express, to the convenience of steam trains and automobiles.

On water, the dangers of untamed rivers gave way to the safety of canals. Slow-moving canoes and flat-boats were replaced by sailing craft, steamboats, and cargo ships.

In air, wishful thinking gave place to the convenience of modern passenger planes and cargo planes.

Communication advanced from Indian signal fires, and the beacon fires of the colonists to the telegraph, telephone, radio, and free delivery of mail.

In the home, the discomfort of primitive methods of living gave way to convenience, comfort, and luxury.

Many of these improvements are memorialized in glassware.

THE COTTON-GIN

A key that unlocked the door to great development, not only of this country but of the whole world, was the invention of the cotton-gin. Machines for weaving cloth by steam power had been invented in England, and this increased the demand for raw cotton. Our southern states were well suited to the raising of this crop, but it was not profitable because not more than a pound of it could be cleaned and seeded and made ready for sale, by one man in one day.

About 1793-1794, Eli Whitney invented a machine that could clean one thousand pounds of cotton in a single day. This caused great excitement. Before all details of the invention were completed, this cotton-gin was stolen from the building in which it was housed, and carried away. (The word "gin" is a shortening of the word "engine".) Soon, several machines were made, on the same principle as Whitney's invention, but with enough change (it was hoped) to evade penalties for imitation, invoked under patent laws.

For many years, Eli Whitney was forced to protect himself against this piracy so that the expense of such protection was more than his profit from sales. Not until the year 1807 was validity settled. After years of struggle the inventor was still a poor man. In a letter to Robert Fulton, he remarked that "the difficulties with which he had to contend originated principally in the want of a disposition in mankind to do justice." Unhappily, that want of a disposition in mankind to do justice seems to remain with humanity. It has been responsible for much of the failure and time-lag encountered by this nation in its quest for better ways, and better things for better living.

Due to the invention of Eli Whitney, cotton became a leading product of the southern states. Its importance was the basis for a great celebration, the World's Industrial and Cotton Centennial Exposition of 1884. It was held in New Orleans, Louisiana. This time was chosen because a bale of cotton, the first known, was shipped to England from this country in 1784.

A park of two hundred fifty acres was laid out and prepared. A feature of the Exposition was found in the avenues winding through vistas of live oaks draped with Spanish moss. Others passed through groves of banana, lemon, and orange trees. Beds of brilliant tropical flowers, and fountains provided beautiful accents. By night, electric lights, at that time a novelty to many visitors, added to the fascination of the Fair.   December 16, was the opening date.   The Main Building was the largest structure ever erected for exhibition purposes, at that time.   Its area was 1,656,030 square feet.

This event gave the South a new sense of its importance and strength, gave the North (through the host of those attending) a friendlier feeling and better understanding for southern affairs.   It is said this influence extended even to the presidential election soon to come.

No. 118   Cotton Bale Box

A rectangular box, shaped like a bale of cotton, may date from the time of this exposition.   There is no knowledge to this effect, but all evidence points strongly in that direction.

The background of the box is stippled to give the effect of a coarse, heavy cloth called "gunny" used for wrapping cotton bales.   Binding straps and inscriptions are of clear glass and stand out in pleasing relief.   Inscribed at one side of the lid are the letters "N. O." meaning (no doubt) New Orleans, which was the great cotton market of earlier times.   Inscribed at one end of the lid are the numerals "520", the weight of a bale of cotton.   At the other end of the lid, the letter "D" is placed within a diamond.   This symbol probably represented the producer.   The entire effect is that of an unusually well-executed piece, showing pleasing perfection of detail.   Size: three and one-half inches long, two and one-half inches wide, and two inches high.   Color: crystal glass.

The McCormick Reaper

The invention of the cotton-gin was followed by inventions of a large number of labor-saving devices.   Reaping and mowing machines were among the number.

No. 118   Cotton Bale Box

No. 119   The Reaper Platter

In 1831 a reaping machine was developed by Cyrus H. McCormick. It was perfected by 1834. After some experience in the states of New York and Ohio, it was evident that better markets for grain reapers existed in the prairie country, so he moved to Chicago in 1847.

At this time he introduced another startling innovation, the selling of his machines on the installment plan.

Information concerning the McCormick reaper is cleverly given on an advertising card, presented to visitors at the Chicago Exposition in 1893, intended to be mailed by them to friends at home.

"I am writing this from the World's Fair headquarters of the McCormick Harvesting Machine Company. Cyrus H. McCormick, you know, invented the reaper in 1831. The Company's display here is very attractive, and I will tell you all about it when I get home. They make binders, reapers, and mowers, and their works (located in this city) are the largest in capacity of any in the world; they have over fifty acres of floor space, employ two thousand men, and have facilities for building a complete machine every minute—and this means an annual output of machines which, if placed end to end, would make a column over five hundred miles long. They annually sell one-third of the world's needs in grain and grass harvesting machinery, and have won the highest awards at every World's Fair and great Exposition held during the last fifty years. The Columbian Exposition, in connection with the McCormick Exhibit recalls the London World's Fair of 1851, at which the early McCormick Reaper was shown. The London TIMES at first ridiculed Mr. McCormick's invention, characterizing it as a cross between an Astley chariot, a wheelbarrow, and a flying machine, but the same paper subsequently said, editorially, that the Reaper was the most valuable contribution to the Exposition, and of sufficient value alone to pay the entire expense of the Exhibition."

No. 119   The Reaper Platter

An oval glass platter, or tray, presents a quaint agricultural scene comprising a grain field and the new-fangled reaper drawn by two lively horses. Two men, and a dog, lend support to the more important features of the design; while trees and buildings are seen in the distance. The border design surrounding this ambitious presentation is, appropriately enough, a picket fence. It is said this platter was introduced to commemorate the McCormick Reaper. Size: thirteen inches long, eight inches wide. Color: crystal glass.

Electricity

The search for better ways of doing things, led many to investigate the subject of electricity; and their experiments brought control of this strange force. Because of the findings of Benjamin Franklin, Joseph Henry, Michael Faraday, Thomas A. Edison, Professor Samuel F. B. Morse, Cyrus W. Field, Alexander Graham Bell, and others, a new and better era was made possible.

No. 120   T.V.A. Bottle

Reference to the control of electrical power is made by a bottle of recent manufacture. The obverse displays a portrait of President Franklin D. Roosevelt. Under this portrait is the Coat-of-Arms of the United States and the date 1936. On the reverse is pictured a large dam over which water is flowing. Below the dam the date 1936 is inscribed. Above the dam, a large muscular hand is tightly clenched around a bolt of lightning. It suggests that the hand of man now has the strange and mighty force called electricity within his control. Above the hand are the letters T.V.A. (Tennessee Valley Authority, the big government-owned hydro-electric project). Capacity: forty-two ounces. Color: aqua.

No. 120
T.V.A. Bottle
OBVERSE

No. 120
T.V.A. Bottle
REVERSE

143

No. 121   ELECTRIC RUNABOUT

No. 122   CHRISTMAS GIFT PLATE

144

No. 121   Electric Runabout Candy Container

Electric vehicles which were dependent on a storage battery for the source of power were developed, and, at one time used to a considerable extent. Distance of travel was limited to battery capacity, and rate of speed was slow. Competition of petrol cars having greater range and speed soon replaced the slow-moving and handicapped electric.

A container shaped like the out-moded vehicle was made for use as a candy container. Size: three and one-half inches long, two and one-half inches high, and one and one-half inches wide. Color: crystal.

No. 122   Christmas Gift Plate

Due to the genius of Thomas A. Edison, electrical power was adapted to the purpose of illumination. It soon passed the stage of ordinary utility and was used extensively as a means of ornamentation, and for advertising purposes. The name of a celebrity, or advertising house and products, or slogan, was formed by incandescent light bulbs to write any name or slogan in "letters of light."

A number of items in glassware show lettering suggestive of this custom. One having unusual appeal carries the inscription "The Compliments of the Season." Sprays of holly and of mistletoe are combined with the lettering to produce a most pleasing effect. Size: ten inches in diameter. Color: crystal.

No. 123   Telephone Blue Bell

An instrument which could carry the tones of the human voice over some distance, to be recognized when heard, as clearly as though speaker and listener were in the same room was constructed by Alexander Graham Bell. The first words transmitted were those of Professor Bell to an assistant in another room: "Mr. Watson, come here, I want you."

No. 123
Telephone Blue Bell

No. 124   General Douglas MacArthur Bottle

A patent, No. 174,465, since called "the most valuable single patent ever issued" was granted and came to Bell on his 29th birthday, March 3, 1876.

This invention was exhibited at the Philadelphia Centennial, but the importance of the instrument was not recognized. The general public had doubts about the success and worth of this "toy" developed by a "crank." Like other men of genius, the inventor was forced to combat the ignorance, the sneers, and the jealousies of others, before his telephone won its way to success. During the lifetime of the original patent (seventeen years) some 600 infringement suits were commenced, but the validity and priority of patent 174,465 was repeatedly upheld.

The "blue bell" of the Bell Telephone Company is the symbol of local and long distance telephone service.

Glass blue bell paperweights have been distributed at various times. Some have inscriptions to identify them, and others have none. The one pictured was distributed to prospective customers of the company named on the bell. Inscriptions read, obverse: "Missouri and Kansas Telephone Company." Reverse: "Local and Long Distance Telephone." It is solid glass of a deep cobalt blue color. Size: three and three-eighths inches in diameter, three inches in height. Colors: various shades of blue glass.

The Telegraph

The telegraph was first brought into practical use by Professor Samuel F. B. Morse. He began his experiments in 1832. For twelve years he was engaged in perfecting his invention and in trying to arouse public interest. He obtained a patent in 1840. Since this undertaking was extremely expensive he asked Congress to supply funds for the purpose of demonstrating its value. Congress did not do so. He then sailed for Europe to take out patents there. In England his application was refused. In France, he obtained a patent but it was appropriated by the French Government without compensation to him. His negotiations with Russia failed, too, and he returned to New York. He continued his efforts with such means as he could provide, and in 1843 Congress granted $30,000 to construct a telegraph from Baltimore to Washington, a distance of 40 miles.

On the morning of May 24, 1844, Samuel Morse sat in the Supreme Court chamber in Washington, ready to test the completed line. Distinguished guests were there with him, and outside, the nation watched, too. Shortly after 8 o'clock, Annie Ellsworth, daughter of the Commissioner of Patents, brought a message to be used for the history-making test. She and her mother had selected it from the Bible. It read: "WHAT HATH GOD WROUGHT." At 8:45 Morse began tapping it out. At the other end of the line, located in the Baltimore and Ohio station in Baltimore, Alfred Vail was ready to take the message. A group of curious watchers was with him. At 8:45 the instrument began to chatter. A code had been arranged. Vail translated the dots and dashes into letters and words, wrote out the message and held it up for inspection. Then he sent the same message back to Washington where it was received with enthusiasm, for the telegraph at long last had become a reality. Its immense value to the public became apparent, but, like other inventors, Morse was compelled to defend his invention in the courts.

He offered the telegraph to the Government for $100,000 but the Postmaster-General felt "uncertain that revenues could be made equal to its expenditures" so the offer was refused. Private capital then furnished the necessary funds and a company was organized. By 1851 fifty companies using Morse telegraph patents were in operation in the United States. His system was adopted throughout Europe, and every European Government honored him with decoration; and finally, through the influence of Napoleon III presented him, as an international gift, in honor of his work, $20,000.

No. 124   General Douglas MacArthur Bottle

No record concerning Professor Morse or the telegraph, in glassware, came to my attention until recent times.

In 1942, a bottle honoring General Douglas MacArthur was made. A portrait of the General ornaments the obverse. Above the portrait "General MacArthur" is inscribed. Below it is a popular wartime slogan "Keep Them Flying." The reverse shows a large letter V and the date 1942. An American flag is flying on either side of this letter. Above, is the inscription "God Bless America" and below, three dots and a dash are placed. These, in telegraphic code, represent the letter V. At that time, "V for Victory" was another wartime slogan in constant use.

While this recognition is indirect, it is, nevertheless, very real. A complete understanding of the mold makers message cannot be realized without knowledge of the work of Professor Morse and the telegraphic Morse code. Capacity: half-pint. Colors: aqua, amethyst, green.

The Atlantic Cable

In simple words, the Atlantic cable was a telegraph line laid on the floor of the ocean instead of on land. There were some differences in the details of construction to be made because the line was placed in water; and there were great difficulties to be overcome in laying this cable in deep water. For some time the subject had been discussed by men of science, but Cyrus W. Field was the first to do something about it.

He formed a company, talked things over with men in England and in 1856 the Atlantic Telegraph Company was

149

No. 125
CABLE PATTERN SPOON-HOLDER

No. 126   CABLE PLATE

organized by them in Great Britain. A government grant of 14,000 pounds for government messages was secured in England, and similar grants were made by the United States Government.

Unsuccessful attempts to lay the cable were made in August, 1857 and again in June, 1858. The complete cable was laid between July 7 and August 5, 1858; but in October the cable became useless, owing to the failure of its electrical insulation.

The "lion-hearted" Cyrus Field did not quit. Guided by his genius, the association composed of leading British and American men continued their tests and trials of improved machinery and cables, and availed themselves of every resource of science. They found what errors had been made in the past and what should be done to win success in the future.

The year 1866 was fixed upon for another effort and the ship "Great Eastern" selected for the purpose. Before the departure from Ireland, a devotional meeting was held, participated in by the company, the officers, and hands, at which the enterprise was solemnly commended to the favor of God.

The cable, 2,000 miles long, was safely stretched across the ocean from Ireland to Newfoundland, and communication proved successful. Messages were immediately exchanged between the Queen of England and the President of the United States; and word of the successful working of the cable soon spread to all the people.

No. 125   Cable Pattern Spoon-Holder

A pattern of glassware was produced to commemorate the laying of the Atlantic Cable. It was made in the usual forms which were popular at the time. The design is simple, consisting of wide panels between which are narrow decorations intended to represent cable. Size: six inches high, base three inches in diameter. Colors: clear glass, a few pieces were made in color.

No. 126   Cable Plate

"Beauty in the commonplace" is an old and trite saying. In this plate we find a demonstration of that fact. The designer fashioned two five-pointed stars, from cable, and intertwined them. Straight lines of varying lengths completed the design. The effect is one of simple elegance. Size: nine and three-fourths inches in diameter. Color: crystal.

No. 127   Mail Box Bottle

A quart bottle made in the shape of a mail box furnishes a measure of uncertainty as to meaning. An inscription "Patented Ent. Dec. 15, 1891" gives information about the time of production but affords no clue concerning why.

In 1691, (according to Funk & Wagnalls) the first official system for transporting mail began. At that time, Thomas Neale was given the privilege of carrying all letters throughout the American Colonies.

In 1791, the Post Office Department (an outgrowth of the Office of Postmaster-General created in 1789) was attached to the Treasury Department as a bureau. The Postmaster-General was not a member of the President's Cabinet until 1829 under President Jackson.

In 1891, the mail box bottle was produced. Whether it was designed as a centennial item, or a bi-centennial item, or both, or neither, is a subject for discussion.

The only design on obverse and reverse of this bottle is a plain rectangular panel. On each end is the inscription "U. S. Mail" and an eagle shown in flight. Color: crystal.

THE COVERED WAGON

The covered wagon was a symbol of migration. From 1788, when General Rufus Putnam (Father of the Northwest) led the colony from Massachusetts which made the first settlement in the Territory of the Northwest at Marietta, Ohio, until emigration was completed to the Pacific Coast more than 100 years later, these slow-moving transports carried owners and freight from the safety and security of the known, to face drama, tragedy, and romance in new frontiers.

The fertility of the soil and genial nature of the climate appealed to those whose pride lay in the possession of land; the summer range for grazing and winter forage of prairie hay made the western country appealing to the raiser of stock; increasing values of property attracted the speculator; the politician anticipated the time when through the ballot-box the West should rule; the young professional man saw a less occupied field of action; and the philanthropist felt a benevolent anxiety for the intellectual, moral, and religious condition of all the people.

Families of all classes removed with large covered wagons; carried and cooked their own provisions and camped out at night. A typical wagon of this period presented a curious and somewhat awkward appearance. Covered over with white sheeting, the front and rear bows were set at an angle of forty-five degrees to the bed of the wagon. The enormous amount of freight that could be stowed away in one of these caverns was astonishing: women, children, beds, buckets, tubs, old-fashioned chairs, and all sorts of household furniture usually used by our log-cabin ancestors. A chicken-coop with a few hens and a jolly rooster, for a start, was tied on behind while, under the wagon, trotted at least one long-eared hound dog, fastened by a short rope to the hind axle.

Fancy one of these wagons on the road; oxen or horses to furnish motive power, probably someone on horseback

No. 127 Mail Box Bottle

No. 128 Covered Wagon Covered Dish

154

plodding along in the rear of the wagon driving a cow and a sow; while others walked ahead with rifles on their shoulders, on the lookout for squirrels, turkey, deer, or Indians. The fear of breaking down was ever present and also danger of being lost on the enormous prairies, but danger of being lost on the enormous prairies too, but hardship, difficulty, and self-denial meant little to the pioneer. He had learned how to banish unreal wants and how to provide for the real. Patience and courage were required of those who trekked to the "land of opportunity" via the covered wagon route.

No. 128   Covered Wagon Covered Dish

The appearance of a "movers" wagon is well presented in this glass dish shaped like the historic vehicle. The wagon cover extends well beyond the wagon bed in front and in rear. The back bow stands slightly higher than the front; the wheels have broad rims and the rear ones are noticeably larger than those in front.

This item offers a challenge to collectors for very few are known to exist.

Size: extreme length, six inches; width, three inches; height, five inches. Color: crystal.

Note: Some covered wagons are pictured with the back bow higher than the front. In others, the front bow stands higher than the rear. The lid of this dish fits in either position but is better as pictured.

The Stage-Coach

This large four-wheeled vehicle, usually with a roomy box swung on straps or springs, and provided with seats within and often on top, was drawn by two to eight horses. Because of its construction, it kept up a continual rocking motion like a ship in a storm. Baggage and mail were stored in a large boot at the back of the stage. This was the principal means of transportation in the

155

East, and also in the early West after the covered wagon went and before the railroad came.

It took six days for a stage-coach to travel from Boston to New York, and three days from New York to Philadelphia. In 1766 the trip between New York and Philadelphia was made in two days. This time was considered so wonderful that the vehicles were called "flying machines."

In 1858, a stage-coach mail route was established between St. Louis, Mo., and San Francisco, Calif. This was a 2,795 mile route. Travel was difficult and dangerous. Drivers were chosen for their ability, courage, and loyalty; and from 700 to 800 were required to man the 100 coaches in use. It required an average of 1500 horses and mules to furnish motive power. The scheduled time for this route was twenty-five days. Breakdowns, bandits, or Indian attacks might cause delay. Good weather, good roads, and good luck often shortened the time by a matter of hours.

The stage driver was highly respected. His swagger, and his ability in handling lines and whip was the envy of small boys. A tavern usually was the stage depot and the arrival of the stage "in clouds of dust and glory" was a great attraction.

No. 129   Stage-Coach Covered Dish

The milk-glass stage-coach is a worthy model of the oldtime vehicle. Coach body, springs, wheels, boot, and driver's seat have been given careful attention. Like the covered wagon, it is notable for its scarcity. Size: five inches long, two inches wide, four and one-half inches high.

Steamboats

The people did not like their means of transportation. It was slow, and it was uncomfortable. They believed something better than the covered wagon and stage-coach could be had, and they thought something better than oars and sails could be provided for water transportation.

No. 129   STAGE-COACH COVERED DISH

After the steam engine had been invented in England, men in France, Scotland, and America tried to build boats that would go by steam. An American, Robert Fulton, built the first steamboat that was really successful. This was in 1807. Steamboats soon served for commerce and travel, and aided greatly in the more rapid development of the country.

No. 130   The Chancellor Livingston Cup-Plate

A noted steamboat was christened the Chancellor Livingston. This was the name by which Robert R. Livingston was generally known. This American statesman had a distinguished record. He helped draft the Declaration of Independence. He was the first Chancellor of the State of New York and in this capacity administered the oath of office to George Washington at his inauguration in 1789. He served as minister to France, and with James Monroe represented the United States in the purchase of the Louisiana Territory. In 1804 he withdrew from public life but retained his interest in public improvements. He met Robert Fulton and was associated with the inventor in developing the first successful steamboat which was named after Livingston's home, Clermont.

The Chancellor Livingston carried sails, so that possible engine failure would not prove disastrous during her voyages between New York and Providence. This custom was continued until 1834.

A cup-plate commemorating this vessel is identified as "lacy Sandwich" and is three and one-half inches in diameter. It was made in clear glass and in some colors.

Canals

Steamboats were a great help to the people in their search for better ways, but they were limited to travel on rivers and lakes. There was need for some connection between the various waterways. Canals had been developed in Europe, so were thought of as connecting links. Many canals have been built and served the country well.

No. 130   CHANCELLOR LIVINGSTON CUP-PLATE

No. 131   GATUN LOCKS WINE GLASS

No. 132   SUCCESS TO THE RAILROAD FLASK

159

The most important of all canals built by the United States is the Panama Canal, connecting the Atlantic and Pacific Oceans through the Isthmus of Panama. Its length from shore line to shore line is about forty miles, and from deep water to deep water about fifty miles.

The canal is elevated above sea level and provided with locks. These locks are "double-barreled" so that ships may proceed in opposite directions simultaneously.

Gatun Locks are the first encountered on the Atlantic side of the canal, and Gatun Locks are pictured on a wine glass. The event commemorated (the building of the Panama Canal) is one of the most important in our country's history.

Preliminary preparations occupied about three years. The thorough sanitation of the Canal Zone was accomplished, yellow fever banished, an operating plant assembled, railways modernized, a working force gathered, living quarters erected, and a food and water supply provided. Actual work of construction then proceeded and was accomplished in about seven more years.

Gatun Locks, as pictured, appears to be a huge dam built of concrete and reinforcing materials, and is shown as it must have looked before being flooded. Size: three and three-fourths inches high, and two inches in width at the top. Color: crystal.

NOTE: This wine glass is not an important looking piece of glassware, and might be rejected by many collectors. However, no one would suggest that the pictures in our homes be confined to rare old masters. No one would wish to limit our books to rare first editions.

Likewise, no one should expect all the glass which we cherish to be rarities of classical beauty. To do so would be to banish true value from places where it should find a warm welcome and add to the joy of wholesome living.

Steamboats and canals brought great changes and improvements, but they were not enough. All over the country there were many communities detached from each other. Machinery, iron products and textiles were made in the Atlantic states but needed in the West, too. Western farms produced grain and food supplies needed in the East. The South had cotton to sell in the North, and needed supplies made in the North. There must be some way to create machinery for interchange, united under one flag. The railroads were developed. They pressed through the wilderness, crossed rivers and mountains, joined seacoast with interior, and the whole course of civilization was changed.

No. 132   SUCCESS TO THE RAILROAD FLASK

The earliest railroads were little cars on iron rails, drawn by horses. They were used to haul coal and stone for short distances. Even the first passenger cars were drawn by horses.

A pint flask commemorates this era. The obverse displays a loaded, horsedrawn cart on rails, and the inscription "Success to the Railroad." This seems to be a toast to the newer and better kind of transportation. The reverse is similar to the obverse. Color: olive green. It was made in other colors also.

NOTE: This flask has been reproduced.

No. 133   PASSENGER TRAIN TUMBLER

A panel on this tumbler pictures an early steam passenger train. The cars seem little more than stage-coaches on rails, while the engine appears anything but trustworthy. It commemorates an early phase of an intercommunication system so vast and comprehensive that it seems impossible for the understanding to really measure its importance in developing the country.

The remainder of the tumbler is decorated with a scroll-like design. It is very heavy. Size: three and one-half inches high, three inches in diameter at top. Color: dull green.

No. 134   Railroad Train Platter

The Union Pacific was the first transcontinental railroad to be completed. It was incorporated in 1862 under an Act of Congress providing for the construction of railroads from the Missouri River to the Pacific Ocean, as a war measure and for the preservation of the Union. It was believed that unless railroad and telegraph connected the two coasts, the Pacific States could not be held in the Union.

Construction proceeded west from Kansas City and Council Bluffs, by way of Denver; and proceeded eastward from San Francisco. The two parts met at a point 53 miles west of Ogden where they were united May 10, 1869.

The Railroad Train platter commemorates the opening of the Union Pacific Railroad and shows the famous engine No. 350. It is twelve inches long and nine inches wide. Color: crystal.

No. 135   Currier & Ives Pattern Tray

In this tray, we find the railroad subject presented with a sense of humor. It was not so unusual in those days for a horse or mule to become stubborn and refuse to go on. Such an animal was termed "balky." A balky mule hitched to a two-wheeled cart, has chosen the railroad track as a convenient place to make his stand. The negro driver and his companion brandish large umbrellas in their frantic desire to move on, out of the path of an approaching train. Two pickaninnies in the back of the cart seem undecided whether to keep their places or jump. The mule looks quite decided about standing just where he is. This

162

No. 133   Panel from Passenger Train Tumbler

No. 134   Railroad Train Platter

163

scene has a landscape background. It is believed to have been taken from a print by Currier & Ives. Size: nine and one-half inches in diameter. The same scene is found on a tray of larger size. Color: crystal. Made also in yellow.

No. 136   NELLIE BLY PLATTER

When the New York World sent Nellie Bly (Elizabeth Cochrane) from New York, November 14, 1889, to beat a fictitious record set by Jules Verne's story "Around the World in Eighty Days" she reached San Francisco January 21st. The Santa Fe Railroad carried her to Chicago in 69 hours. The run from Chicago to New York was slow. Even so, she arrived 72 days, 6 hours, 11 minutes out, on the 25th.

This was an amazing show of speed for the years 1889-90. It made people realize how far transportation had advanced during the preceding fifty-odd years.

A platter was produced in commemoration. A full length picture of the heroine, in her traveling outfit, occupies the center. The name "Nellie Bly" is inscribed below. Above is: "Around the World in 72 D's, 6 H's, 11 M's." Other inscription reads: "New York, Nov. 14, '89; Southampton Nov. 22; Brindisi Nov. 24; Suez Nov. 27; Colombo Dec. 8; Singapore Dec. 18; Hong Kong Dec. 23; Yokohama Dec. 28; San Francisco Jan. 21, '90; Chicago Jan. 24; Pittsburgh Jan. 25; New York Jan. 25."

Size: twelve and three-fourths inches long, six and three-fourths inches wide. Color: crystal.

No. 135   CURRIER & IVES PATTERN TRAY

No. 136   NELLIE BLY PLATTER

165

No. 137   THE OCTOPUS BOTTLE

The story of the railroads is not all of great and happy evolution. One of the bitter chapters was written in the State of California where financial trouble developed between the ranchmen and the railroads.

In 1901 Frank Norris published a book, "The Octopus," a novel that dealt with the war between the wheat grower and the Railroad Trust.

A small bottle refers to this subject. It has the shape of a large American dollar. An eight-armed octopus has secured a strangle-hold on the coin. On the obverse the head of Liberty is shown with her mouth open as though screaming with pain. The reverse shows the American eagle under which the date 1901 is molded in the glass.

The octopus figuratively represents the organized power of the many-armed railroads and their far-reaching capacity for harm to the financial welfare of the producer.

Capacity: four ounces. Color: milk-white glass originally decorated with gold and red, the coin being gold and the octopus red.

No. 138   RAILROAD ENGINE

This covered container has the form of an outmoded railroad engine. Size: six inches long, three inches wide, and the extreme height is four and one-half inches. Color: green. Probably made in other colors.

No. 139   RAILROAD GONDOLA

An open dish made in the form of a railroad gondola. It shows two inscriptions on each side of the car: "Capacity 50,000 lbs. No. 2353." "No. 2353, Wt. 18,000." Size: eight inches long, six inches wide, two and one-half inches high. Colors: clear, blue, amber.

No. 140   THE PULLMAN "AMERICA"

In 1892-3 an ideal passenger train was exhibited at the Chicago World's Fair, by the Pullman Company.

No. 137
THE OCTOPUS BOTTLE
OBVERSE

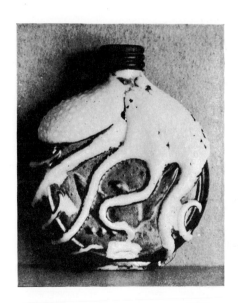

No. 137
THE OCTOPUS BOTTLE
REVERSE

No. 138   Railroad Engine

No. 139   Railroad Gondola

It included eight cars, each having a name suggestive of some incident in the career of Columbus.

At the head stood a large locomotive. The smoking car was named the "Marchena," the observation car was "Isabella," the mail car was "U. S. Railway Post-Office," the dining car was "La Rabida," day coach was "1893," parlor car was "Santa Maria," compartment sleeping car was "Ferdinand," and the standard Pullman sleeper was "America."

A covered dish having the appearance of a Pullman sleeping car is inscribed "150 America 150" and may have some association with this Pullman exhibit. Size: nine and one-half inches long, four inches wide, and four inches high. Color: crystal.

No. 141 Automobile Roadster

The search for better ways, in transportation, continued. Many men, in different places, were working on the problem of self-propelled vehicles that could run on ordinary roads. It is difficult to give definite names and dates for events in the progress of this development; for the motor car is not the product of a single invention or year. The effect of the automobile, however, was profound. It revolutionized the lives of the people so that distance became thought of in terms of minutes rather than in miles.

A glassware novelty represents an early type of roadster, with the top laid back. Size: five inches long, two and one-half inches wide, and two and three-fourths inches high. Color: crystal.

No. 142 Automobile Sedan

This container for small candy is made in the form of a closed car, a four door sedan. Size: four and one-fourth inches long, one and one-half inches wide, two and one-fourth inches high: Color: crystal.

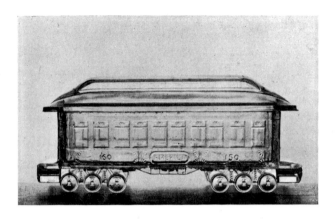

No. 140   The Pullman "America"

No. 141   Automobile Roadster *(left)*
No. 142   Automobile Sedan *(right)*

Conquest of the air was the next step in the development of transportation. No other means of transport receives so much attention from the public and from experts as the aeroplane. The aim has been, and is, to establish air transport of passengers, freight, and the mails, upon a self-supporting commercial basis. Trans-continental and trans-oceanic flights have aroused eager interest. The flights of Charles Lindbergh were received with greatest enthusiasm. In May, 1927, in the plane "Spirit of St. Louis" he flew from San Diego to New York to Paris. This was in competition for the $25,000 prize offered by Raymond B. Ortig for a New York to Paris non-stop flight. This flight claimed world-wide attention.

Upon invitation from President Calles of Mexico he made a non-stop flight from Washington, D. C., to Mexico City, in December of the same year. The "Good Will" mission, as it was called, continued, to include the countries of Central America, northern South America, and the West Indies. He visited sixteen countries and flew 7,860 miles.

No. 143   Lindbergh Candy Container

A candy container is fashioned in the shape of an aeroplane and includes the head and shoulders of a man, intended to represent Charles Lindbergh. The body of the plane carries an inscription: "Spirit of Good Will." Size: five inches long, three and three-fourths inches wide, two and three-fourths inches high. Color: crystal.

No. 143   CHARLES LINDBERGH CANDY CONTAINER

No. 144
THE CASH REGISTER

The effect of improved transportation has been to create better conditions of living, increase economic activity, stimulate wider intellectual interest, and raise the standards of living to the highest point ever achieved by any people at any time.

The change has not been entirely advantageous, and it remains for man to adjust to the changed order of things and successfully meet the social problems that have arisen.

No. 144   The Cash Register Candy Container

The search for better ways has been so continuous and so prolonged that it is sometimes referred to as "an American custom."

In 1879, James Ritty, of Ohio, invented the first cash register. For business establishments, it supplies a record of sales, makes the giving of change speedy and accurate, and prevents loss due to dishonesty.

A novelty container for candy is made in the form of a cash register. It is inscribed "Cash Register" and "Patd. Appd. For." Size: base is three by one and one-half inches; height is two and three-fourths inches. Color: crystal.

Better Firearms

When Eli Whitney became convinced he never could obtain just recognition and the compensation due him from his invention of the cotton gin, he decided on a new enterprise.

He decided to manufacture firearms, and undertook the production of muskets for the United States Army. His contract called for ten thousand arms to be delivered within a period of about twenty months. His workers must do what had never before been tried in this or in any other country. Whitney designed machines and tools. He tested woods, metals, alloys.

173

When work was well under way he found his greatest difficulty lay in the poor quality of his workmen. In order to overcome this handicap he separated the various tasks necessary in making a musket. Then he simplified each of these operations as much as was possible, and kept individuals and groups working, each at some special and simplified unit of work.

When parts produced in this manner were assembled, the finished muskets were superior to those produced by any previous method. An advantage was apparent too, in case of repair. A new part could exactly replace an old one, and at low cost. This, in 1798, was the beginning of mass production, and mass production made production of better firearms a possibility and a reality.

Glassware offers several representations of firearms.

No. 145   Pistol Bottle

A dueling pistol seems to have been used as a container for some fluid, probably liquor. Metal parts are represented in clear glass, and wooden parts are shown in frosted finish. It is almost ten inches long.

No. 146   Revolver Bottle

This represents a type of revolver in common use during the latter part of the nineteenth century. Containers of this sort were used for liquor and also to hold small candy. It is crystal glass, eight inches in length.

No. 147   Cannon Covered Dish

The lid of this novelty container displays a cannon and its accompanying bunch of "grape," a type characteristic of the Civil War period although the item may have been made at a later time. The base represents a snare drum. It is of milk-white glass, four and one-fourth inches in diameter.

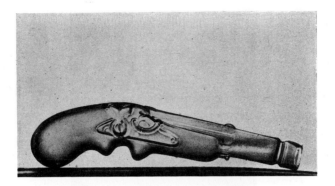

No. 145   Pistol Bottle

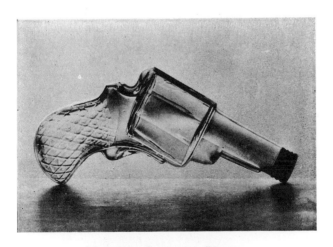

No. 146   Revolver Bottle

175

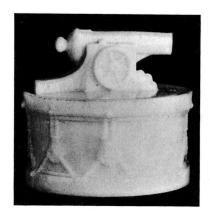

No. 147
CANNON COVERED DISH

No. 148
CIVIL WAR TUMBLER

176

No. 148   Civil War Tumbler

A tall beverage glass, with Civil War ordnance decoration, prominently displays a cannon, with its "grape" ready for use. "Grape" was a term commonly used for a stack of cannon-balls, since they bore some resemblance to a bunch of grapes. A trench mortar is shown too, with its large ball near by. The mortar is a short piece of ordnance used for firing large-calibre shells, at great angles of elevation. A flag flies from a staff in the background.

On the reverse, an American eagle with a shield on its breast, holds an unfurled flag in one talon and a long sword in the other. There are 34 stars in the flag.

On each side of the tumbler, a liberty pole bearing the traditional liberty cap, extends from top to bottom.

This is an unusually well-made piece. It has a good bell tone, and the designs are skilfully executed. It is crystal glass, four and three-fourths inches high. Diameter at the top is three and one-fourth inches.

Other Firearms

The emblem sugar-bowl, chapter III, shows cannon and shell of Spanish-American War days; and the Volunteer plate, chapter IV, shows muskets and cannon of the Mexican War era.

Better Things for Better Homes

It was not until about 1827 that manufacturers began to experiment with a new method of making glassware: the pressing or molding process. In 1828 Deming Jarves was granted a patent in connection with this method. Pressed glassware superseded the blown after 1830 and the method was well perfected by 1835.

Machine-made pressed glassware made articles cost so much less that more people could afford to buy more of them. This made it necessary to employ more people to handle the machines that made glass articles cost less, so glass manufacture became a rapidly expanding and important business. Then, as now, necessity was the mother of invention, and it was necessary for all glass companies to meet this competition. Factories for making pressed glassware sprang up like mushrooms. At first, the more essential articles of tableware only, were made. But as the population increased and financial matters improved, there was a general rise in refinement and in the furnishings of homes. There came to be a demand for things formerly considered luxuries. The fruit of the American plan of LIBERTY AND FREEDOM for every man was beginning to mature in the shape of mass production industries that made the good things of life circulate among all the people. Never before had the cupboards of the average family been able to boast of goblets, pitchers, creamers, spoon-holders, sauce-dishes, compotes, sugar-bowls, relish dishes, plates and platters, and other forms of glassware in anything approaching such bounty. And these things were satisfying too, both in quality and beauty of form.

The pride of the people in their possession of this attractive glassware was but the forerunner of the pride of the people in their possession of good automobiles and radios. This pride of possession led to a desire for more glassware, for decorative glassware, a type that glass houses had not been able to produce by means of the blowing process.

To meet this demand, mold makers were called on for new ideas; new ideas in both decorative treatment and in new forms for tableware, and for novelties.

The Home in Glassware

The home was a fruitful source of inspiration for items that combined utility with novelty. Familiar things within the house, the kitchen stove and the coal bucket, the skillet and flat iron, the dustpan, the rolling-pin, the iron pot, the washtubs and washboard, were copied in glass. A chest of drawers, chair, couch, the family Bible, the

178

parlor album, cradle, trunk, and bathtub, served as patterns.

Personal possessions, too, were used. The fan, the parasol, hat, slippers, corset, satchel, thimble, hairbrush and whisk-broom, were created in glass miniature forms. Objects outside the home were utilized, too. The wagon, the sleigh, and wheelbarrow, the pump and log watering trough, saddle and horseshoe, anvil, lantern, bucket, bushel baskets, and other familiar things had a secondary use as models.

As a group, these suggest something of the rise of refinements in household furnishings and utensils, and show how something new, regarded as a luxury, soon becomes commonplace and accepted as a necessity.

This is especially true of the kitchen stove. At an early time the fireplace with its Dutch oven and other utensils was the only available source of heat for cooking. One pioneer who knew this way, told me how biscuits were made in the Dutch oven, and how they were kept warm by placing them between feather beds until enough had been made for all, when company came. Another pioneer related how excited her family was when they secured their first cook-stove. Her father drove to a city more than 150 miles away and brought the precious thing back with him. It was called the "Jenny Lind." People came to see it "from far and near" for no one else in those parts had one. They looked it over and talked it over and said how different kinds of pans and things would have to be made to use in the new-fangled oven. Utensils they had for fireplace cooking would not do for the stove.

That a luxury is soon accepted as a necessity is shown as well in the case of the bathtub. The bathtub is very much an American innovation, for the extent of the bathtub vogue in America is not shared by any other nation. Of the world's approximately twenty-four million bathtubs, considerably more than twenty-one million are in use in the United States of America.

These glassware objects had a variety of uses. Some served a general, or some special purpose of table utility. Others were suited to parlor purpose, a whimsy for the what-not, an ink pot, match holder, pin or card tray, or purely as decoration. Today they are sought for as eagerly as when first made. They may now serve the purpose for which originally intended, or as holders for candy, nuts, and flowers; or as before, purely decorative usage. They serve, too, as a reminder that nowhere in the world has the home of the average man held so much of material comfort, so much to provide for necessity and fulfill desire, as in the American home.

No. 149   Kitchen Stove

A covered dish shaped like an old-fashioned kitchen stove has a cover finial in the form of an iron. This is a highly decorative item and as popular as it is decorative. It is six and three-fourths inches long, four and one-half inches wide, and four and one-half inches high. The one shown is crystal glass, but several colors were made.

Nos. 150-151   Pump and Trough

Companion pieces represent a pioneer type of pump and log watering trough. Just what purpose they were designed to serve is not clear at this time, although a number of uses may readily be found. They are interesting and justify their present popularity.

The pump is seven inches high, and two inches wide at the top. The trough is five inches long, two and one-half inches across, and two and one-fourth inches high. The ones pictured are of clear glass, dotted with small hobnails. Rims of both items are opalescent. They were made in several other colors. Reproductions have been made.

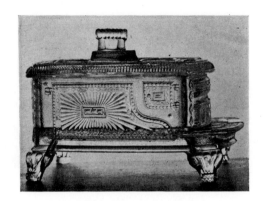

No. 149   Kitchen Stove

No. 150   Pump
No. 151   Log Watering Trough

No. 152 THIMBLE
No. 153 CRADLE
No. 154 CUSPIDOR

No. 155 IRON KETTLE
No. 156 LANTERN
No. 157 CHAIR (INKWELL) WITH CAT ON CUSHION LID

No. 152   Thimble

The thimble pictured was intended, it seems, for a liquor glass. It is shaped like a thimble, and carries the inscription: "Just a Thimbleful." At one time this was the correct reply to make when asked to "have a little drink." Capacity: one ounce, although it was made in at least one other size. Color: crystal.

No. 153   Cradle

The rock-a-bye-baby appeal of this item must have made it a happy choice for the what-not, although it might well have been used to hold table salt too. It is two and one-half inches long, two and one-half inches wide, and two inches high. The one pictured is a beautiful blue color.

No. 154   Cuspidor

Quite some time ago, the cuspidor was a standard piece of household furnishing. It appears in glass, in miniature form, being two and three-fourths inches in diameter, and one and five-eighths inches high. The one shown is blue.

No. 155   Iron Kettle

A glass replica of the old time iron kettle having three small feet was used for various household purposes. This one served as a toothpick holder. It is two and one-half inches in diameter, and two and one-fourth inches in height. Color: crystal.

No. 156   Lantern

This lantern represents the kind used by country folk and others who had need for an out-of-doors light. It is quite different from the ones used by the railroads. The base is removable, and the item was a container for small candy. Color: crystal. It is five and three-fourths inches high, and three inches wide.

No. 157   Chair

An inkwell is concealed in this chair, made in the Daisy and Button pattern. There are three separate pieces: the chair, the ink pot, and a cover for the inkwell. This cover represents a cat sitting on a chair cushion. It is four and one-half inches high, two and one-half inches wide at the front. It was made in crystal, and in several colors.

No. 158   Basket

This basket is a faithful representation of a woven farm basket which held the standard bushel. Two stout handles were provided. These were not for ornamental purposes either, since a bushel basket filled with corn or fruit weighs about sixty pounds. The glass basket is provided with a cover. It holds seven fluid ounces. The one pictured is green in color. It was made in crystal, too, in opaque white and in opaque blue.

No. 159   Dustpan

This is a replica of an instrument resembling a short handled shovel into which dust was (and is) swept. It measures three and three-fourths inches in height and three and three-fourths inches in width. Color: light amber.

No. 160   Washboard

This represents a frame containing corrugated metal upon which wet clothes were rubbed when washing by hand. The crystal glass miniature is four inches long and two inches wide.

No. 161   Washtub and Washboard

In this item the tub and board are made in one piece. Several articles of clothing are molded in the glass inside the tub. Handkerchief, socks, collar, a "fine" shirt, knitted long underwear, and a cake of soap are represented. It

No. 158   BUSHEL BASKET
No. 159   DUSTPAN
No. 160   WASHBOARD

No. 161   WASHTUB AND WASHBOARD
No. 162   WASHTUB
No. 163   CART

is crystal glass, four and three-fourths inches in diameter, and two inches high.

No. 162   Washtub

Another crystal tub is shown without a washboard. High wooden handles are a distinctive touch. It is four inches in diameter and two and three-fourths inches high to top of handles. (See also No. 166)

No. 163   Cart

A small wagon, or farm cart, is represented here. It is three and three-fourths inches long, one and seven-eighths inches wide, and two inches high. Color: crystal.

No. 164   Wheelbarrow

A wheelbarrow, the type made of wood, with removable sides, is represented here. The sides are decorated with the Barley pattern. On the base, "Pat. Apl'd. For" is inscribed. Axle and wheel are metal. It is eight inches long, four inches wide, and two and three-fourths inches high. Color: crystal.

No. 165   Chest of Drawers

The appearance of an old time article of furniture (perhaps a butler's desk) is well presented in this crystal glass item. Wear marks on the bottom suggest it may have been used as a spoonholder. It is four and one-fourth inches high, three and one-fourth inches wide, and two inches in depth.

No. 166   Bathtub

The first American bathtubs were improvised from common round wooden tubs, used in washing clothes and illustrated in No. 162.

No. 164   Wheelbarrow

No. 165   Chest of Drawers
No. 166   Bathtub

The type of bathtub represented here came into popularity only after plumbing and sewers came into general use. It was about 1872 that the first iron bathtub covered with enamel was manufactured. Such a bathtub is represented by a glass novelty shaped like the old fashioned tub, resting on four feet. It is five and one-fourth inches long, two and one-half inches wide, and two and one-eighth inches high. The one pictured is a deep green but other colors were made.

No. 167   Rolling-Pin

A rolling-pin was much used in former times, by cartoonists and comic strip artists, as a weapon in the hands of woman. It came to represent more than an article used in the kitchen. The blown glass ones, which represented real ones, were used for ornamental purposes. A ribbon or cord was tied to the ends of a rolling-pin so that it might be hung on a wall. They were made in various sizes and colors, including amethyst. The one pictured is blue, and is smaller than most. It is ten inches long, and one and one-half inches in diameter.

No. 168   Iron on Trivet

A covered dish represents a flat iron resting on a three-legged stand, or trivet. Since it is both decorative and useful, it has become a choice collectors item. Size: nine inches long, five inches wide, and four inches high to top of handle. It may be found in several choice colors. The one pictured is blue.

No. 169   Satchel

A crystal candy container represents an old time leather satchel. It is a faithful reproduction. The surface is finely stippled. Metal parts and leather straps are clear. One end carries the inscription: "Pat. Appld. For." It is four inches long, two inches wide, and four inches high to top of metal handle.

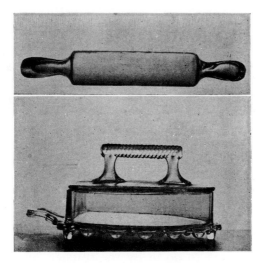

No. 167   Rolling-Pin
No. 168   Iron on Trivet

No. 169   Satchel
No. 170   Wooden Pail

No. 170   Wooden Pail

At one time, the pail was a household necessity. No kitchen could be without one. Cedar wood was commonly used and the staves were held together by brass hoops. A metal handle, or bail, was securely attached. An empty pail was carried to a spring, probably some distance from the house, or to a well where it often was filled by means of "the old oaken bucket." A dipper, many times made from a gourd, was a companion item.

The wooden pail was an essential of rural schoolhouse equipment too, usually placed on a shelf or a bench at the back of the schoolroom. Many school grounds had no well, and water must be carried from the nearest farm house. In such cases a pail of fresh water brought by older pupils, appointed to do so by the teacher, was most welcome. The pail was passed around and all drank from the same dipper.

In glassware, a cream pitcher has the essential form of a wooden pail, with pouring spout and a handle added. Several other forms were made too, in which a pail provided the basic idea. Size: four and one-half inches high, three inches in diameter at base. Color: blue. Clear, amber, vaseline, and amethyst colors are all to be found in wooden-pail glassware.

No. 171   Parasol

A light weight sunshade has always been popular with the ladies. Highly decorative parasols are treasured above others. Glassmakers created a novelty representing a lace parasol of the late nineteenth century, which might serve to ornament the parlor what-not, or be used on a hanging-lamp to hold matches. The one illustrated represents a parasol partly opened and is made in the Daisy and Button pattern. It has a metal handle, six and one-half inches long. The parasol is three and one-fourth inches in

No. 171   Parasol

No. 172   Folding Fan

diameter. Color: amber. It was made in clear glass and in some other colors.

No. 172   Folding Fan

Fans, too, always have been popular feminine accessories. Several types are represented in glassware. A folding fan, spread out, Daisy and Button pattern, is large enough to serve as a utility dish for table use. The "stick" of the fan is seven inches long, and the "spread" is ten and three-fourths inches. This fan has been reproduced in clear glass and in several colors.

No. 173   Iron Skillet

One can hardly think of an old-fashioned deep skillet of iron, without thinking of fried chicken and gravy, fried potatoes, fried mush and maple syrup, fried ham and eggs, fried doughnuts, and pancakes.

A glassware version of the skillet is attractive and realistic. It is small enough to be "cute" and large enough to be useful. An all-over pattern decorates the bottom of the dish and the short handle. The side is ribbed, and has two pouring spouts. It rests on three small feet. Size: six inches in diameter; one and one-half inches deep. Color: crystal.

No. 174   Palm Leaf Fan

The palm leaf fan was made from the dried leaf of the palm or palmetto. It was plain and tough, it was durable, and it was cheap. These virtues made it a favorite fan for general use.

The glassware palm leaf fan is considerably dressed-up. It has a dewdrop border. Stippled floral sprays ornament a large part of the surface. A curved band, showing small dewdrops and a stippled, conventional pattern, adds to the decorative effect. The surface of the dish is curved.

No. 173   Skillet

No. 174   Palm Leaf Fan
No. 175   Whisk-Broom

193

Three small feet serve as flower centers and insure stability. Size: six inches in diameter, three-fourths of an inch in depth. Color: crystal.

No. 175 Whisk-Broom

A small, short handled broom was (and is) used to "whisk" dust from clothing and other cloth surfaces. The glassware whisk-broom is a dressed-up example because of the Daisy and Button pattern used on the upper part. An inscription on the handle reads: "Pat. Apld. For." Size: seven and one-half inches long, five inches wide, and one inch deep. Color: amber.

No. 176 Coal Hod

A very commonplace article of household equipment was lifted from its state of humble service when glassmakers produced a miniature form of the coal hod. In its natural state, the coal bucket is always dirty. In a glass representation, it is lily white. Other types are found too, in crystal glass and in colors, and in various shapes and patterns.

The one pictured is of milk-white glass, and is four inches high to top of the metal handle. It may serve to hold toothpicks, matches, cigarettes, flowers, nuts, or candy.

No. 177 Bushel Basket with Chicks on Lid

This basket is identical in form and size with No. 158, but a story told by the lid sets it apart. This basket, filled with straw, must have been chosen by a broody hen for a nesting place. The background of the lid represents straw. Ten eggs are clustered thereon. Chicks are emerging from five of these while two others show definite cracks, forecasting future activity. This basket comes in milk-white glass.

No. 176   Coal Hod
No. 177   Bushel Basket with Chicks on Lid
No. 178   Parlor Album

No. 179   Corset
No. 180   Couch

No. 181   Trunk

No. 178 Parlor Album

The family album was second in importance to the family Bible, only. Most albums were made to hold what was known as the "cabinet photograph" being four and one-fourth by six and one-half inches in size. Photograph albums were popular Christmas gifts for mother, and when filled with pictures of the family and friends, became highly prized possessions.

The glassware album represents a photograph album of the cabinet type, with front and back covers firmly held in place by a metal clasp. The base measures one and one-fourth by two and one-fourth inches. It is three inches high. The top is open so it may conveniently hold matches, cigarettes, or other small articles. It is of milk-white glass, but has a decided bluish tinge.

No. 179 Corset

The heavily boned and tightly laced Victorian corset, like the rolling-pin, was a subject of much jesting. It is not surprising to find it presented in glass. Perhaps it could be used for matches, or toothpicks, or salt, but no doubt it more often found rest as a novelty on some parlor what-not.

It is three inches in height, and the base is two and one-half inches in diameter. Made of milk-white glass, decorated with gold, and with green and red floral sprays.

No. 180 Couch

A small covered dish is made in the form of a couch. This couch was a successor of the earlier day-bed, and a fore-runner of the modern davenport. It is made of milk-white glass, with top colored green and the sides brown. Extreme dimensions are five by two inches. The headrest is one and three-fourths inches high.

No. 181 Trunk

The rectangular form of a trunk is well adapted to the shape of a useful covered dish. The one pictured is of a fine quality of milk-white glass and seems to represent a trunk of the late nineteenth century. Plain surfaces of the trunk are finely stippled, while wooden, metal, and leather parts are plain. It is six and one-half inches long, four inches wide, and three inches high.

The Log Cabin Home

Ours is a nation of humble homes. Most of our important men have known the pinch of poverty. Most of our presidents have come from humble or modest homes; six were born in log cabins. This could have happened in no country save the United States of America. It is a commonplace, here, for men born in humble surroundings, to travel the rough road known to those who have gone from the bottom to the top of the prosperity ladder under the protection of a Constitution that says all men shall have an equal chance to climb; and may go as high as their brains, and hard work, and good character will carry them.

The log cabin has become a symbol. It was a valuable asset in one of our famous presidential campaigns. Log cabin homes of famous men are preserved, and are visited by millions of persons annually. Other log cabin homes have been restored and provide shrines where people of today may better understand and evaluate the meanings of yesterday.

The log cabin found a place in glassware too. Several log cabin items commemorate the William Henry Harrison presidential campaign. The log cabin appears in the Westward-Ho design. A small night lamp is fashioned in the form of a log cabin. A log cabin covered dish serves as a coin bank; and the Log Cabin pattern is quaint and interesting.

197

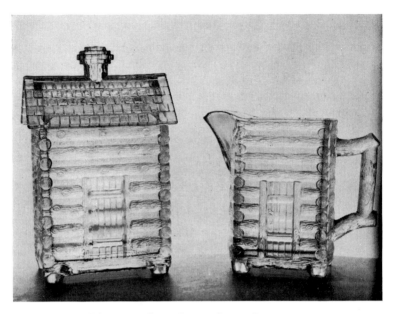

No. 182   Log Cabin Sugar-Bowl
No. 183   Log Cabin Cream-Pitcher

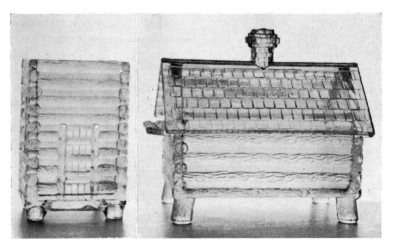

No. 184   Log Cabin Spoon-Holder
No. 185   Log Cabin Butter-Dish

The Log Cabin Pattern

A rectangular form is not well adapted to all forms of tableware, so it is not surprising to find a limited number of forms in the Log Cabin pattern. Most items are of clear, stippled glass. A few may be found in color: blue, amber, or vaseline.

No. 182   Log Cabin Sugar-Bowl

The sugar-bowl is realistic. It has a front door and a latch string "hanging out." There are two windows, one in each end, but no back door. It rests on four small log feet. The lid is in the form of a roof. A chimney on the roof provides a knob. The rectangular part measures four and one-fourth, by four, by three inches.

No. 183   Log Cabin Cream-Pitcher

The cream-pitcher has a front door similar to one on the sugar-bowl. The back wall has a window. A log handle is attached to one side-wall and a pouring spout is provided on the opposite side. It is four and one-fourth, by three, by two and one-half inches in size.

No. 184   Log Cabin Spoon-Holder

The spoon-holder has a front door and two side windows, as in the sugar-bowl; but there is no roof. It has the same rectangular size as the cream-pitcher.

No. 185   Log Cabin Butter-Dish

The butter-dish was designed without door or window. It is a low dish, so this may have been a matter of necessity rather than choice. The log walls rest on four log feet that are much larger than those on the other forms. Log handles are provided at each end. The lid, with chimney knob, is similar to the one on the sugar-bowl. The base is six inches long, four inches wide, and two inches deep.

No. 186   Log Cabin Water Pitcher

In general, the water pitcher is a larger edition of the cream-pitcher. Five boards are used to form the door, where there are but four in the cream-pitcher. There is some difference in detail work of the latch string. It is eight, by five, by four inches in size.

No. 187   Log Cabin Compote

Various sizes of covered compotes are found. The one pictured shows a front door and window. Two windows are on the opposite side. End walls show no openings. The roof is identical with the one on the butter-dish. The cabin is supported on a standard made to represent the trunk of a tree. It measures six, by four inches; and the over-all height is nine and one-half inches.

No. 188   Log Cabin Sauce-Dish

A sauce-dish represents log cabin side-walls resting on four small feet. It measures four, by three, by one and one-fourth inches.

No. 189   Log Cabin Sauce-Dish

A smaller sauce-dish has log handles, and is one inch, by three and one-fourth, by two and one-half inches in size.

No. 190   Log Cabin Bank

This milk-white covered dish does not belong to the Log Cabin pattern. It seems to have been a container for some commercial product, probably mustard. There is a front door and one window. Other walls show no openings. It has a slotted chimney top, through which coins may be dropped. It measures three, by three and one-half inches; and is four inches high.

No. 186   Log Cabin Water Pitcher

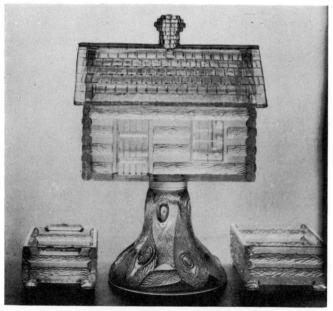

No. 187   Log Cabin Covered Compote
No. 188   Log Cabin Sauce-Dish *(right)*
No. 189   Log Cabin Sauce-Dish *(left)*

No. 190   Log Cabin Bank   No. 191   Log Cabin Lamp

No. 192   Westward-Ho Compote

A small night lamp, in the form of a log cabin, of translucent glass, in an amethystine shade, holds a scant eight ounces of fluid. The base measures three and one-eighth, by two and three-fourths inches. It is three and one-half inches from base to top of the metal collar. This collar carries an inscription: "Patd. Apr. 18, 1875; Mch. 21, 1876." It may be found in crystal, blue, amber, and milk-white glass.

Westward-Ho (pe)

In early times "Pioneer" was an important word. A pioneer is an early leader. A pioneer leader usually clears away obstacles and prepares the way for those who come after him.

During the 1870's a pattern of glassware was produced, honoring the pioneer, and this name was used by the manufacturer. Today it is known as Westward-Ho. In meaning, these words are closely related for the phrase "Westward-Ho" was a rallying cry of our pioneers. Its meaning is: Westward lies hope.

The history connected with this oft-repeated phrase is interesting. A poem from which the idea was taken was written by Bishop George Berkeley in 1726. The Bishop felt that religion was losing ground in the old world and that America seemed to be the likeliest place wherein to make up for what had been lost in Europe. One line of his poem lives on: "Westward the course of empire takes its way;" westward lay hope for the survival and revival of religion.

The rallying cry of Westward-Ho was heard many times in the early history of the United States. It became a siren call when gold was discovered in California. Until this time California had been a place to talk about, to guess and wonder about. In 1848 the story was excitedly told of how, in a week, ten men shook gravel through hand-screens and found a million dollars worth of gold. Wild times followed. The excitement reached everywhere. Should they go? Should they stay? Adventure called. WESTWARD-HO! Many answered. Westward lay hope for riches.

When government lands west of the Mississippi River were opened, at various times, to homestead settlement, WESTWARD-HO became the popular slogan. Again, long trains of covered wagons trekked westward towards the land of opportunity. Westward lay hope, for homes and happiness.

THE WESTWARD-HO PATTERN

In this design, the story of the western frontier being pushed backward is plainly shown. A pioneer log cabin has been established in the wilds. Deer and bison are seen fleeing from encroaching civilization. The sun, rising from behind the hills, brings its message of hope, for each new day brings a new chance to the waking world. Those west-bound travelers needed the tonic of that hope. They had learned how weary feet, aching backs, and heavy hearts, are sisters to success. Their fears and dangers are symbolized in the Westward-Ho pattern too, shown by a crouching Indian which serves as a knob to all covered pieces.

This glassware was freely purchased by women of the 70's. They knew the story of pioneer experiences in person, or had learned about them at mother's knee. And now, we who inherit the benefits paid for by pioneer daring and toil, rightly treasure the remnants of this pattern which have survived to the present time.

No. 192 WESTWARD-HO COMPOTE

The bowl of this oval, covered dish, presents the scene just described. On one side, two deer (buck and doe) are in full flight. On the other, a frightened looking bison rushes away from a sturdily built log cabin. Near the cabin is a well, and "old oaken bucket" type of well-

No. 193   WESTWARD-HO CELERY HOLDER

No. 194   WESTWARD-HO ROUND COMPOTE
No. 195   WESTWARD-HO PITCHER

205

sweep. Trees, hills, and rising sun combine to form a pleasing background. The lid has a finial in the form of a stealthy, kneeling Indian, with feather head dress. A tomahawk is held in his right hand. Size: four and three-fourths inches, by seven and three-fourths inches. Extreme height is ten and one-half inches. Crystal glass, design in frosted finish.

No. 193   WESTWARD-HO CELERY HOLDER

This presents most of the symbols previously mentioned; log cabin, well, bison, one buck deer, trees, hills, and sun. It is three and three-fourths inches in diameter, and eight and one-half inches high.

No. 194   WESTWARD-HO ROUND COMPOTE

This small compote, too, shows a log cabin, well, bison, buck deer, trees, hills, sun, and Indian. It is five inches in diameter, and is extremely scarce in this size. Height is nine and one-half inches.

No. 195   WESTWARD-HO MILK PITCHER

In addition to the usual symbols, the pitcher shows a dog's head at the lower part of the handle. Its extreme height is seven and one-half inches.

HOME SWEET HOME

So much depends on the way we learn to look at life. We require some steadying influence. We require a sustaining power. We require inspiration. We require a sense of security. These are timbers with which to build faith, courage, confidence, morale. They insure a belief that we can build tomorrow better than we did today. Nowhere in the world, since the beginning of time, has this need been supplied so abundantly as it has in the American Home. Perhaps emotion connected with the word "home" has been more completely expressed in the verses of that famous song "Home Sweet Home" than in any other way.

A paperweight is a small thing to hold so much of meaning, but we find one dedicated to that purpose. It is the door-knob type, and the workmanship is plain. The maker evidently intended to present the thought: "Be It Ever So Humble" as well as "There's No Place Like Home."

A path in the foreground leads to a two-story building. Smoke pours from the chimney and suggests a "warm" welcome. A bit of fence on each side of the house provides enclosure for a tree. Above all, in large letters, are the words, in color: "Home Sweet Home." The letters h-o-m-e are inscribed in red; s-w-e-e-t are in green, and h-o-m-e in blue. These same colors are used throughout the design. Background is of milk-white glass, and the dome is crystal. In size it is three and one-fourth inches in diameter, and two inches in depth. It is reported in other color combinations, too.

No. 196   HOME SWEET HOME PAPERWEIGHT

CHAPTER VI

CHAPTER VI

SOMETHING BEYOND SUBSTANCE

The influence of religion on glassware is evident . . . the Bible . . . angels . . . Mephistopheles . . . The Creation . . . Rebekah . . . Jacob . . . Moses . . . Ruth . . . the birth of Christ . . . the Lord's Prayer . . . the Golden Rule . . . mottoes of Biblical origin . . . Faith, Hope, and Charity . . . Calvary . . . I.H.S. . . . the Lord's Supper . . . Rock of Ages . . . religious bodies . . . John Taylor . . . the Mormon Temple . . . Sir Moses Montefiore . . . Pope Leo . . . Henry Ward Beecher . . .

Ay, call it holy ground,
  The soil where first they trod:
They have left unstained what there they found—
  Freedom to worship God.
      "Landing of the Pilgrim Fathers"—Mrs. Hemans

Worship, in its best sense, is not defined as just a ceremony. It covers more ground than that. Worship is a
living. Worship is also a giving. And worship, sometimes, is a giving-up, too. Freedom of worship implies
some form of worship. "Absence of worship" is not
synonymous with "freedom of worship." A survey of
glassware has something to say concerning the worship of
our people. From this evidence we may safely declare they
were essentially a religious class. From cellar and attic,
from cabinet and cupboard, from closet and chimney-
place comes a shimmering host to bear silent witness and
direct proof of this assertion.

Life, in those days, held little but struggle and weariness
for even the richest. There was little hope for physical
comfort, such as we know, in the land of the living. Compensation for a good life was hoped for in the next world.
Desire for the rewards of a religious life kept people interested in religious ways and means, crystallized the will
to follow religious roads, and made them eager for new
ideas concerning religious subjects. Desire is naturally the
fore-runner of fact.

Commercial interests are quick to recognize what the
general public wants or needs, and to supply such things
as are required; so glassware factories created glassware
patterns and forms which were symbolic of religious
themes. That such designs were appreciated and freely
purchased is shown by the many specimens that have survived to the present time. Examination of these is an
index to the Bible stories that were favorites.

It has always been the custom for Christian people to gather in groups and to build churches. The desire to have appropriate buildings in which to worship led to the development of a great type of architecture, the Gothic. It was not only ecclesiastic in origin, but has always been bound up with the church. The devotional atmosphere of such a structure owes much to the window, pointed arch in shape; the form of human hands in the attitude of prayer. Often the glory of saints as well as the suffering of sinners was shown on the richly colored window-glass and helped provide a religious feeling that impressed unbelievers as well as Christian worshipers. Our early glassware shows two patterns that are symbolic of this idea; one called Gothic, and one Cathedral. Both are found in the usual forms needed for table service, although single pieces may be used alone quite satisfactorily.

No. 197   Gothic Sugar-Bowl

This form, like others of the pattern, is bright and shining, and "rings like a bell" indicating a fine quality of metal. It is an early pattern, probably produced before the Civil War. None of the forms are plentiful at the present time. It is found only in clear glass. Size: four and one-eighth inches in diameter, seven and one-half inches high.

No. 198   Cathedral Spoon-Holder

Cathedral is a much later pattern. It is of good quality, though not so fine as Gothic. Collectors who delight in color will find much to satisfy them in this pattern for it was made in clear glass, in yellow, amber, blue, and a lovely amethyst. Size: three and one-fourth inches in diameter; six inches in height.

No. 197

GOTHIC SUGAR-BOWL

No. 198

CATHEDRAL
SPOON-HOLDER

213

The Bible is the oldest book in existence. Men have tried by every known means to destroy it. They have hidden it, ridiculed it, banished it, burned it, and made it a capital crime to own one. But the Book lives. It has out-ridden the storms of centuries. It has found its way into every nation and language of earth. It has been the torch of civilization and liberty. Its influence for good has been recognized by all classes and countries. Our people were no exception. They believed with Locke, that the Bible has "God for its author, salvation for its end, and truth—without any mixture of error—for its matter; it is all pure, all sincere; nothing too much, nothing wanting." And with Webster "The Bible is a book of faith, and a book of doctrine, and a book of morals, and a book of religion, of special revelation from God; but it is also a book which teaches man his own individual responsibility, his own dignity, and his equality with his fellow-man."

THE BOOK

"We search the world for truth, we cull
The good, the true, the beautiful,
From graven stone and written scroll—
From all old flower-fields of the soul;
And, weary seekers for the best,
We come home laden from our quest
To find all that the ages said
Is in the Book our mothers read."
—John Greenleaf Whittier

The Bible influences our every-day conversation to a great extent. Many phrases in ordinary use stem from its pages. They are used without a thought concerning their origin. A handicap is a "thorn in the flesh." Unpleasant things are "gall and worm-wood." A burden is "a millstone around the neck." Escape or success by a narrow margin "by the skin of the teeth." To earn a living by working is "by the sweat of the brow." A worrier, is, like

214

No. 199
BIBLE MATCH-HOLDER

No. 200   BIBLE BREAD-TRAY

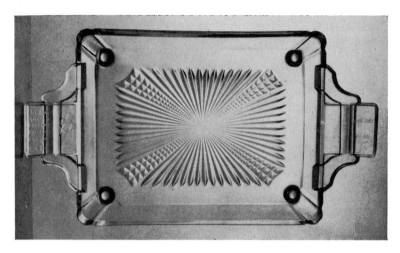

No. 201   The Bishop's Bread-Plate

No. 202   Flower-Pot Pattern Bread-Tray

216

Martha, "troubled about many things." An unreasonable person "strains at a gnat and swallows a camel." A task too heavy may mean "the spirit is willing but the flesh is weak." Self control is proper, for a "soft answer turneth away wrath." Evil living is suggested by "sowing the wind to reap the whirlwind." A measure of moral value is "worth far above rubies." A good person is "the salt of the earth." An outstanding Christian "a shining light." To return good for evil is to "heap coals of fire on their heads." Peace is a time "when swords are beaten into plough-shares and spears into pruning-hooks." Other familiar phrases are: "It rains on the just and unjust." "Cast thy bread upon the waters." "A good Samaritan." "A house built on the sand."

No. 199   Bible Match-Holder

The Bible is represented in glassware. Quaint book match-holders are fashioned like a certain type of old-fashioned Bible, so it seems reasonable to assume they are symbolic of that Book. They are found in clear, amber, and blue glass, and in opaque. One in blue and white marble glass is the rarest specimen.

No. 200   Bible Bread-Tray

At least two bread-trays showing Bible sentiment were made. Both are oblong in shape. One shows an open Bible in the center of the tray, on which is inscribed "Give Us This Day Our Daily Bread." This particular platter belongs to a pattern group sometimes called "curtain tie-back." The Bible, however, appears on the bread-tray only. In size, it is ten and one-half inches by seven and one-half inches.

No. 201   The Bishop's Bread-Plate

The central portion of this rectangular bread-tray has a decorative design of no special importance. The significance appears on the handles, for each one represents

217

an open Bible. A Greek inscription is found on one, and the "daily bread" motto, in small letters, on the other. It rests on four small feet, each being about one-half inch in height. The Bishop's bread-plate was a name given the tray in my possession, by the original owner. In her childhood home it was so called because it was always used when the Bishop came to visit her clergyman father and had dinner with the family.

No. 202. Flower-Pot Pattern Bread-Tray

The motto "In God We Trust" is a plain statement of faith in the power and wisdom of the Creator of all things, to preserve and govern all things: of faith that this eternal and incomprehensible Being is the only proper object of worship by mankind. Since the time of Adam, human beings have tried to create some man-made scheme for successful living and have found all such efforts incomplete. It seems that God's way has been used as sort of an amendment to man's plan. In the course of time, perhaps more perfect trust will be placed in God's plan for humanity.

An oblong shaped bread-tray which belongs to the flower-pot pattern of table glassware, shows this motto in stippled lettering along the sides. Each end is ornamented with an urn of flowers against a heavily stippled background. The center of the tray shows a design much like the one in the Bishop's bread-plate. Perhaps the same individual designed both items. It is twelve by eight inches in size.

No. 203 Angel Border Plate

To speak, with confidence, of anything so obscure as angels is a delicate matter indeed. It is possible to speak with confidence, however, of man's conception of angels at a given period in the world's history. At the time when angel border plates were produced, angels were considered to be God's messengers, bearing communications between

218

No. 203   ANGEL BORDER PLATE

No. 204
ANGEL CREAM-PITCHER

No. 205
ANGEL PLATE

the heart of man and his God. They were thought of, rather vaguely, as a Heavenly Host . . . the glorified spirits of deceased persons . . . possessing immortal life . . . engaged as attendants at the throne of God . . . ministering to man's need . . . keeping records of human events . . . guarding and protecting the helpless . . . or attending and guiding the destinies of the righteous.

The prevailing idea concerning angels was expressed in a favorite hymn of the times: "I want to be an angel and with the angels stand." If one wished to be an angel after earth life was done, it was necessary to be good, useful, helpful; and to try for perfection. There was no other, no "royal" way.

The angel border plate shows the head of a youthful person, with wings, combined with flowers and scrolling, as the prevailing motif of an openwork border. It suggests a poignant story of man's desire for, his hope for, and his faith in, immortality. I have found these nine-inch plates in frosted glass, in transparent amber, opaque white, and opaque blue.

No. 204   Angel Cream-Pitcher

Figures of angels were used on other dishware, too. A cream-pitcher offers an unusual decoration consisting of angels and blossoms. The busy little figures carry musical instruments and no doubt are supposed to be producing "angelic harmony." The design is etched on a clear glass background. Extreme height is five inches.

No. 205   Angel Plate

A small plate, with dainty forget-me-not border, shows a central decoration composed of three angelic figures and a few flowers. These seem to be the angels of quite young children and are not occupied in any way. The plate is five and one-half inches in diameter.

This mug is said to represent Mephistopheles. In old demonology, Mephistopheles ranks next to Satan as one of the seven chief devils (Funk & Wagnalls). Without doubt, this horned creature is someone's conception of the spirit of evil. According to general usage, the culprit seems to be identified by several aliases: the dragon, the serpent, the devil, Satan, etc.; thought of as continually tempting mankind to do wrong.

The obverse and reverse sides of the mug are identical: a strange looking and rather terrifying head, placed within a medallion. The handle represents a dragon. It is a well executed piece, and the surface is all frosted, inside and outside. Size: three and one-fourth inches high; three inches diameter at top.

No. 206
Mephistopheles Mug

221

No. 207 EDEN PLATTER

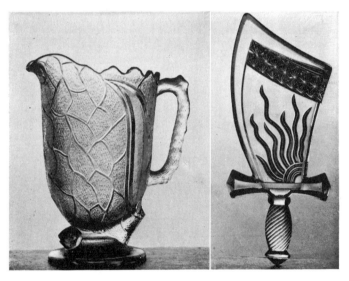

No. 208
EDEN PITCHER

No. 209
FLAMING SWORD DISH

The Garden of Eden

The miracle of Creation was an accepted fact. The Garden of Eden was a dream-place of beauty wherein man yielded to sin, was expelled from the Garden, and heard the sentence: "In the sweat of thy face shalt thou eat bread, till thou returnest unto the ground." The story of the serpent tempter, too, and its association with the tree of knowledge, was a commonplace.

No. 207   Eden Platter

Tradition tells that a pattern of tableware is symbolic of the story of the Creation as found in the Bible. All pieces show a heavily stippled design suggestive of leaves which have been sewed together. This seems to refer to the passage "and they sewed fig-leaves together and made themselves aprons." The bread-tray shows a central fig-like ornament, log handles, and designs resembling the cross-section of a tree. It is inscribed with the daily bread motto.

No. 208   Eden Pitcher

The water pitcher, too, is decorated with the fig-leaf all-over design, and has a log handle beneath which is a protuberance resembling a tree stump. At the base of the pitcher, underneath the pouring spout, the head of the serpent tempter appears. This figure has sometimes been called a frog, and also, a fish; but the nose seems much too pointed for that. While tradition must, in most cases, be termed unreliable, I see no reason to doubt the report concerning this unusual glassware. How else explain the combination of fig, fig-leaves, tree branch and stump, and serpent? The pitcher is eight and one-half inches high, and the largest diameter is five and one-fourth inches.

No. 209   Flaming Sword Dish

The story of the Creation includes mention of the flaming sword which turned every way, guarding the gate (after the expulsion) and preventing man from returning into the Garden, eating of the fruit of the tree of life, and living forever in a sinful state.

A relish dish shaped like a sword of olden times, has a flame-like design on its surface and is known as the Flaming Sword relish dish. I have found it in clear and in blue glass. It is ten inches long and the widest part measures four and one-fourth inches.

No. 210   Rebekah Compote

When Isaac was forty years of age, his father Abraham sent Eliezer, a steward, into Mesopotamia, to procure a wife for him, from his brother-in-law's family. Rebekah was pointed out by God himself. The meeting of Rebekah and Eliezer "at the well" is one of the best known of Bible stories. It has been a favorite subject for artistic portrayal, so that "Rebekah at the well" (represented as a fair maiden with a pitcher upon her shoulder) has become a familiar figure to most everyone.

In glassware, a fruit compote which represents Rebekah at the well is an outstanding example of the glassmaker's art. It is classically lovely, and must be seen to be fully appreciated. Fortunate, indeed, is the collector who is able to secure "Rebekah" at this time.

The bowl of the compote is engraved in a pleasing design and rests on the water pitcher held by the maiden. It is crystal glass, acid finish. The height is twelve and three-eighths inches. Diameter of the bowl is ten inches.

No. 211   Jacob's Ladder Celery Holder

Jacob and Esau, twin sons of Rebekah and Isaac, became celebrated Bible characters too. A story from the life of Jacob is memorialized in glassware.

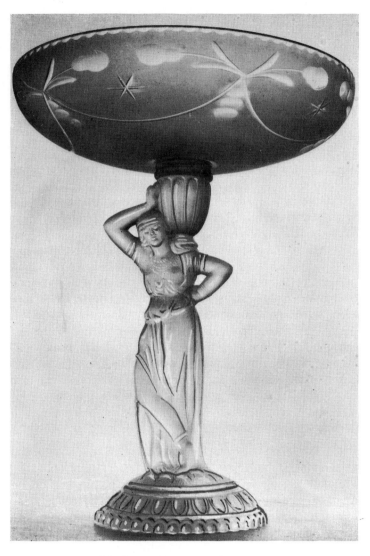

No. 210   Rebekah Compote

Jacob, alone, started to the house of his Uncle Laban, that he might seek a wife from among his own kin-folk. One night, sleeping on the ground in the open air, with a stone for a pillow, he dreamed of a ladder set upon the earth, the top of which reached to Heaven. On this ladder he saw angels of God ascending and descending. The vision affected him, being lonely and sad, and doubtful of his future. It revealed to him that his prayers were like angels ascending to Heaven and to God . . . that God's promises, strength, comfort, and protection were coming down to him. Longfellow, Whittier, and Tennyson used this theme in literature; artists presented the idea on canvas; and the hymn: "Nearer My God to Thee," makes reference to this vision.

A pattern of glassware, well and favorably known, is called Jacob's Ladder. The name seems fitting because of a suggestion of the steps of a ladder which is a prominent feature of the design. This may not have been the original name of the pattern, and the application made at a later time. But the association was made, and the name is in general use. When it was made, or by whom made, is not so essential for our purpose as it is to understand its symbolism. The Jacob's Ladder pattern of glassware is especially brilliant, and is usually found in crystal though specimens may be found in amber and in amethyst. The celery holder is nine inches high, and the base is four inches in diameter.

No. 212   Jacob's Coat Bowl

It is but a short step from this story to one matchless in interest and pathos; a story concerning Jacob's son. Class distinction, with its ever-present envy and ugliness existed even at that early time. It brought tragedy and woe into Jacob's family circle, for Joseph, the finest child and favorite son, was envied by all his brothers. He was a victim of their cruelty, cowardice, falsehood, and insolence, but steadily grew to be a better individual in spite of all his strange and bitter experiences.

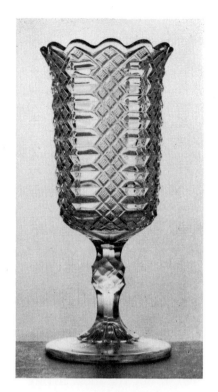

No. 211   Jacob's Ladder
Celery Holder

No. 212   Jacob's Coat Bowl

227

One cause of his brothers' hatred was their father's gift of "the coat of many colors" to Joseph. This sort of robe was worn only by princes, by the wealthy and noble, and by those who had no need to toil. All who worked for a living wore short, colored garments that did not readily show soil, or cramp free movements of the body. Such was the clothing of all Jacob's sons excepting Joseph, whose gift coat, we are told, was made of fine Egyptian linen, richly embroidered. When about seventeen years of age, he was sent as a messenger to his brothers who were tending their flocks in a pasture some fifty miles away. As the brothers caught sight of Joseph riding on his camel, clothed in his handsome coat, their envy so crystallized that they determined to wreak vengeance on him. He was sold as a slave into Egypt. A kid was killed, the coat dipped in blood, and sent to Jacob who accepted it as proof of Joseph's death.

The complete story of Joseph's life has been called the most perfect short story in all the world's literature; and the symbol by which it is commonly suggested is a coat; the coat of many colors which Jacob gave to Joseph.

Some may feel that the suggested pattern of a coat worn so many years ago, is not the most fitting design that can be selected for a piece of tableware; but the Jacob's Coat pattern of glassware is highly decorative and dainty in effect. This name, too, may have been supplied after the time of production. If so, it must have been used because it was more fitting than any other. It is classic in its symbolism and may well be treasured for that reason as well as for its ornamental features and utility. I have found it in clear glass, in white opaque, and in some colors. The bowl is nine and one-fourth inches in diameter, and three and one-eighth inches high.

No. 213   Moses in the Bulrushes Tray

No. 214   Moses in the Bulrushes
Covered Dish

The finding of an abandoned baby is a touching and memorable circumstance, so the story of "The Divine Lawgiver" has always been a favorite. A distracted mother sought to save her baby boy from death according to a decree of King Pharaoh that all male Hebrew children should be destroyed. He was placed in a sort of shallow vessel made of rushes, with clay, and laid on a bank of the River Nile. Here, the King's own daughter found him, adopted him, and named him Moses (meaning, saved out of the water). Unknowingly, she chose the infant's own mother to care for him. Moses lived as an adopted son in the palace of a King and was taught everything a King's son should know. His teacher-mother secretly instructed him about God and his own people, so that when grown he preferred to share their lot and endure their afflictions, rather than be a member of the court of Pharaoh. Eventually, he conquered Pharaoh and led the Children of Israel out of bondage to freedom and to the Promised Land. Fifty days after their departure out of Egypt, on Mount Sinai, Moses received, for his people, the law which we call the Ten Commandments; and it is upon this moral law that the Civil Laws of our land, today, are based. All this, and more, is suggested to us when we look upon glassware items commemorating the "Divine Lawgiver."

A tray, commonly referred to as Moses in the Bulrushes, shows the baby Moses against a background design suggestive of the vessel made of rushes in which he was placed by his mother. This tray is eight and three-fourths inches in length, and six and five-eighths inches in width. It rests on three small feet. I have found it in clear glass, amber, translucent blue, and opaque white.

No. 214 Moses in the Bulrushes Covered Dish

A small covered dish is said to represent the baby Moses, too. The base is ornamented with a design resembling rushes, while the lid shows a full length figure of an infant.

230

This dish is five and one-half inches long, four inches wide, and three inches deep. I have seen it in opaque white, only.

No. 215   Moses Bottle

As Moses led his people out of bondage, many hardships were met. At Rephidim, the people suffered greatly from thirst. Their suffering was so intense they began to whisper among themselves, to "murmur against Moses" and doubt the presence of the Lord among them. Moses, following the Lord's command, smote the rock of Horeb with his rod, and water came out of it, to supply their needs.

This event is commemorated by a bottle which shows Moses holding the rod in his hands. The bottle was used as a container for mineral water and the obverse is inscribed "Poland Water." Inscriptions on the reverse read: "H. Ricker & Son's Proprietor's." Capacity: one quart.

No. 216   Ruth Statuette

Ruth was a woman of the country of Moab, and a daughter-in-law of the Israelite Naomi. After the death of her husband she left her own people and went to live with Naomi at Bethlehem. Here she gleaned grain, after the reapers, in the field of Boaz. Eventually, she married Boaz and became the mother of Obed, and an ancestress of Mary, Mother of Jesus.

Ruth, the gleaner, is represented in glassware by a small statuette. She is shown as a gleaner, resting on one knee, with wisps of grain in each hand. The figure is four and one-half inches high, and the base is two and one-half inches in diameter. An inscription on the base reads: "Gillinder & Sons Centennial Exhibition." Clear glass, satin finish.

No. 215
MOSES BOTTLE

No. 216
RUTH STATUETTE

The world's most famous holiday commemorates the birth of the world's most famous baby; the Baby who changed the whole current of world affairs; the Baby whose coming brought the message of "Peace on Earth, Good Will to Men."

The Christmas season of many years ago was different from that of today in superficial respects, yet those things essential to the celebration of the day were present. Christmas carols, Christmas cheer, Christmas trees and holly, Christmas gifts and Christmas joy were blended as an offering to HIM, symbolic of "The Remembrance of Others." No one has ever been too poor and humble to make life more abundant for those about him through some gift of service. No one has ever been too rich and powerful to need to learn that "Peace on Earth" does come to those who show "Good Will to Men" through service. This is the Spirit of Christmas-time.

In glassware, we find dishes ornamented with mistletoe and holly, as in Christmas Gift Plate, No. 122, and several novelties representing Santa Claus, who is the personification of the Christmas Spirit and dear to the hearts of everyone.

No. 217   Santa and Sleigh

A covered dish featuring Santa and his sleigh is popular. The base is in the form of a sleigh. Santa's head provides a knob for the lid. It comes in clear glass and in opaque white. Extreme length is five and one-fourth inches. Width is three and one-fourth inches. Height is four and one-half inches.

No. 218   Santa Claus Bottle

A bottle shaped like a full length figure of Santa, wearing his fur coat and cap, is pleasing. Pleasing, possibly, because of its association with the Christmas Spirit more than its merits otherwise. On the reverse, near the base, is

No. 217 Santa and Sleigh

No. 218
Santa Claus Bottle

inscribed in small letters "M. G. Husted." It is crystal glass, with surface mostly stippled. Capacity is twenty-four ounces.

No. 219   Christmas Eve Plate

An alphabet border plate shows Santa making his Christmas Eve rounds. He has used a ladder to reach the top of a brick chimney and is just stepping inside the flue. He carries a pack full of toys slung over one shoulder. Snowshoes, a saddle, a drum and drumsticks, dolls, and other gifts are fastened about his waist. A clown wearing a neck ruff and cap suggestive of those worn by a court jester, an elephant, and a horn, top the pack. Unless that chimney is flexible, Santa should have lightened his pack before attempting to descend, for it looks as though a rescue squad might be needed. The words: "Christmas Eve" are inscribed just above Santa Claus. The background of border and design is finely stippled, and the central part is frosted. Diameter: six inches. Color: crystal.

No. 122   Christmas Gift Plate

This large plate must have provided Christmas joy for someone, many years ago. A design, fashioned from sprays of holly, mistletoe, and berries, are combined with large "letters of light" to create a handsome gift. "Letters of light" are made up of small dewdrops, and are intended to represent letters fashioned by incandescent light bulbs.

One feels a great respect for the mold maker's skill, when studying this design. More than one thousand perfectly round dewdrops and berries; a garland of Christmas greens with leaves finely stippled; a sunburst center; a scalloped and ribbed border, all combine to produce a silvery effect that rivals much of the lacy Sandwich glassware. Lucky lady who first received this plate. Lucky lady, now, who secures a surviving specimen. See No. 122 (pages 144 and 145) for further details and illustration.

No. 219
CHRISTMAS EVE PLATE

No. 220
LORD'S PRAYER TUMBLER

A religious feature of real importance, from the gospel of St. Matthew, is the Sermon on the Mount, wherein is found the law of the Kingdom of Heaven. Prayer is the heart of that law, and at its best becomes the world's greatest art. It was in prayer that these earlier people found their loftiest moments. In the Lord's Prayer, the perfect prayer, but one of the seven petitions concerns an earthly need: "Give us this day our daily bread."

Many patterns of glassware had daily bread mottoes on bread-plates. Most cupboards held at least one of these. Three times each day, at table, grace was said, and the bread-tray passed. Three times each day, the thought of man's need and God's care, was presented. In "Give us this day our daily bread" we acknowledge that our daily bread is a gift from God. The fact seems to imply that the means by which we earn our living must be, in its daily routine and nature, something of which we are not ashamed in prayer. No doubt this was partially responsible for the common belief that in business, a man's word should "be as good as his bond." If it failed to measure up to this standard his community standing suffered accordingly. The people probably didn't know it, but they were just as surely advertising religion in this way, as are present day advertisers presenting modern products by means of oft repeated, appealing slogans.

No. 220 Lord's Prayer Tumbler

The bread-tray was not the only form of tableware that advertised religion by means of being brought to mind, many times, at mealtime. A water tumbler is etched with the entire Lord's Prayer. The head of an angel is pictured at the top. It is four inches high, and two and three-fourths inches in diameter.

No. 221   Golden Rule Plate

No. 221   Golden Rule Plate

Inspiration for another motto, came from the Sermon on the Mount: "Do unto others as you would have them do unto you." The Golden Rule is a command to "play fair" stated in words so simple that anyone who has the will to understand them can do so. Be fair, and no exceptions are allowed; be fair, to those above you as well as those below you in the financial scale; be fair, to those whose learning surpasses your own as well as to those who are less intelligent; be fair, to those on your own level; be fair, to yourself, and do not let selfishness so color circumstances that you condemn in others what you condone in yourself; be fair, to the "ins" and the "outs"; be fair, in work and in play. It is a Divine command that, if carried out, would create harmony in all human relationships.

The Golden Rule motto plate belongs to a pattern group sometimes called stars-and-bars; is appealing, lovely, and useful. It is a large plate, being eleven inches in diameter; and is found in a crystal glass of good quality.

Motto Tumblers

Other mottoes of Biblical origin are found etched on tumblers. Each motto is accompanied by some decorative feature, usually a floral spray.

No. 222   Motto Tumbler

Inscribed: "Trust in the Lord."

No. 223   Motto Tumbler

Inscribed: "The Lord Hath Been Mindful of Us."

No. 224   Motto Tumbler

Inscribed: "Rock of Ages."

No. 225   Motto Tumbler

Inscribed: "My God Shall Supply All Your Need."

MOTTO TUMBLERS

No. 222
TRUST IN THE LORD

No. 223
THE LORD HATH BEEN
MINDFUL OF US

No. 224
ROCK OF AGES

No. 225
MY GOD SHALL
SUPPLY ALL
YOUR NEED

No. 226
FEAR THOU NOT FOR
I AM WITH THEE

No. 227
ROCK OF AGES

No. 228
MAKE HASTE TO LIVE
AND CONSIDER EACH
DAY A NEW LIFE

No. 229
THE FLOWER FADETH
BUT THE WORD OF
GOD SHALL STAND
FOREVER

240

No. 226   Motto Tumbler

Inscribed: "Fear Thou Not for I Am With Thee."

No. 227   Motto Tumbler

Inscribed: "Rock of Ages."

No. 228   Motto Tumbler

Inscribed: "Make Haste to Live and Consider Each Day a New Life."

No. 229   Motto Tumbler

Inscribed: "The Flower Fadeth But the Word of God Shall Stand Forever."

No. 230   Faith Hope and Charity Plate

Perhaps no one has journeyed long among the joys and sorrows and perplexities of life and not asked himself some serious questions concerning its mysteries. Probably the most common query is this: What is the best and most lasting thing I can find in the world? No one has found an answer more satisfying than that found in the Bible, "and now abideth faith, hope, and charity; these three, but the greatest of these is charity." No writer has stated the meaning more clearly than Drummond when he wrote: "Covet, therefore, that everlasting gift, that one thing which it is certain is going to stand, that one coinage which will be current in the Universe when all other coinages of all the nations of the world shall be useless and unhonored." The coin of love, or charity.

When shops offered for sale, round, deep plates, ornamented with three maidens posed as the Three Graces, Faith, Hope and Charity, it was natural for people who accepted charity as the supreme good, to prize an article wherein the greatest thing in the world was symbolized through the medium of the clearest thing in the world (glass) and to purchase freely.

241

No. 230   Faith, Hope and Charity Plate

Opaque White Inlay Center in a
Rare Form of No. 230

242

Three inscriptions are found on this plate. The pedestal on which the maidens are posed is inscribed "Three Graces." Above the figures, on the rim, are the words "Faith Hope." Below the figures, on the rim, are "and Charity." It also carries the information "Patd. Nov. 23 1875." It comes in clear glass, and a rare specimen is found with milk-glass inlay. In this rarity, the central part showing the posed figures and pedestal, forms an in-set of opaque white glass. Diameter of the plate, which seems to have been intended for cake, is ten inches. Depth, one and three-eighths inches.

CALVARY

The story of Calvary is the story of a crucifixion, of a resurrection, and of redemption. It is a story so powerful that its force cannot be judged. The measure of its meaning is the measure of an individual's understanding.

They crucified Him, on a day which is the saddest in human history, a crime which stands alone in all history, an atonement without parallel, a triumph never equalled, the central event in the history of the world. The fateful hour in the life of Him who was called the "Light of the World" is symbolized in glassware, by an article used in giving light to the world, the candlestick.

Cruciform candlesticks show the design of a cross bearing an effigy of Christ crucified. They may be found in clear glass and several colors, and in slightly varying forms.

No. 231   CRUCIFORM CANDLESTICK

A rare, vaseline-colored cruciform candlestick. Height, eleven and one-half inches.

No. 232   CRUCIFORM CANDLESTICK

Cruciform candlestick, ten and one-fourth inches high. Found in opaque white, also in clear glass with acid finish.

243

No. 231
CRUCIFORM CANDLESTICK

No. 232
CRUCIFORM CANDLESTICK

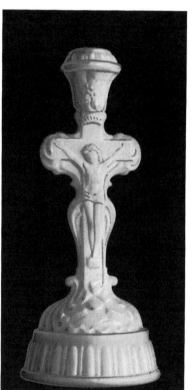

No. 233
CRUCIFORM CANDLESTICK

No. 234
CRUCIFORM CANDLESTICK

NO. 235   THE LORD'S SUPPER BREAD-PLATE

Figures, left to right, represent:

1 Bartholomew
2 James the Younger
3 Andrew
4 Judas
5 Peter
6 John
7 The Christ
8 Thomas
9 James the Elder
10 Philip
11 Matthew
12 Thaddeus
13 Simon

No. 233 Cruciform Candlestick

Cruciform candlestick, nine inches high. Found in various sizes and in a number of colors. I have found it in clear glass, cobalt blue, amber, and opaque white. This form is the one most commonly found.

No. 234 Cruciform Candlestick

Cruciform candlestick, eight and three-fourths inches high. I have found it in clear glass only.

No. 235 The Lord's Supper Bread-Plate

One of the Church sacraments ordained of Christ is the "Supper of the Lord." It is a sacrament of our redemption by Christ's death. It signifies the love Christians should hold among themselves, for "the nearer to Christ, the nearer to each other." The uplift received through the sacrament of the Lord's Supper has been an essential in the progress and success of the Church through all the time since its institution.

The Lord's Supper bread-tray presents the scene recorded in a famous painting, and includes the figures of the Christ and the twelve apostles. Its appeal is universal and constant. I have found this item in crystal, in crystal with acid (or satin) finish, and in clear glass "backed" with gold and colors. It measures seven by eleven inches.

No. 236 Rock of Ages Bread-Plate

Music is an essential of formal worship, and there is evidence to suggest that glass buyers "knew their hymns."

The Methodist movement in hymnody began about 1738 and became divided between the Wesley, the Moravian, and the Calvinist groups. Each of these sections had its own hymn writers. Among these, Charles Wesley is said to have ranked first, in a general way, but the Calvinists' contribution was also of great value.

The Reverend Augustus Toplady (1740-1778) an English clergyman, editor, and hymn writer, was of the Cal-

247

No. 236 Rock of Ages Bread-Plate
(two lines are used for the inscription on the cross)

Opaque White Inlay Center
in a Rare Form of No. 236
(three lines are used for the inscription on the cross)

vinist group. He is especially remembered as the author of "Rock of Ages," by some, esteemed as the finest hymn in the English language.

This hymn is memorialized in glass, by an oval bread-tray. "Give Us This Day Our Daily Bread" in stippled letters, appears around the border. In the center, a human figure with uplifted face is shown clinging to the base of a stippled cross. An angel lends support. At the top of the cross is written "Simply to Thy Cross I Cling" and at the foot "Rock of Ages." The tray also bears the inscription "Patented Dec. 7, 1875." It is usually found in crystal glass, but comes also, in a very deep blue. Another is of crystal glass with the central portion consisting of an inset, or inlay, of opaque white. This inlay is similar in workmanship to the inlay mentioned in No. 230, the Faith, Hope and Charity plate.

Religious Bodies

Four religious bodies are represented in glassware: the Mormon, the Jewish, Catholic, and Protestant.

No. 237   President Taylor Bread-Tray

When Brigham Young, Mormon leader, died in 1877, he was succeeded by John Taylor. A bread-tray commemorates President John Taylor. His portrait ornaments the center. The words "President Taylor" are inscribed below the picture. The remainder of the tray is identical with No. 168, the Bible bread-tray.

No. 238   Mormon Temple Bread-Tray

This temple stands in Temple Square, Salt Lake City, Utah. It was built of granite (1853-'93) and no "gentile" may enter there. Only Mormons are admitted. The walls are six feet thick. There are six spires, the highest of which is surmounted with a copper statue of the angel Moroni.

No. 237
PRESIDENT TAYLOR BREAD-TRAY

No. 238   MORMON TEMPLE BREAD-TRAY

According to the story of Joseph Smith, founder of the sect, the angel Moroni was a messenger from the Lord who appeared before him in a vision and announced the divine will that he (Smith) should become a spiritual leader.

A likeness of the temple ornaments the center of the bread-tray, and the words "Salt Lake Temple" are inscribed below it. The border of the tray is identical with the one included in the Egyptian pattern. It carries the daily bread motto.

No. 239   Sir Moses Montefiore Plate

Sir Moses Montefiore was born in Italy, of a family of Jewish merchants, who settled there long before. An uncle purchased for him the right to practice as one of the twelve Jewish brokers licensed by the City of London, and he entered the Stock Exchange. By the time he was forty he had made a fortune. In making this fortune he was helped by having a close business connection with the house of Rothschild, since Montefiore's wife and Nathan M. Rothschild's wife were sisters.

From 1827 until his death, fifty-eight years later, Montefiore devoted his life to relieving the hardships of the Jewish people. He made seven pilgrimages to the Holy Land. He was knighted in 1837, and at a later date was made a baronet by Queen Victoria. His philanthropy included the peoples of Britain, Syria, Damascus, Turkey, Russia, Morocco, and Rumania. He counselled with all manner of men, including the Pope, Mohammed Ali, the Russian Tsar, Turkish rulers, Queen Victoria, and Prince Charles of Rumania.

This Jewish philanthropist, who lived one hundred years, is honored in glassware by a crystal plate. His portrait occupies the center. The border is highly decorative and includes the inscription, in poster-size letters: "Sir Moses Montefiore." Diameter: ten and one-half inches.

No. 239   Sir Moses Montefiore Plate

No. 240   Pope Leo XIII Plate

No. 240   Pope Leo Plate

Pope Leo XIII (1810-1903) was crowned in 1878. Under his direction the papacy acquired a prestige unknown since the Middle Ages. It has been said he would have become a statesman of the first rank had he held office in a secular government. On March 3, 1903, he celebrated his jubilee (twenty-five years of service) with marked grandeur and ceremony. He died on July 20, following.

Pope Leo is honored by a plate of crystal glass. His portrait ornaments the center, and the name "Pope Leo XIII" is inscribed below it. The rim is decorated with a hobnail design alternating with church symbols. It is ten inches in diameter.

No. 241   Pope Leo Covered Dish

Pope Leo is also featured on an opaque white covered dish. It is a very scarce dish. A well modeled head of the Pope forms the knob of the cover. It carries the inscription "Leon XIII." Diameter: five inches. Height: five and one-half inches.

No. 242   I.H.S.

An oval dish bears the letters I.H.S. This is a monogram signifying Jesus Christ, being the first three letters in the name of Jesus, in Greek. Obviously, it is a dish set apart for the service of the church. It is about nine by five inches in size.

No. 243   Henry Ward Beecher Plate

Henry Ward Beecher (1813-1887) won fame as a Protestant pulpit orator of the nineteenth century. In 1847 he became pastor of Plymouth Congregational Church in Brooklyn, N. Y., and at once became a recognized leader. He was a preacher with an almost unrivaled following. John Hay called him "the greatest preacher the world has seen since St. Paul preached on Mars Hill."

253

No. 241
POPE LEO XIII COVERED DISH

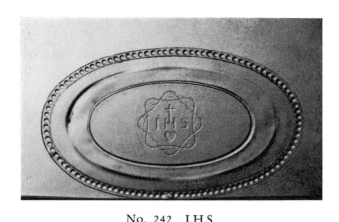

No. 242   I.H.S.

254

No. 243   HENRY WARD BEECHER PLATE

No. 244
HENRY WARD BEECHER BOTTLE

255

A plate honors his memory. His portrait occupies the center. A decorative border consists of a "victor's wreath" and dewdrop designs, and the initials H.W.B. Diameter: nine and one-fourth inches. The plate illustrated is a very lovely shade of amber. It comes also in clear glass.

No. 244   Henry Ward Beecher Bottle

This bottle presents a fairly good (at least a recognizable) likeness of the noted preacher. The obverse is inscribed "Beecher." The reverse carries the inscription "Pat. June 9th, 1874." On the base "T. P. Spencer & Co. N. Y." It is six and one-half inches high.

★ ★ ★

Yes, greatness flourished in this country. Great men lived who knew the feel of a sword in battle.

Great men and women, too, lived, who exercised a weapon said to be "more mighty than the sword."

Great men dreamed; men who conquered hardships for other men through the development of science.

Statesmen and editors, philosophers and orators, preachers, teachers and historians, made great thoughts to become uncommonly common.

We are able to gather fruits growing on the high branches of civilization because we stand on the "blood, toil, sweat, and tears" of men and women who lived before us. They believed that future generations would cherish, defend, protect and preserve such human rights and benefits as have come about under the guidance and shielding arm of moral and civil law. It is our high privilege to justify that faith.

CHAPTER VII

A survey of historical glassware gives one a feeling that Uncle Sam kept a record book, in glass, in somewhat the same spirit that we keep family records in albums. There are gaps in Uncle Sam's record, but it shows how a nation was carried from an intangible desire and hope, to fruition as the mightiest power in the world. It is one of the most colorful stories in human history.

The record is colorful, too. Most commemoratives are found in aristocratic crystal, but numerous examples, some of them rarities, are available in a multitude of colors. There are blues and greens, amber and amethyst, black amethyst and vaseline, reds and yellows, and mixtures.

Portraits of the children are plentiful, clever children who achieved fame. There are presidents, vice-presidents, statesmen, heroes of the army and navy, writers, preachers, and others. There are large plates, medium sized plates, small plates, platters and plaques. Other forms were used to show portraits too, but platters and plates predominate. Some are wonderful examples of the sculptor's skill, some are just average in execution, while others are poorly done. Some members of the family have been raised above the plates and platters level and appear in statuette form. These trophies are not plentiful. They are highly desirable, deserving of respect and appreciation. Other children whose stature and popularity were less, but who built a future for themselves and us, are represented. They could think hard and come up with the right answers. Their ability to analyze a subject and originate better things was astonishing.

Glassware evidence shows the general public gave applause most generously to military men and to presidents. These classes merge, since many presidents had military records, too. Of the eighteen presidents whose commemoratives I have encountered, twelve were army men. All but one were elected to office as presidential candidates. Although the other, C. A. Arthur, became President, he took office following the death of James A. Garfield, so was not elected directly by vote of the people. His name therefore, does not appear in the list of elected presidents, in the table which follows.

The twelve having military records are George Washington, William H. Harrison, Andrew Jackson, Zachary Taylor, Abraham Lincoln, Ulysses S. Grant, James A. Garfield, Chester A. Arthur, Benjamin Harrison, Rutherford B. Hayes, William McKinley, and Theodore Roosevelt.

Presidential and Vice-Presidential items should be considered the most important of all in the historical field since these offices stand highest on the ladder of fame.

The following table shows the election records of forty-five presidents, vice-presidents, and defeated candidates honored in glassware, whose commemoratives the author has been able to secure. Additional items relating to some of these individuals, and some honoring Presidents John Quincy Adams, Millard Fillmore, James Monroe, and John Tyler, have been reported by others.

ELECTED		Year	DEFEATED	
PRESIDENT	VICE-PRESIDENT		PRESIDENT	VICE-PRESIDENT
George Washington	John Adams	1789	John Hancock	
			S. Huntington	
George Washington	John Adams	1792	Thomas Jefferson	
John Adams	Thomas Jefferson	1796	Samuel Adams	
Thomas Jefferson		1800	John Adams	
Thomas Jefferson		1804		
	Elbridge Gerry	1812		
		1824	Andrew Jackson	
			Henry Clay	
Andrew Jackson		1828		
Andrew Jackson		1832	Henry Clay	
		1836	Daniel Webster	
			Wm. H. Harrison	Francis Granger
Wm. H. Harrison		1840		
		1844	Henry Clay	
Zachary Taylor		1848		
Abraham Lincoln		1860		
Abraham Lincoln		1864		
J. S. Grant		1868		
J. S. Grant	Henry Wilson	1872	Horace Greeley	B. G. Brown
R. B. Hayes	W. A. Wheeler	1876		T. A. Hendricks
J. A. Garfield	C. A. Arthur	1880	W. S. Hancock	W. H. English
Grover Cleveland	T. A. Hendricks	1884	J. G. Blaine	John A. Logan
Benjamin Harrison	L. P. Morton	1888	Grover Cleveland	A. G. Thurman
Grover Cleveland	A. E. Stevenson	1892	Benjamin Harrison	Whitelaw Reid
Wm. McKinley	G. A. Hobart	1896	W. J. Bryan	
Wm. McKinley	Theo. Roosevelt	1900	W. J. Bryan	A. E. Stevenson
Theo. Roosevelt		1904		
W. H. Taft	J. S. Sherman	1908	W. J. Bryan	J. W. Kern
	Tom Marshall	1912	W. H. Taft	J. S. Sherman
			Theo. Roosevelt	
	Tom Marshall	1916		
	Calvin Coolidge	1920		F. D. Roosevelt
Calvin Coolidge		1924		
F. D. Roosevelt		1932		
F. D. Roosevelt		1936	A. M. Landon	
F. D. Roosevelt		1940	Wendell Willkie	
F. D. Roosevelt		1944		

Table showing the election records of forty-five presidents, vice-presidents, and defeated candidates. These are honored in one hundred thirty-three glassware items, pictured and described in the following pages.

259

No. 245   WASHINGTON GEORGE PLATE

No. 50   WASHINGTON FLASK
OBVERSE

No. 246   WASHINGTON FLASK
REVERSE

George Washington

George Washington (1732-1799) was the first President of the United States, under the Constitution (1789-1797). He has a record of many other firsts. He was "first in war, first in peace, and first in the hearts of his countrymen." He seems first in the number of glassware trophies dedicated to his memory, and he is first, also, in the number of forms used to present his fame. He is first again, as a companion to other celebrities seen on items. He is reported on no less than sixty-one flasks, and there are bottles, plates, platters, goblets, mugs, hatchets, paperweights, and statuettes to be found, keeping alive his memory. He is shown with Columbus, Lafayette, Andrew Jackson, Zachary Taylor, Abraham Lincoln, J. A. Garfield, and Henry Clay; and the names of Adams, Jefferson, and Captain Bragg, are inscribed on Washington portrait flasks. This overlapping makes repetition unavoidable in giving rightful credit to all individuals represented. More or less overlapping is noticeable in much of the commemorative portrait glassware and complicates the organization of material in a simple and concise manner; in fact, it *defeats* organization of material in a simple and concise manner.

No. 245   Washington George Plate

A tea-plate in lacy Sandwich glass honors Washington. A small profile portrait bearing no resemblance to him, is surrounded by a wreath of acorns and leaves, supported by a scroll. A star at the top completes the wreath. Border is an elaborate design of scrolls and flowers. Inscribed: "Washington George." It is six inches in diameter. Possibly issued in 1832, the centennial year of his birth. This is a popular item and must have been widely distributed since it is not too scarce today.

No. 50   Washington Flask

In 1826, a pint flask honoring Washington had been placed in circulation. His portrait ornamented the obverse. An American eagle was on the reverse. The obverse

261

No. 247
WASHINGTON FLASK
OBVERSE

No. 248
WASHINGTON FLASK
OBVERSE

was inscribed "General Washington" above the portrait. On the reverse "T.W.D." was placed within an oval beneath the eagle. The initials were those of Dr. Dyott of the Kensington Glass Works. It must have been a popular flask for this was the mold selected to be re-cut for commemorating the deaths of John Adams and Thomas Jefferson. Above the eagle, "E Pluribus Unum" was inscribed, and in the edges, the words: "Adams and Jefferson July 4 A.D. 1776. Kensington Glass Works, Philadelphia" were cut. Probably no flask holds greater dramatic significance than this. It is found in several colors. (For further details concerning the flask and its story, see item No. 50.)

No. 246 Washington Flask

The obverse of this pint flask shows a portrait of Washington in military uniform, with the word "Washington" inscribed above it. A portrait of Andrew Jackscn in uniform decorates the reverse, with "Jackson" inscribed above. Reported in several colors, but not too easily found. It may have been circulated during one of Jackson's campaigns in 1824, 1828, or 1832.

No. 247 Washington Flask

A smaller flask, half-pint in size, aquamarine in color, honors Washington, and features his classical bust portrait on the obverse. He is not in uniform here. "The Father of his Country" is inscribed in a semi-circle above the portrait. The reverse presents a likeness of General Zachary Taylor, in uniform. "General Taylor Never Surrenders" is inscribed in a semi-circle above his portrait. An anecdote concerning General Taylor is kept alive by this inscription. At the Battle of Buena Vista during the Mexican War, Lieutenant Crittendon, aide to General Taylor, had gone to Santa Anna's headquarters. He was told that if General Taylor would surrender he should be protected. Crittendon replied: "General Taylor Never Surrenders." This was a favorite motto used during the

No. 27   Washington Platter

No. 249   Three Presidents Platter

campaign of 1848. General Taylor became presidential candidate Taylor in 1848 and this flask may date from that time.

No. 248 WASHINGTON FLASK

In this quart-size flask, a portrait of Washington similar to the one described above, adorns the obverse. A portrait of Taylor, similar to the one described above, is on the reverse. "A Little More Grape Captain Bragg" is inscribed in a semi-circle above the portrait of Taylor. Another anecdote of Taylor is recalled by this inscription. During the same battle, the situation had become desperate due to our smaller number of troops. Bragg's artillery was sent to the rescue. They dashed up to within a few yards of the enemy. A single discharge made them waver. Taylor shouted "A Little More Grape, Captain Bragg." A second and a third discharge followed and the Mexicans broke and fled. This flask, too, probably figured as an item of the presidential campaign in 1848, and was made in a number of colors.

No. 27 WASHINGTON PLATTER

When death ended the career of the first President, his intimate friend, General Henry (Lighthorse Harry) Lee, pronounced before Congress and a large assembly, the funeral oration, December 26, 1799. It was in this address that George Washington was first proclaimed "first in war, first in peace, first in the hearts of his countrymen."

An oval platter bears Washington's portrait and this inscription. It is framed by a border in the Centennial pattern, so named because this pattern was produced in the centennial year, 1876. On some specimens, plain spaces within the bear-paw handles are inscribed "Centennial 1776-1876." (See item No. 27.)

No. 250
THREE PRESIDENTS GOBLET

No. 251
WASHINGTON-LAFAYETTE MUG

No. 2
WASHINGTON-COLUMBUS MUG

No. 249 Three Presidents Platter

The platter must have been issued after the death of President Garfield, and suggests that, in public esteem, this martyred President is held on the same high plane as Washington and Lincoln.

Three oval medallions show bust portraits of James A. Garfield, George Washington, and Abraham Lincoln. A shield and laurel branches are decorative features. Stippled leaves ornament the border. Inscribed on the border: "In Remembrance." Inscribed beneath medallions: "God Reigns" "First in Peace" "Charity for All." Crystal glass with center frosted or clear. It is ten by twelve and one-half inches in size.

While this platter is primarily a Garfield item, it suggests that George Washington, its central figure, is the yardstick measure of greatness in our nation. This idea must be recorded along with other honors awarded to the Father of His Country.

No. 250 Three Presidents Goblet

Like the platter just described, this goblet honors Presidents Washington, Lincoln, and Garfield, and must have been made after Garfield's untimely death. Bust portraits of the trio are framed in medallion settings. Washington is placed in the center, with Garfield and Lincoln at his left and right. An eagle, supported by flags, is placed above the portrait. It is suggestive of the idea that, in public esteem, Garfield had reached the level of Washington and Lincoln. It is three inches in diameter, six and one-fourth inches in height, and is difficult to locate.

No. 251 Washington-Lafayette Mug

Tradition says that portraits on this mug represent Washington and Lafayette. They bear slight resemblance to these men and so the intention may be questioned. Had it borne a suitable inscription, as was given the Washington George plate, we could then speak with assurance. The

267

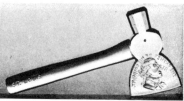

No. 252
WASHINGTON HATCHET

No. 253
WASHINGTON HATCHET

No. 254 WASHINGTON
CENTENNIAL
BITTERS BOTTLE

No. 255 WASHINGTON
MONUMENT
PAPERWEIGHT

mug is rather plain in effect, showing profile portraits placed in oval beaded medallions, flanked with laurel branches, and placed on opposite sides. It must have had a large sale, for many specimens in varying sizes and colors are reported. Just why an ordinary mug should have enjoyed so wide a distribution unless it had some special message of significance is difficult to understand. Perhaps it *was* intended to represent Washington and Lafayette. The close friendship of these men was a suitable theme for commemoration, but worthy of a much better article.

No. 2   Washington-Columbus Mug

Another mug has profile bust portraits of Columbus and George Washington on obverse and reverse, respectively. An inscription on the base reads: "World's Columbian Exposition 1893." (See item No. 2.)

No. 252   Washington Hatchet

This replica of a hatchet shows a bust portrait of Washington on the blade. Above the portrait is inscribed "The Father of This Country." Reverse of the blade has "World's Fair 1893." On the handle is "Libbey Glass Co. Toledo, Ohio." The item is most often found in all clear glass. The one pictured is more rare. It is milk-white glass, and another rare one is crystal with the obverse, or portrait side, frosted, excepting the portrait, which is clear. This specimen also has "World's Fair 1893" in clear letters against the frosting, above the portrait. The length is eight inches.

No. 253   Washington Hatchet

A hatchet similar to the preceding one has profile bust portrait of Washington on obverse. Inscribed aboye portrait, "The Father of His Country." On reverse of blade, inscribed "World's Fair 1904." On the handle "St. Louis." It is crystal glass, eight inches in length.

No. 256
WASHINGTON PAPERWEIGHT

No. 257
WASHINGTON PAPERWEIGHT

No. 258   WASHINGTON BI-CENTENNIAL PLATE

270

No. 254 Washington Centennial Bitters Bottle

A quart-size bottle appears in the shape of Washington, wearing a uniform. An inscription on front of base reads: "Simon's Centennial Bitters." "Trade Mark" is on back of base. The bottle illustrated is amber, but other colors were made. Unfortunately, it has been reproduced, in many colors.

No. 255 Washington Monument Paperweight

A small paperweight replica of the Washington Monument has a square base. At one corner is an oval medallion ornamented with a profile bust portrait of Washington. At the opposite corner another medallion has an ornamentation of the square and compass. Sides of the base are sloping. On one side is the inscription "Top 35′ Sq. Base 55′ Height 555′." Another side reads "81200 Gross Tons." The third reads "Born Feb. 22d 1732." The fourth reads "Died Dec. 14th 1799." Top of the base is inscribed "Cornerstone July 4th '48 Dedicated Feb. 21st '85." It is amber glass, and difficult to secure. The base is two and three-fourths inches square. It is five and one-half inches in height.

No. 256 Washington Paperweight

A medallion paperweight honoring Washington appears as a clear block of glass, made in a round shape, and having a portrait bust pressed in the base. The portrait is in frosted finish. Rims are slightly beveled. A rare weight probably dating from the 1850's. It is three and one-half inches in diameter, and three-fourths of an inch in depth.

No. 257 Washington Paperweight

Another fine crystal medallion paperweight honoring Washington, has a profile portrait that originated with the sculptor Houdon. It is round and flat, has turned sides and a beveled rim. The portrait and turned sides are

271

No. 259 Washington Statuette

frosted. In some cases the rim is frosted. In some there is a circular frosted background around the portrait. In the writer's opinion, these variations add interest to the items. The base of the weight is shaped almost to the rim in concave form. It was sold at the Philadelphia Centennial in 1876. Diameter is three and one-eighth inches. Depth is one inch.

No. 258 Washington Bi-Centennial Plate

A portrait of Washington fills the center. Border design consists of thirteen large, bright stars, placed against a stippled background. Inscribed beneath portrait "G. Washington 1732-1932." A commemorative item issued during the Washington bi-centennial celebration in 1932. Crystal glass, eight inches in diameter.

No. 259 Washington Statuette

This paperweight is in the form of a portrait bust of Washington, made in opaque white glass with satinized finish. It closely resembles marble. Made also in clear glass with frosted finish. Some specimens are inscribed on back of base "Centennial Exhibition Gillinder and Sons." It is very heavy, weighing three and three-fourths pounds. Its height is five and three-fourths inches. Rare, in either form.

No. 260 Washington Bi-Centennial Bottle

A crystal, pint bottle shaped like a full figure of Washington shows him in military coat and tricorn hat. A sabre is held in the right hand. It is inscribed on front of base "Washington." The height is nine and one-half inches. Issued for the bi-centennial of his birth.

No. 261 Washington Bi-Centennial Bottle

Another pint bottle commemorating Washington is calabash shaped. A profile bust portrait is on the obverse. Reverse shows a small tree, or the bough of a tree, in leaf.

No. 260 WASHINGTON BI-CENTENNIAL
BOTTLE

No. 261 WASHINGTON
BI-CENTENNIAL
BOTTLE

No. 262 WASHINGTON
BI-CENTENNIAL
BOTTLE

Probably intended for the "Liberty Tree," a tree or green bough dedicated to liberty and set up in some public place; used during the Revolutionary War. An inscription beneath the Liberty Tree reads: "1732-1932." A bi-centennial item, eight inches in height.

No. 262   Washington Bi-Centennial Bottle

A quart-size bottle honoring Washington has an oval medallion portrait on the obverse. The inscription "1732 George Washington 1932" follows the oval line above portrait. Reverse shows an oval medallion containing an American eagle with olive branches and thunderbolts in his talons. Twelve stars outline the lower part of the oval. Edge is heavily ribbed. Neck is threaded for a metal screw cap. Issued for the celebration in 1932. Crystal.

No. 40   John Hancock Platter

John Hancock (1737-1793) received four electoral votes in the presidential election of 1789. His public life dated from 1766. He served as a soldier as well as a statesman. He held many responsible positions but is best remembered as President of the Continental Congress and signer of the Declaration of Independence. He wrote his name in poster-size letters, and remarked: "I guess King George can read that without spectacles." The platter honoring him bears his signature as it appears on the document. (See item No. 40.)

No. 42   The Signers Platter

The Signers platter honors many men. It bears the names of all signers of the Declaration of Independence, and the states from which they came. Six of these men became President or Vice-President or were candidates for those offices.

John Adams (1735-1826) served as the first Vice-President and was the second President (1797-1801).

Thomas Jefferson (1743-1826) served as Vice-President

No. 40   Hancock (John) Platter

No. 42   The Signers Platter

with Adams, and was the third President (1801-1809). The political theories of Thomas Jefferson have had more influence upon the public life of the nation than those of any other man. He is called the author of the Declaration of Independence, and founder of the Democratic Party. He was a defeated Presidential candidate in 1792 and in 1796. He won in 1800.

John Hancock was a contender for the Presidential office in 1789.

Samuel Huntington (1732-1796) also lost to Washington in that year. He received two electoral votes. Like Hancock, he had served as President of the Continental Congress. He signed the Declaration in company with three others from Connecticut.

Samuel Adams (1722-1803) second cousin to John, was a candidate for President in 1796. It is said no one did more to bring about the Revolution than he.

Elbridge Gerry (1744-1814) served as Vice-President with James Madison in the second term (1813-1814). He signed the Declaration, and aided in framing the Constitution but refused to sign it, believing too great powers were given to the National Government. Gerry is given credit for the coining of the word "gerry-mander." In politics, it means to change the political map so that voting districts are unfairly or abnormally arranged, for the purpose of advancing interests of a particular party or candidate. As Governor of Massachusetts, his administration was notable for a re-division of senatorial districts in such a manner as to consolidate the Federalist vote. This word has come to mean also, the garbling of facts in an argument in order to achieve a desired conclusion. Vice-President Gerry died in office.

Richard Stockton, who signed the Declaration, from New Jersey, has been mentioned as a defeated candidate for Vice-President, but this could not be so. He died in 1781, so the Richard Stockton who ran for Vice-President in 1820 could not have been this man. (See also, No.42.)

No. 263   Jackson Tumbler

No. 264   Henry Clay
Cup-Plate

No. 265   Daniel Webster
Paperweight

Andrew Jackson

In flask No. 246 George Washington shares honors with Andrew Jackson (1767-1845), seventh President of the United States (1829-1837). He had been defeated for the presidency in 1824. Jackson was the first man of the common people to become President. He was the first President to build a party machine and introduce patronage into national politics. (See No. 246, under Washington items.)

No. 263   Jackson Tumbler

Beginning in 1825 and continuing for approximately a quarter of a century, cameo incrustations came into favor. They were popular in medallion paperweights, in cup-plates, and appear in more limited form as decoration for tumblers. Bakewell, Page and Bakewell of Pittsburgh, Pennsylvania, began producing these tumblers in 1825, honoring a group of famous persons. A likeness of the subject was formed of a composition and imbedded in the bottom of a tumbler while the glass was hot. When finished, the cameo took on an attractive silvery sheen. One such tumbler has a profile portrait of Jackson in the heavy bottom of the glass. He is shown in civilian clothing. This suggests the item may have been circulated during his second or third Presidential campaign, 1828 or 1832, when military dress had been put aside. The under side of the portrait is lettered "Gen. Jackson." Lower portion of the tumbler is ribbed, by cutting. Height: three and one-fourth inches. Top diameter: three inches.

No. 264   Henry Clay Cup-Plate

Henry Clay (1777-1852) was prominent in public life for nearly half a century. His activities were many, constructive, and important; but of all causes, Clay's career was connected most intimately with the subject of slavery. Though he constantly denounced slavery as an evil, custom led him to keep slaves on his own plantation in Kentucky.

279

While he opposed slavery in principle, he disliked the abolitionists, and felt they increased the strife which menaced the Union. This attitude caused the abolitionists to denounce him as a slave-holder, and slave-holders to regard him as an abolitionist. Such straddling was a major cause of his loss of the presidency which he long coveted. In 1824 he was a candidate and received thirty-seven electoral votes. In 1832 he lost again, and in 1844 he lost for the third time. In a speech made about 1850, Clay remarked: "I would rather be right than be President." This quotation, often repeated since that time, is almost as familiar as the name "Clay" so that when one thinks of Henry Clay he thinks also: "who would rather be right than be President." Henry Clay was one of the great men who helped mold this nation to a pattern of greatness.

The Great Compromiser, or The Great Pacificator, as he was known, is honored in several items of glassware. A cup-plate in lacy Sandwich has a profile portrait in center. It bears small likeness to Clay but his name frames the portrait. It is regarded as an item of the 1844 campaign. The one pictured is crystal glass, three and one-half inches in diameter.

No. 265   Daniel Webster Paperweight

Daniel Webster (1782-1852) was a contemporary of Henry Clay. He won distinction as a statesman but was more appreciated for his oratory. Among his great speeches, three were outstanding: at Plymouth, 1820, on the bicentennial celebrating the landing of the Pilgrims; at the laying of the cornerstone of the Bunker Hill Monument, 1825; the eulogy on Adams and Jefferson, 1826. He ranked chief among the orators known as the "giants" in Congress. It has been said that Webster was the incarnation of common sense and that he gave common sense and human truth a dignity of expression that has never been equaled nor forgotten. In 1836 he received the electoral vote of Massachusetts for President, but the political seal of success as President of the United States was denied him.

No. 266   Granger Bottle

No. 267   Industry Bowl

The highest office which he held was Secretary of State under Wm. Henry Harrison and John Tyler, and again under Millard Fillmore.

Webster is honored in glass, by a paperweight; a clear block of glass in hexagonal shape, beveled on the upper rim. A profile portrait of Webster is molded in the base and has a frosted finish. This portrait is reported as being from a bronze medal signed by Wright. Some specimens have the word "Webster" beneath the portrait. Diameter: three inches. Depth: one and one-half inches. It is an early weight, probably 1852, and rare.

No. 266   Granger Bottle

Francis Granger (1792-1868) was a member of Congress in 1836, when he became a candidate for Vice-President on the Whig ticket, with William Henry Harrison. He lost, and continued in Congress, where he served a total of six years. He was Postmaster-General in 1841.

A bottle is shaped like the bust of Francis Granger. The word "Granger" is on front of base. Some believe the bottle may represent Gordon Granger, (1821-1876) a veteran of the Mexican War who was brevetted Major-General during the Civil War. In either case, it probably is a memorial item. Height: six and one-half inches. It has been said, also, that the bottle represents Dr. Granger, a British subject.

William Henry Harrison

William Henry Harrison (1773-1841), ninth President of the United States (March 4-April 4, 1841), was an old hero of the Indian Wars in which he earned the nickname "Tippecanoe" in allusion to his victory over the Indians on Tippecanoe River, Indiana. He was a Presidential candidate in 1836, and lost to Van Buren; but he was nominated again and won the next election.

The campaign of 1840 was the famous "log cabin and hard cider" campaign, in which the homely virtues and simplicity of Harrison were contrasted with Van Buren's

No. 269 HARRISON
CAMPAIGN
BREAST-PIN

No. 268 HARD CIDER BOTTLE

No. 270 TAYLOR-RINGGOLD FLASK

more aristocratic and luxurious background. Democrats scornfully pointed out that Harrison was born in a log cabin, and was satisfied to drink cider in place of wine. The Whigs turned this criticism into an asset and rushed their candidate into office in a colorful campaign during which a log cabin and cider barrel were prominent symbols, and the campaign cry was "Tippecanoe and Tyler too." The joy of victory soon turned to grief for the aging Harrison died one month after his inauguration, the first death of a President while in office.

Glassware went into politics with a rush at this time, featuring the Whig Harrison. Factories turned out flasks, bottles, cup-plates, tumblers, bowls, and a breast-pin setting, to help elect him.

No. 267   Industry Bowl

An item of Sandwich origin is the Industry Bowl. In center, it shows the usual log cabin, with a cider barrel at the right-hand corner of the house. Border design shows a man plowing, a sailing ship, and a factory (agricultural, commercial, and industrial symbols) against a stippled background. The plowman is supposed to symbolize Harrison, who sometimes was called "The Cincinnatus of the West." The factory represents the New England Glass Factory. The bowl may have been made here as well as at Sandwich. Four variants of the Industry Bowl are found. The border is scalloped on many specimens. Crystal glass, six and one-fourth inches in diameter.

No. 268   Hard Cider Bottle

A small bottle, barrel shaped, has, in raised letters "Hard Cider" on one side and "Tippecanoe Extract" on the other. It must have been made in profuse quantity for the Harrison campaign, but is hard to locate at the present time. It holds one and one-fourth ounces.

No. 269   Harrison Campaign Breast-Pin

Another Harrison campaign item might be referred to as "cute." It is a small, thin, rectangularly shaped piece

284

of glass which shows a log cabin with the door ajar, a tree, cider barrel and pitcher, a flag flying from a staff beside the house, and the words "Harrison and Reform." It is said to have formed the setting for a breast-pin of the 1840 campaign. Like the hard cider bottle, it must have been produced in quantity but now is hard to secure. When one does appear, it usually is found in a button-box, in company with old buttons.

Zachary Taylor

Zachary Taylor (1784-1850), twelfth President of the United States (1849-July 9, 1850), was a military man. His forty years of service extended from the War of 1812 to the War with Mexico. The Whigs had discovered that a popular hero was the best qualified man to win votes. In this respect "Old Rough and Ready" was an outstanding figure. He might have been an able executive, but he died before he had time to prove himself.

A number of flasks were made to honor Taylor. He shares honors with Washington on flasks No. 247 and 248. (See these items, under Washington.)

No. 270   Taylor-Ringgold Flask

A pint flask honors President Taylor and Major Ringgold. A profile portrait of Taylor, in uniform, within an oval, is on the obverse. Below it the words "Rough and Ready" are placed. A profile portrait of Ringgold is on the reverse, with the word "Major" above it, and "Ringgold" beneath.

Major Samuel Ringgold (1800-1846) of the Artillery, at an earlier time had served as aide-de-camp to General Winfield Scott, Commander-in-Chief of the U. S. Army. He was killed at the Battle of Palo Alto, the first important battle of the Mexican War.

The flask was made in many colors. The one pictured is aqua.

No. 271   The Martyrs Platter

No. 272   The Martyrs Mug

ABRAHAM LINCOLN

Abraham Lincoln (1809-1865), sixteenth President of the United States (1861-1865), is held in national esteem that is second to none. His renown is perpetuated by many memorials. His memory is enshrined in the hearts of the nation. His fame is celebrated in many glassware trophies.

He shares honors with Washington and Garfield in No. 249 and in No. 250. (See these numbers, under Washington.)

No. 271   The Martyrs Platter

Lincoln shares honors again, on a platter which must have been produced after the death of Garfield. In the center, oval medallion portraits of these martyrs appear against a stippled background. An American eagle, with outstretched wings, stands guard above them. Below, an inscription reads: "Our Country's Martyrs." The border is ornamented with a simple design. Handles are unique, showing a figure which resembles the head of Christ, the greatest martyr. It is crystal glass, twelve and one-half by seven and three-fourths inches in size.

No. 272   The Martyrs Mug

Lincoln shares honors with Garfield, in a small commemorative mug. A bust portrait of Garfield is on the obverse. Inscribed beneath portrait: "Garfield died Sept. 19th, 1881." Inscribed at left of portrait: "Born Nov. 19th 1831." Inscribed at right of portrait: "Assassinated July 2nd 1881." A bust portrait of Lincoln is on the reverse. Inscribed beneath portrait: "Lincoln died April 15th, 1865." Inscribed at left of portrait: "Born Feb. 12th, 1809." Inscribed at right of portrait: "Assassinated April 14th, 1865." The handle is decorated with a laurel wreath and stars. The base is inscribed: "Our Country's Martyrs." It is crystal glass, two and three-fourths inches in diameter, and two and five-eighths inches in height.

No. 273
LINCOLN PAPERWEIGHT

No. 274
LINCOLN PAPERWEIGHT

No. 275
LINCOLN PAPERWEIGHT

No. 276
LINCOLN PAPERWEIGHT

No. 273   LINCOLN PAPERWEIGHT

A crystal medallion paperweight honoring Lincoln is similar to the Washington item No. 257. It is round and flat, with turned and frosted sides. A frosted, profile bust of Lincoln is molded in the base, and the base is shaped almost to the rim, in concave form. The background is all clear (no frosted circle) and the beveled rim on the upper surface is clear. The top surface is flat. Diameter is three and one-eighth inches, and the depth is one inch. Probably another 1876 centennial item.

No. 274   LINCOLN PAPERWEIGHT

This paperweight is similar to No. 273. It, also, is round and has turned sides, and a beveled rim on the upper surface. The same familiar bust of Lincoln, within a frosted circle, is molded in the base. Sides, and rim of the top surface are frosted. The base is shaped almost to the rim in concave form. The top surface is slightly convex. It is three and one-eighth inches in diameter, and one and one-eighth inches in depth.

No. 275   LINCOLN PAPERWEIGHT

A paperweight honoring Lincoln is slab type, rectangular in shape, and features a large head of Lincoln, in profile, molded in the base. It is crystal glass, three by four and one-half inches in size. The depth is seven-eighths of an inch.

No. 276   LINCOLN PAPERWEIGHT

Another paperweight featuring Lincoln is oval in shape, has turned sides, and a large head of Lincoln pressed in base. Sides and base are all-frosted. It is three and three-eighths by four and seven-eighths inches in size. The depth is one and one-eighth inches. Probably an item of the 1876 centennial.

No. 277　Lincoln Statuette

No. 278　Lincoln Logs Plaque

No. 277   Lincoln Statuette

A portrait bust of Lincoln is a companion to the Washington item No. 258. It strongly resembles marble. The one illustrated is made of opaque white glass, with satinized finish. It was made also in clear glass, with frosted finish. Some specimens are inscribed on back of base: "Centennial Exhibition Gillinder and Sons." It is very heavy, weighing three and three-fourths pounds. Its height is six inches. A rare and desirable item.

No. 278   Lincoln Logs Plaque

An opaque white plaque suitable for hanging on the wall or for use on a table easel, has a likeness of Lincoln molded in high relief. The portrait center is framed in an openwork design resembling rails. These rails are stippled to resemble tree bark.

There seems little doubt that this is an 1864 campaign item. The beard is very short, and the hair is parted on the right side. These details report it as of that year. All pictures of Lincoln with a beard were made between November 1860 and April 1865. When he came to Washington, his beard was full. Barbers gradually shortened it until in 1865 it became very short. All pictures made from the time of his first inauguration until February 9, 1864, show his hair parted on the left side of his head. After February, 1864, the parting was on the right side, until 1865 when he went back to the left side parting. The plaque measures six and three-fourths by eight and one-fourth inches.

No. 279   Lincoln Lithophane

A rectangular plaque of milk-white glass, a transparency, also bears a well executed portrait of Lincoln. The border is plain, simulating a wooden frame. It, too, shows the short beard, and hair parted on the right side. The portrait seems to be a Brady profile, taken February 9, 1864. The personal history of this particular piece also establishes it as a campaign item of 1864. It was

No. 280   Lincoln Drape with Tassel Pattern Goblet

No. 281   Lincoln Drape Pattern Compote

brought by a Union soldier, in the War between the States, as a gift to his parents, when he came home on furlough. It is eight by eleven inches in size. A handsome, but elusive item. (See frontispiece.)

No. 280 Lincoln Drape with Tassel Pattern Goblet

A crystal goblet honoring Lincoln, is one form in the pattern named Lincoln Drape with Tassel, issued after the death of the President. Although the pattern is suggestive of funereal drapery, the glass is not depressive in effect. It is clear and lovely, and of fine quality. Its height is six inches, and the diameter is three and one-fourth inches.

No. 281 Lincoln Drape Pattern Compote

An open compote honoring Lincoln, is one form in the pattern named Lincoln Drape, issued after the President's death. The design suggests funereal drapery, and is graceful and significant. It is crystal glass of fine quality. Its diameter is eight inches and the height is five and one-fourth inches.

No. 282 Lincoln's Tribute Tumbler

Lincoln's famous and oft repeated tribute to his mother is etched on this tumbler: "All I am or can be I owe to my angel mother." A graceful spray of flowers adds interest to the decorative effect. It is crystal glass, three and three-fourths inches in height, and the top diameter is two and three-fourths inches.

No. 283 Lincoln's Home Paperweight

A doorknob type paperweight has a crude picture of a log cabin, such as sheltered Lincoln. A tree grows beside the house. A squirrel sits in its branches. "Lincoln's Home" is inscribed at the top. The background is a thick layer of cobalt blue glass. The picture is outlined in white. The dome is crystal. It is three and one-fourth inches in diameter.

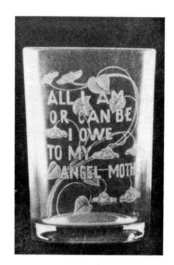

No. 282 Lincoln's Tribute Tumbler

No. 283 Lincoln's Home Paperweight

ULYSSES S. GRANT

Ulysses S. Grant (1822-1885), eighteenth President of the United States (1869-1877), won popular favor as a military man. He was a graduate of West Point (1843) and General of the Union Army in the War between the States. He won admiration for his modesty, calmness, and patience, and for great moral and physical courage as well as for his military successes. The trust which he placed in others sometimes was a disadvantage to him. Some of his advisers proved unworthy and created difficulties for him during his administration and for his personal affairs at a later time. In 1868 and again in 1872 he was elected President by overwhelming majorities. In the election of 1872 Grant received 292 electoral votes, the largest number that had ever been given to a presidential candidate.

No. 284   Grant Paperweight

A simply made paperweight is of the doorknob type. A profile bust of Grant is pressed in the base. "U. S." is inscribed at the left of this portrait, and "Grant" at the right side. The base is slightly constricted. It could have been a campaign or a memorial item. It is two and three-fourths inches in diameter.

No. 285   Grant Tumbler

A water tumbler has a bust of Grant pressed in the base. "Let Us Have Peace" is inscribed beneath the portrait. Sides are plain. It is three and one-half inches in height. Top diameter is three and one-eighth inches.

No. 286   Grant-Wilson Goblet

A crystal goblet is clearly an item of the 1872 campaign. A bust portrait of Grant within a star-bordered oval medallion, is on the obverse. "Grant" is inscribed beneath the portrait.

A bust portrait of Henry Wilson (1812-1875), Vice-President with Grant (1873-1877), within a star-bordered

No. 284
Grant Paperweight

No. 285
Grant Tumbler

No. 286
Grant-Wilson Goblet

No. 287
Greeley-Brown Goblet

medallion is opposite Grant on the reverse. "Wilson" is inscribed beneath his portrait. His correct name was Jeremiah J. Colbath (or Colbaith) but for some reason he changed his name, by act of legislature, when twenty-one years old, to Henry Wilson.

The goblet is six and one-fourth inches in height, and top diameter is three and five-eighths inches. It must have been distributed in quantity, but one is hard to locate after the seventy-five years interval since it was issued.

No. 287   Greeley-Brown Goblet

Horace Greeley (1811-1872) was the defeated candidate for President in 1872. He was an outstanding editor, and U. S. Congressman, frank and open-minded, firm in his convictions, and sincere in his efforts for the welfare of the nation. He was eccentric, too, in his habits and in his thoughts. He advocated the abolition of slavery during the war, supported impartial suffrage during the period of reconstruction, but became a bondsman for Jefferson Davis in 1867. He lived but a short time after his defeat by Grant.

B. G. Brown (1826-1885), defeated Vice-Presidential candidate, was a military man, a Congressman, and Governor of Missouri. With the exception of portraits this goblet is identical with the one honoring Grant and Wilson.

No. 288   Grant Memorial Plate

A plate shows the portrait of Grant, in civilian dress. "Grant" is inscribed beneath the portrait. A laurel wreath against a stippled background provides a decorative border which carries the word "Memorial" at top. It is crystal glass, ten inches in diameter.

No. 289   Grant Peace Plate

A circular memorial plate presents a bust of Grant in uniform. The memorial dates: "Born April 27, 1822 Died July 23, 1885" appear in semi-circular form above the portrait. A stippled maple-leaf border provides a frame

No. 288   Grant Memorial Plate

No. 289   Grant Peace Plate

and carries the inscription: "Let Us Have Peace, U. S. Grant."

General Grant had known the horror and misery of war. He wanted no more of it. In his acceptance speech in 1868, he pictured the havoc of war and coined the phrase "Let Us Have Peace" which has been associated with his name ever since. The plate is found in several colors, crystal, two shades of amber, yellow, and green. It is ten and one-half inches in diameter.

No. 290   Grant's Tomb Bottle

This unusual piece of glassware is made to represent the tomb of Grant, in Riverside Park, New York City. It was built by voluntary contributions of the people, representing free offerings from grateful hearts. Dedication ceremonies on April 27, Grant's birthday, were lengthy and impressive.

The tomb is square in shape, 90 feet on a side; and is of Grecian-Doric order. Its height to the parapet is 72 feet. The circular cupola, 70 feet in diameter, terminates in a pyramidal top 150 feet above ground level. An inscription above the entrance reads: "Let Us Have Peace."

The bottle is opaque white glass. The base is three and one-fourth inches square. Height is eight inches. A rare item.

No. 291   Grant Square Plate

A deep plate features a medallion profile portrait of Grant, in uniform, in the center. "The Patriot and Soldier" is inscribed above, and "Gen. Ulysses S. Grant" below the portrait. A decorative pattern border covers the remainder of the plate. It is found most readily in crystal, but was made in amber. The amber one is extremely rare. It measures nine and one-half inches across and the depth is one and one-half inches. A memorial item.

No. 290 Grant's Tomb Bottle

No. 291 Grant Square Plate

RUTHERFORD B. HAYES

Rutherford B. Hayes (1822-1893) was the nineteenth President of the United States (1877-1881). The Presidential campaign of 1876 was so hotly contested that Congress referred the contested election returns to a joint Electoral Commission composed of five senators, five representatives, and five judges of the Supreme Court. These men decided that 185 electoral votes had been cast for Hayes and Wheeler, and 184 for Tilden and Hendricks.

William A. Wheeler (1819-1887) was a U. S. Congressman, prominent for many years in state and national politics. Nominated for Vice-President on the ticket with Hayes, he was elected and served (1877-1881).

No. 292   HAYES-WHEELER MUG

One glassware item refers to this exciting campaign. A mug, small in size, has a Liberty Bell molded on each side. One bell carries the name "Hayes," the other "Wheeler." Between the bells, a ribbon bears the dates "1776-1876." The base is inscribed "Adams and Co. Glass Works." This bell was produced, without the names, for the Nation's Centennial at Philadelphia in 1876. By adding the names of the Republican candidates, the mug doubled as a campaign item. It is crystal glass, two inches in height, and one and three-fourths inches in diameter. It was also made (without the names) in opaque white. Both are rare.

JAMES ABRAM GARFIELD

James Abram Garfield (1831-1881) was the twentieth President of the United States (1881). He brought to this high office an understanding of humanity, born of varied experiences. He was born in a log cabin, he taught school and became President of Hiram College; he preached the Gospel; he acquired the title of Major-General in the War between the States; he was a self-made statesman; he became leader of the Republican Party and in the campaign of 1880 was elected President. His sound principle and solid character promised well for the nation, but a few

301

No. 292   Hayes-Wheeler Mug

No. 293   Garfield-Arthur Mug

No. 294   Garfield Memorial Mug

months after his inauguration he was shot by a fanatic, and died.

Garfield is shown in company with other notables, on several items of glassware. He is seen with Washington and Lincoln, on a platter. (See item No. 249, under Washington.) He is shown again with these men, on a goblet. (See item No. 250, under Washington.) He appears with Lincoln, on a platter. (See item No. 271, under Lincoln.) And he is placed with Lincoln, once more, on a small mug. (See item No. 272, under Lincoln.)

No. 293   GARFIELD-ARTHUR MUG

This mug evidently was produced for the political campaign of 1880. A bust portrait of Garfield appears on the obverse, with "James A. Garfield" inscribed beneath the portrait. The figure of a raccoon, which once was an emblem of the Whig Party and also used by Republicans, decorates the reverse. The animal is thumbing its nose at opponents and is rather humorous in effect. "Garfield" is inscribed on the handle, obverse; and "Arthurs" on the opposite side. On top of the handle "1880" is placed. An inscription on the base reads "Adams and Co. Glass Mfgrs." The mug is very small, being one and seven-eighths inches in diameter, and two and one-fourth inches in height. Made in crystal glass, and not easy to secure.

No. 294   GARFIELD MEMORIAL MUG

The molds of this mug must have been re-cut from the campaign mug. The raccoon was replaced by a memorial scroll. Candidates' names were erased from the handle, but the date 1880 remains and provides the clue to the mug's origin. The figures are small and are placed where easily overlooked. The inscription was erased from the base, and beading was added. The memorial scroll is inscribed "Born Nov. 19th 1831. Assassinated July 2nd 1881, Died Sept. 19th, 1881." Made in crystal and in amber. Amber is rare.

303

No. 295
GARFIELD TUMBLER

No. 296
GARFIELD TUMBLER

No. 297
GARFIELD CUP-PLATE

No. 298
GARFIELD PAPERWEIGHT

No. 295   Garfield Tumbler

A crystal water tumbler has Garfield's likeness pressed in the base. Sides are plain. It is three and seven-eighths inches in height. Top diameter is three and one-sixteenth inches. It could have been a campaign item or a memorial piece. Since the date of his assassination was less than a year from the time of his election, it could be that some items served both purposes.

No. 296   Garfield Tumbler

Another tumbler has a smaller bust of Garfield pressed in the base. His name is inscribed beneath it. A laurel wreath frames the whole. Sides are plain. It is three and seven-eighths inches in height and the top diameter is three and one-fourth inches.

No. 297   Garfield Cup-Plate

A small receptacle honoring Garfield probably is a cup-plate, although sometimes called a pin-tray or ash-tray. A portrait of Garfield fills the base. Remainder of the item is plain. The sides are flaring. Diameter at top is three inches. Diameter at base is two and one-fourth inches. Depth is seven-eighths of an inch.

No. 298   Garfield Paperweight

A crystal paperweight, doorknob type, has the bust of Garfield pressed in a frosted base. Its diameter is three inches.

No. 299   Garfield Star Plate

A small plate has a bust portrait of Garfield in its center, surrounded by a border showing thirteen stars, a shield, and two flags. His name is inscribed beneath the portrait. Crystal glass, with bust clear or frosted. The diameter is six inches.

No. 299   Garfield Star Plate

No. 300   Garfield One-O-One Plate

No. 300   Garfield One-O-One Plate

On a larger plate, having integral handles, a frosted bust of Garfield ornaments the center.   The border is known as egg-and-dart pattern; also as one-o-one.   It is crystal glass, nine inches in diameter.

No. 301   Garfield ABC Plate

Another small plate has Garfield's likeness in the center, surrounded by an alphabet border.   Crystal glass, with frosted bust.   Diameter is six inches.

No. 302   Garfield Memorial Plate

Again, the portrait of Garfield decorates the center of a plate.   A laurel wreath against a stippled background forms the border.   "Memorial" is inscribed at top of border.   It is crystal glass, ten inches in diameter.

No. 303   Garfield Drape Pattern Plate

A large circular plate, with portrait bust of Garfield in the center, is surrounded by a circle of stars, and inscriptions: "We Mourn our Nation's Loss. Born Nov. 19, 1831. Shot July 2, 1881. Died Sept. 19, 1881." The Garfield Drape pattern forms a border.   The rim is scalloped.   It is crystal glass, eleven and one-half inches in diameter.

No. 304   Garfield Statuette

A portrait bust, or statuette, representing Garfield, was made in crystal glass, with satinized finish.   The base is unusual, being very large, and hollow.   Probably a memorial item.   The height is six and one-half inches.   Diameter of base is four and one-fourth inches.

No. 305   Garfield Drape Pattern Pitcher

The pitcher shown is one form in a pattern issued in honor of President Garfield.   Garlands for Garfield, might be called the theme of this design.   It is a long established

No. 301 GARFIELD ABC PLATE

No. 302 GARFIELD MEMORIAL PLATE

custom to use strings of leaves, flowers, or the like, as decoration in honor of some success won by an individual; and affection of this nation for the martyr-teacher-preacher, President Garfield, was suggested in the Garfield Drape. A festoon of flowers and foliage against a lightly stippled background is arranged in three swags around the body of the pitcher. It is crystal glass, milk-size. Extreme height is eight and three-fourths inches.

No. 306   Garfield Monument Plate

The Garfield Monument in Lake View Cemetery, Cleveland, Ohio, is shown here. It was completed in 1890, and is built of Ohio sandstone. The tower rises to a height of 165 feet. In the base is a chapel containing a statue of Garfield; and a crypt below the statue holds his remains.

The plate is opaque white glass. The monument is molded in high relief, and accented with brown paint. Brown paint is used also on the leaf border. Trees and grass are shown in green. "Garfield Monument" is lettered near the top. Diameter: seven and one-fourth inches.

No. 307   Garfield Shaving-Mug

Both President and Mrs. Garfield are honored in this unusual shaving-mug. Lucretia Randolph and the President were married about the time that he became president of Hiram College. At this time, Garfield was a leading preacher of the gospel as well as a popular teacher. Mrs. Garfield was well fitted for her position. She had been a teacher and was able to give assistance in preparing lectures as well as being the capable wife and mother. Until the President's death, she was an active companion in the events that brought to them the highest honor a nation can bestow. During his last long illness, she was the most untiring of all the attendants who cared for him. Her heroic years well earned for her the esteem given when laurel sprays were used in connection with her portrait, to suggest honor. They are placed on either side of her portrait,

309

No. 303   Garfield Drape Pattern Plate

No. 304
Garfield Statuette

No. 305
Garfield Drape Pattern Pitcher

on the reverse side of the mug. Garfield's likeness is on the opposite side, with sprays of ivy, signifying an evergreen memory, on either side of the portrait. It is opaque white glass. Height: two and three-fourths inches. The width is five inches. A memorial item of 1881.

No. 308   Hancock Paperweight

Winfield S. Hancock (1824-1886) was the Presidential candidate of the Democratic Party in 1880, but he lost to Garfield. His popularity was due to a military career. He graduated from the U. S. Military Academy in 1844. He was a veteran of the Mexican War. He was made a Major-General in the regular army during the War between the States. General Grant said of him: "Hancock stands the most conspicuous figure of all the general officers who did not exercise a separate command. He commanded a corps longer than any other one, and his name was never mentioned as having committed a blunder for which he was responsible."

The Hancock paperweight shows a likeness of the man pressed in the base. He wears civilian clothing. It is crystal glass, three and one-fourth inches in diameter. Depth is seven-eighths of an inch. Probably an item of the 1880 campaign.

311

No. 306   GARFIELD MONUMENT PLATE

No. 307   GARFIELD SHAVING-MUG

312

Wm. H. English (1822-1896) won political popularity in his home state, Indiana. He became Congressman in 1852, and was a strong opponent of secession. In 1880, he was nominated by the Democratic Party, for Vice-President on the ticket with Hancock, and lost.

A bottle probably is intended to honor English. It is shaped like the bust of him and bears a strong resemblance to his pictures. Some think it may represent General Robert E. Lee. These men do bear a strong resemblance to each other, and there is no inscription for identification. The resemblance to English is stronger, and the flowing tie, as seen in pictures of English, supports this theory. It is a large bottle, being eleven inches in height, and it is extremely rare. The writer has seen no more than two and heard of no others. This also suggests the English identity since the universal popularity of General Lee should have given a commemorative bottle representing him, a larger distribution.

No. 308 Hancock Paperweight

No. 309 English Bottle

THE CAMPAIGN OF 1884

The political campaign of 1884 was one of the most hotly contested elections ever held. The Democratic Party nominated Grover Cleveland and Thomas Hendricks. The Republican Party named James G. Blaine and John A. Logan. The contest was marked by bitter recriminations, both nominees Blaine and Cleveland suffering unparalleled attacks that produced one of the most extraordinary and exciting personal campaigns on record.

Some Independent Republican voters bolted the nomination of Blaine and were called "mugwumps." Mugwump is a word of Indian derivation (meaning a great personage) that after long use in localities, and occasional use in politics, now came into prominence through being applied to all Independent Republicans.

Republican campaign clubs were called "Plumed Knights" because Blaine was popularly known as the "Plumed Knight." The name was derived from a speech of Colonel Robert Ingersoll, in which he gave that designation to Mr. Blaine.

This campaign, too, gave rise to the phrase, "Rum, Romanism, and Rebellion." At a meeting of clergy, in which all denominations were supposed to be represented, held in New York City, Reverend R. B. Burchard described the Democrats as the party of Rum, Romanism, and Rebellion. This remark was unfortunate and the opposition made ready capital of the bracketing of Roman Catholicism with the liquor traffic and Rebellion. Blaine, as well as many others, believed the loss of the Roman Catholic vote in this way, was responsible for his defeat. He lost the State of New York, and so lost the electoral college.

All four of the office-seekers had enviable records of worthy service over a long period of time.

No. 310   CLEVELAND CLASSIC PATTERN PLATE

No. 311   HENDRICKS CLASSIC PATTERN PLATE

No. 312   BLAINE CLASSIC PATTERN PLATE

No. 313   LOGAN CLASSIC PATTERN PLATE

Thomas A. Hendricks

T. A. Hendricks (1819-1885) was a native of Ohio. He was elected to the Indiana House of Representatives in 1848 and became Senator in 1849. Was a prominent member of the convention for the revision of the State Constitution in 1850-51. Was a Representative in the United States Congress from 1851 to 1855. Was a Commissioner of the United States General Land Office 1855 to 1859. A United States Senator 1863-1869; Governor of Indiana from 1873 to 1877. From 1868 until his death in 1885 he was put forward for nomination for the Presidency at every Democratic Convention, save in 1872. In 1876, and in 1884, after he failed to receive the nomination for President, he was nominated for Vice-President. In 1876, he lost the disputed election by the decision of the electoral commission. He was elected with Grover Cleveland in 1884 and died during his term of office.

John Alexander Logan

Hendricks' opponent in this memorable campaign, was John A. Logan (1826-1886), a native of Illinois. He saw service during the Mexican War. He entered politics as a Douglas Democrat. Left politics to engage in the War between the States, became known as "Black Jack" Logan, and was one of the most noted non-West-Pointers. After the War, he resumed politics, as a Republican. Served as United States Congressman 1867-1871, and Senator 1871-1877, and 1879-1886. He had an influential part in legislation relating to the reconstruction of the South, and from his activity in promoting measures for the benefit of the soldiers, came to be regarded by them as their special champion and friend. He was one of the founders of the Grand Army of the Republic and was its first national commander (1868-1871). He also first instituted Memorial Day which is now observed on the 30th day of May, every year. It is believed the idea originated with him. He received some votes for Presidential nominee at the convention of 1884, and was nominated for Vice-President on the Republican ticket.

James Gillespie Blaine

Logan's running-mate, James Gillespie Blaine (1830-1893), was one of a long list of Americans whose ability and political qualifications have led them close to the presidency of the United States. Mr. Blaine was a native of Pennsylvania, but in 1854 became a resident of Maine and was elected to the State Legislature in 1858. Was elected to the United States Congress in 1862 where he served in the House of Representatives until 1881, when he resigned to become Secretary of State. In 1869 he was elected Speaker of the House of Representatives, at that time one of the most powerful positions in the American Government. He served in this capacity for six years. In 1876, Blaine was the leading candidate for the Republican nomination for the Presidency but suffered a sunstroke on the eve of the convention. Rumors of his illness (even of his death) were circulated freely and probably contributed to his losing the nomination to Hayes, by 28 votes. In 1880, Blaine was again a candidate for the Presidential nomination but lost to Garfield. During the short administration of President Garfield, Blaine was Secretary of State, and on the death of his chief he resigned office and retired to his home in Maine. In 1884, Blaine was finally nominated for the Presidency by the Republican convention. His campaign was brilliant and his election seemed sure until the incident in New York City previously mentioned, and he lost the election to his opponent, Mr. Cleveland.

Grover Cleveland

Grover Cleveland (1837-1908) was born in New Jersey. When the War between the States began, the three Cleveland brothers drew lots to see which should remain at home to support their mother; the lot fell to Grover and when he was drafted he hired a substitute. His first great oppor-

No. 314 Cleveland-Hendricks Tray

No. 315 Blaine-Logan Tray

tunity came in 1881, when a reform movement made him the Mayor of Buffalo. In 1882 he received the Democratic nomination for Governor of New York. The prestige won in this office made him a national figure. In 1884 the Democratic Party had been out of power in national affairs for twenty-three years. Upon a platform which called for radical reforms in the administrative departments, the civil service, the tariff, and the national finances, he was nominated for President and subsequently elected. He was re-nominated for the Presidency in 1888 but lost to his Republican opponent in a campaign which had the tariff as its leading feature. In 1892 he was again the successful Democratic candidate, and was the first of our Presidents to serve a second term without being elected as his own successor. In 1886, he was married in the White House, to Miss Frances Folsom. Mrs. Cleveland was the first wife of a President married in the White House and their daughter Esther was the first child to be born in the Executive Mansion.

Four companion plates commemorate the campaign of 1884. The name "P. J. Jacobus, Scul." in small letters, is inscribed on one shoulder in the Blaine, and also in the Hendricks plate. It could be that some Cleveland and Logan items might also be found so labeled. They are large plates, eleven and one-half inches in diameter. They represent the highest in artistic merit of all glassware portraiture.

No. 310 Cleveland Classic Pattern Plate

A finely modeled bust portrait of Cleveland is in the center. Border is of the Classic pattern. Crystal glass, all-frosted center.

No. 311 Hendricks Classic Pattern Plate

A finely modeled bust portrait of Hendricks is in the center. Border is of the Classic pattern. Crystal glass, all-frosted center.

321

No. 316   Cleveland Reform Plate

No. 317   Blaine-Logan Flask

322

No. 312   Blaine Classic Pattern Plate

A finely modeled bust portrait of Blaine is in the center. Border is of the Classic pattern. Crystal glass, all-frosted center.

No. 313   Logan Classic Pattern Plate

A finely modeled bust portrait of Logan is in the center. Border is of the Classic pattern. Crystal glass, all-frosted center.

No. 314   Cleveland-Hendricks Tray

A rectangular tray honors Cleveland and Hendricks. Bust portraits of these men form an all-frosted center. Names of each are inscribed on the busts. Stippled ivy leaves form an attractive border, and well-designed handles give a finished effect. It is eleven and one-half by eight and one-half inches in size, and is a campaign item of 1884.

No. 315   Blaine-Logan Tray

This tray honors the defeated candidates Blaine and Logan, and matches the Cleveland-Hendricks item in all respects excepting the portraits.

No. 316   Cleveland Reform Plate

A circular plate has the bust portrait of Cleveland in its center. His name is inscribed beneath it. A hobnail pattern forms the border, with the word "Reform" at top. It is crystal glass, ten inches in diameter. Probably a campaign item of 1884 although it could refer to later years. Cleveland always ran for office on a reform platform.

No. 317   Blaine-Logan Flask

A pint flask has the bust of Blaine within a depressed circle, on the obverse. A matching bust of Logan is on the reverse. Names of the men are on the busts. Crystal glass.

No. 318   Cleveland Bottle

No. 319   Cleveland Campaign Horn

No. 318   Cleveland Bottle

A bottle is shaped like a bust of Cleveland.   According to N. Hudson Moore in the Collector's Manual, this bottle was "brought out in the Cleveland campaign."   Since this type of bottle was popular in the 1870's and for some years later, perhaps it should be attributed to his first campaign in 1884.   His name is inscribed on front of base.   Base and neck are clear glass, with the remainder in acid finish.   The Cleveland bottle is larger than most bottles of this type, being ten inches in height.   The base is three and one-fourth inches in diameter.

No. 319   Cleveland Campaign Horn

The Cleveland horn is in a color class all by itself.   It isn't blue and it isn't green, yet it is of a blue-green cast.

Workmen in the lamp-room at Whitall-Tatum and Co., Millville, New Jersey, sometimes made these horns for their own amusement.   They were never made for the market. When the men finished celebrating, horns were dashed to bits as is sometimes done with champagne glasses.   It would require a glass-blower's lung power to tootle this horn, for fun, throughout an evening's celebration.   An average person soon would become exhausted.   This one is a lone survivor of Cleveland's campaign in 1884.   It is ten and one-half inches in length.

No. 320   Cleveland Tumbler

In a tumbler honoring Cleveland, a bust portrait is placed on one side of the glass.   "Our Next President" is inscribed above the portrait.   The word "Marie" is etched on the opposite side.   This is the name, no doubt, of the original owner.   Probably a campaign item of 1884, although it could refer to a later campaign.   Crystal glass, three and three-fourths inches in height.

No. 321   Blaine Tumbler

A tumbler honoring Blaine has a portrait of the man on one side, and his autograph beneath.   Crystal glass, with

No. 320
CLEVELAND TUMBLER

No. 321
BLAINE TUMBLER

No. 322
LOGAN TUMBLER

No. 323
BLAINE TUMBLER

portrait and autograph in red transfer. Height: three and five-eighths inches. Diameter: two and five-eighths inches.

No. 322   Logan Tumbler

A tumbler honoring Logan has the name "Logan" engraved in Old English letters, within a wreath. Probably a memorial item, but could have been issued during the 1884 campaign. Crystal glass. Height: three and one-half inches. Diameter: two inches.

No. 323   Blaine Tumbler

Another tumbler honoring Blaine has the bust portrait of him pressed in the base against a stippled background. It is crystal glass, three and five-eighths inches in height. The top diameter is three and one-sixteenth inches.

Benjamin Harrison

Benjamin Harrison (1833-1901), twenty-third President of the United States (1889-1893), was a grandson of the ninth President, William Henry Harrison. He was named for his great-grandfather, Benjamin Harrison of Virginia, who was a signer of the Declaration of Independence. He became famous in his own right. He was a veteran of the War between the States, and was popular with his men who nicknamed him "Little Ben." He had served in the United States Senate and won distinction as an impromptu orator. He was nominated by the Republicans for President in 1888 and won the election against the Democratic candidate, Grover Cleveland.

Levi P. Morton

Levi P. Morton (1824-1920) won popularity as a banker and politician. His banking firm was fiscal agent of the United States Government from 1873 to 1884. He served as a United States Congressman and as United States Minister to France. In 1888 he was elected Vice-President of the United States with Benjamin Harrison and served from

327

No. 324　Harrison-Morton Tray

No. 325　Cleveland-Thurman Tray

1889 to 1893.   At a later date he was Governor of New York.

ALLEN G. THURMAN

Allen G. Thurman (1813-1895) was a statesman who gave many years of service to his country.   He was a Congressman, from Ohio; he was Chief Justice of the Supreme Court; and he was the minority party leader for some time. He received votes in the Democratic National Conventions of 1876, 1880 and 1884.   In 1888 he was nominated by acclamation for second place on the ticket with Cleveland but was defeated in the election.

No. 324   HARRISON-MORTON TRAY

A rectangular tray honors Harrison and Morton.   Bust portraits of these men form an all-frosted center.   Names of each are inscribed on the busts.   Stippled ivy leaves form an attractive border.   It is crystal glass, nine and one-half by eight and one-half inches in size.

No. 325   CLEVELAND-THURMAN TRAY

A rectangular tray honors Cleveland and Thurman, defeated candidates in the campaign of 1888.   Bust portraits of the contenders are framed by an ivy leaf border.   Each portrait is inscribed with the subject's name.   Center is all-frosted, and ivy leaves are stippled.   It is nine and one-half by eight and one-half inches in size, and matches a tray honoring the winning candidates.

No. 326   HARRISON-MORTON MUG

A mug was issued in honor of Harrison and Morton. Bust portrait of Harrison is on the obverse, within a stippled medallion.   Bust portrait of Morton is placed opposite on the reverse.   It too, is within a stippled medallion.   It is three inches in diameter, and three and one-eighth inches in height.   Made for the campaign of 1888, in crystal and blue.   Blue is scarce.   The mug illustrated shows many large bubbles in the glass.

329

No. 326   Harrison-Morton Mug

No. 327   Cleveland-Thurman Mug

No. 327   Cleveland-Thurman Mug

Mug honoring Cleveland and Thurman.   Bust portrait of Cleveland ornaments the obverse.   Bust portrait of Thurman is shown on the reverse.   Crystal glass, three inches in diameter, three and one-eighth inches in height. A campaign item of 1888.

No. 328   Harrison Statuette

A portrait bust of Harrison was made.   It is of frosted crystal glass, and rests on a special base, a tall column of fluted black amethyst glass.   The bust is five and three-fourths inches in height.   The base measures eleven inches, and largest base diameter is four and one-fourth inches. It may have been a campaign item of 1888, or of 1892, or possibly a memorial piece.

Whitelaw Reid

Whitelaw Reid (1837-1912) was a journalist, editor, and diplomat.   He was a war correspondent during the War between the States.   He became editor and proprietor of the New York Tribune.   He was Minister to France, and in 1892 was the candidate of Republicans for Vice-President on the ticket with Harrison but was defeated.

No. 329   Harrison-Reid Paperweight

A doorknob type, crystal paperweight, pictures a high hat done in gold, against a frosted background.   "The Harrison Hat" is on the hat-band.   "One Good Term Deserves Another" is placed above the hat.   Below it is: "In hoc signo vinces" and "Harrison and Reid."   Campaign item of 1892.

In hoc signo vinces (by this sign thou wilt conquer) was the motto of the Roman Emperor Constantine, first Christian Emperor.   During one of his campaigns it is said, he saw in the heavens, a luminous cross with this inscription: "With This Sign You Will Conquer."   He made the cross the royal standard and his soldiers for the first time marched under the emblem of Christianity.

331

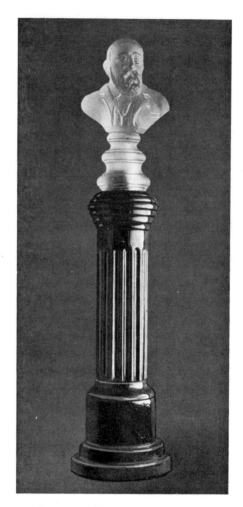

No. 328   Harrison Statuette

No. 330   Cleveland Hat

A toothpick or match holder is shaped like a high hat. It usually is called the Cleveland hat. It also is called the Harrison hat. Both parties used the high hat theme in this campaign. In Republican parades, marchers wore black high hats. In Democratic parades, they wore grey high hats. An inscription on one side of the glass hat reads: "The Same Old Hat." This could apply to either candidate, since Cleveland won the 1884 election, and Harrison won in 1888. Another slogan on the opposite side: "He's All Right" might be claimed by either side, too. In parades, the campaign cry "What's The Matter With Cleveland" or "What's The Matter With Harrison" was answered with a lusty "He's All Right." The hat is crystal glass, two and one-fourth inches in height. A campaign item of 1892.

Adlai Ewing Stevenson

Adlai Ewing Stevenson (1835-1914) was an attorney and legislator, and Congressman from Illinois. He was First Assistant Postmaster-General in President Cleveland's first administration. In 1892, he received the nomination for Vice-President on the ticket with Cleveland, was elected, and served with him (1893-1897).

No. 331   Cleve-Steve Flask

A flask honors Cleveland and Stevenson. It is a pint size flask, made in the form of a wooden keg, flattened. Staves and hoops are clearly defined. On one side, bust portraits of the men are placed within a rectangular panel. Above these portraits is the inscription "Our Choice." Below, "Cleve and Steve, November 8th 92, March 4th 93." The only decoration on the opposite side is the figure of a crowing rooster which is a symbol often used by the Democrats. Color is aqua. A smaller size in amber is reported. A scarce item of the 1892 campaign.

No. 329
HARRISON-REID PAPERWEIGHT

No. 330
CLEVELAND HAT

No. 331   CLEVE-STEVE FLASK

William McKinley

William McKinley (1843-1901), twenty-fifth President of the United States (1897-1901), was a veteran of the War between the States. He was Governor of Ohio, and served seven terms in Congress. He won popular attention by the protective tariff bill which bore his name. He was the Republican choice for President in the campaign of 1896, and won the election largely by defending the gold standard against the free coinage of silver, advocated by his Democratic opponent. His conduct of the Spanish-American War had popular approval and he was re-nominated by acclamation, in 1900. In 1901 he met an untimely death at the hands of an anarchist, and his name was added to the list of our martyr Presidents.

Garret A. Hobart

Garret A. Hobart (1844-1899) was a statesman who was long conspicuous in New Jersey politics, and in Republican national nominating conventions. In 1896 he accepted the nomination for Vice-President on the ticket with McKinley and was elected. He died during his term of office.

William J. Bryan

William J. Bryan (1860-1925) was a Congressman who won popularity by his eloquence in debate. Though he never was in the White House, he was the recognized moving spirit and leader of the Democratic Party for thirty years. He was the Democratic Presidential nominee in 1896, but lost to McKinley. He was nominated again in 1900 and was again defeated by McKinley. He was nominated for the third time in 1908 and lost to Theodore Roosevelt. It was largely due to his influence that Woodrow Wilson received the nomination in 1912, and he served as Secretary of State in Wilson's cabinet.

Free silver coinage was advocated by Bryan, as well as tariff and voting reforms. His sympathy for the masses

335

No. 332   McKinley Gold Standard Tray

336

who had been neglected in legislation made him popular with his party and with the general public, but he could not win the votes required for election success. He often was referred to as The Great Commoner, and the silver-tongued orator. He was the youngest candidate ever named for the Presidency by any party in United States history.

No. 332   McKinley Gold Standard Tray

In the center, a full length figure of McKinley stands on a plank inscribed "Gold." "The Gold Standard" expressed the attitude of the Republican Party with respect to the coinage only of money which would be worth its face value anywhere in the world. In his right hand he holds a scroll inscribed "Sound Money Policy." On the base of this scroll is his autograph "W. McKinl." The letters "ey" are supposed to be concealed by his coat. The border pattern is identical with that of a tray in the pattern called Feather Duster. It is crystal glass, seven and three-fourths by ten and one-fourth inches in size. Evidently a campaign item of 1896.

No. 333   McKinley Protection and Plenty Plate

A circular plate has McKinley's portrait framed by a shield within a circle. "Protection and Plenty" is beneath the portrait. The phrase, protection and plenty (or prosperity), referred to the doctrine of a protective tariff advocated by Republicans. Democrats favored free trade. Forty-five stars, one for each state in the Union at that time, ornament the border. It has a rope edge. Crystal glass, and made in several sizes. The one pictured is seven and one-fourth inches in diameter. A campaign item of 1896.

No. 334   McKinley Plaque

A round plaque shows McKinley's portrait in relief, within a simulated picture-frame border. The rim is pierced for hanging. Inscribed on coat, "Wm. McKinley."

No. 333   McKinley Protection and Plenty Plate

No. 334   McKinley Plaque

It is opaque white glass of fine quality and is an unusually well executed piece. Diameter is seven and one-half inches. Perhaps a campaign item but could be memorial. Rare.

No. 335   McKinley Covered Cup

A covered cup, or mug, honors McKinley. A bust portrait is placed opposite the handle. His name is beneath the portrait. "Protection and Prosperity" is lettered above it. This slogan was commonly used during the campaign, and refers to the McKinley protective tariff law which was passed by Congress, to protect American working-men against low wages, by holding back low priced foreign goods made by cheap labor. The remainder of the mug is covered with scrolls and conventional patterns against a stippled background. A domed cover repeats the decorative motifs on the mug. It is crystal glass, five inches in height, and three and three-fourths inches top diameter. A campaign item of 1896.

No. 336   Bryan Covered Cup

The Bryan covered cup matches the McKinley cup, with the exception of portraits and inscriptions. Bryan's name is beneath his portrait, and "The People's Money" is lettered above it. This referred to the gold versus silver controversy which high-lighted the campaign.

No. 337   McKinley Tumbler

A water tumbler has McKinley's likeness pressed in the base. The slogan "Protection and Plenty" above and below the portrait proves it to be a campaign item. Plain sides. It is three and seven-eighths inches in height, and three inches top diameter.

No. 335
MCKINLEY COVERED CUP

No. 336
BRYAN COVERED CUP

340

No. 338   McKinley-Hobart Tumbler

This tumbler honors both McKinley and his Vice-President Hobart. Bust portraits of the men, in oval medallions, are placed on the side. The name of each is inscribed beneath his portrait. U. S. flags are seen in the background. The words "Protection" and "Prosperity" are part of a decorative effect between the medallions. The reverse is etched with the name "Orie" (no doubt the owner's name) and the date "1896." It is crystal glass, three and one-half inches in height.

No. 339   McKinley-Hobart Tumbler

Another tumbler honors McKinley and Hobart. Bust portraits of both men are placed in oval medallions on the side. Wreaths frame the medallions. Inscribed beneath portraits "Integrity" "Inspiration" "Industry." Crystal glass, three and three-fourths inches in height. Thin glass, straight sides. Campaign item of 1896.

No. 340   McKinley-Hobart Tumbler

A third tumbler honors the winners of the 1896 campaign. Portraits of McKinley and Hobart, in oval medallions, are placed on the side. The name of each individual is inscribed above his portrait. Flags, stars, a wreath, and a shield, are used for decoration. Crystal glass, and very thin. Height: three and three-fourths inches.

No. 337
McKinley Tumbler

No. 338
McKinley-Hobart Tumbler

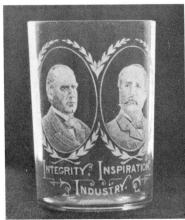

No. 339
McKinley-Hobart Tumbler

No. 340
McKinley-Hobart Tumbler

No. 341   McKinley Gothic Border Plate

A circular plate has Gothic pattern border framing the bust portrait of McKinley. His name is inscribed on the coat. Found in opaque white glass, and in black amethyst. The black amethyst is rare. Diameter is nine inches. A campaign item of 1896 or 1900.

No. 342   Bryan Gothic Border Plate

This plate matches the McKinley one, excepting the portrait, which is that of Bryan, and his name inscribed on his coat. It is the same size, and is found in the same colors.

No. 343   Bryan E Pluribus Unum Plate

A circular plate honoring Bryan has his portrait in center framed by a circle of thirteen stars, the date 1896, and words "E Pluribus Unum." Inscribed on his right shoulder "Bryan," and on the left shoulder "16 to 1." 16 to 1 referred to the Democratic demand for free coinage of silver at a ratio of 16 to 1 as compared with gold. Forget-me-not border. Crystal glass. Diameter: nine inches.

No. 344   McKinley Forget-Me-Not Plate

A small plate has forget-me-not border framing Mc-Kinley's portrait. It is crystal glass, five and one-half inches in diameter. Probably a campaign item of 1896 or 1900.

No. 345   Bryan Forget-Me-Not Plate

A plate matches the one above, excepting the portrait which is that of Bryan. Both plates are five and one-half inches in diameter.

No. 346   McKinley Cup-Plate

A cup-plate has McKinley's portrait in center. The rim is petal shaped. It is opaque white glass, and the portrait is in red transfer. The diameter is three and one-eighth inches. Probably an item of 1896 or 1900.

No. 341 McKinley Gothic Border Plate

No. 342 Bryan Gothic Border Plate

344

No. 343   Bryan E Pluribus Unum Plate

No. 344
McKinley
Forget-Me-Not Plate

No. 345
Bryan
Forget-Me-Not Plate

No. 347   McKinley Sailor Hat

A novelty in the shape of a sailor straw hat has Mc-
Kinley's portrait in black transfer inside the crown. The
wide ribbon hat-band is gold. It matches a hat honoring
Bryan, that has a silver hat-band. It is four by three and
one-half inches in size. Depth is one inch. Opaque white
glass. A campaign item of 1896 or 1900, possibly both.

No. 348   McKinley Plate

A small plate has leaf border, framing McKinley's likeness. It is of opaque white glass, with portrait in black
transfer. The diameter is five and one-fourth inches.
Probably a campaign item.

No. 349   McKinley-Roosevelt Plate

A small plate has portraits of McKinley and Vice-President Roosevelt, within a wreath. It is opaque white glass.
Portraits are in reddish brown transfer. The rim is decorated in blue. Five and one-half inches in diameter. A
campaign item of 1900.

No. 350   McKinley Tumbler

McKinley's likeness is on the side. "Our President 1896
to 1900" is inscribed beneath. Probably a campaign piece
of 1900, and suggests candidate McKinley who first was
nominated in 1896. He did not become President until
1897. Crystal glass, very thin. It is three and three-fourths
inches in height.

No. 351   McKinley Tumbler

A tumbler is identical with the foregoing one, excepting
the dates. On this, they read "1897 to 1901." Because of
the date 1901, this seems to be a memorial tumbler, and no
doubt was a re-issue of the other, with only a change of
dates.

346

No. 346
McKinley Cup-Plate

No. 347
McKinley Sailor Hat

No. 348
McKinley Plate

No. 349
McKinley-Roosevelt Plate

No. 352   McKinley Tumbler

A memorial tumbler has McKinley's portrait on the side, framed by a wreath of small flags. His autograph is beneath his portrait. Inscribed at top "Our Martyr President." Inscribed at bottom "Assassinated Sept. 6, Died Sept. 14, 1901." Crystal glass, very thin. Height: three and seven-eighths inches.

No. 353   McKinley-Roosevelt Tumbler

McKinley and Vice-President Roosevelt are honored here. Portraits of them, in oval medallions, are placed on the side. Laurel wreaths frame the medallions. The name of each is placed beneath his portrait. A spread eagle, with shield, hovers between and above the medallions. Three stars within a small wreath are placed between the medallions, near the base. Crystal glass, very thin. The height is three and three-fourths inches. A campaign item of 1900.

No. 354   McKinley Statuette

A portrait bust, or statuette, of McKinley, was made in crystal glass, with satinized finish. Probably a memorial item. The height is five and one-half inches.

No. 355   McKinley-Roosevelt Canteen

Portraits of McKinley and Roosevelt are placed on the obverse. Their names are beneath their portraits. Other decoration consists of an eagle, a shield, and a building representing the Capitol. "U. S." in large red letters, is on the reverse. The neck is threaded for a metal screw cap. A red, white, and blue cord is attached by means of metal hoops. Capacity: one-half pint. A campaign item of 1900.

No. 350
McKinley Tumbler

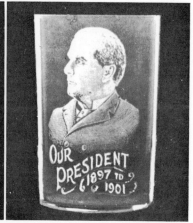

No. 351
McKinley Tumbler

No. 352
McKinley Tumbler

No. 353
McKinley-Roosevelt Tumbler

No. 354
McKinley Statuette

No. 355
McKinley-Roosevelt Canteen

No. 356   McKinley Memorial Platter

No. 356   McKinley Memorial Platter

This platter shows the same figure of McKinley used in the Gold Standard Platter. The scroll and gold plank have been removed, and memorial dates added. The center is framed by a laurel wreath border, and inscriptions: "It is God's Way" "His Will be Done." These were the President's last words. It is crystal glass, ten and one-half by eight inches in size.

Theodore Roosevelt

Theodore Roosevelt (1858-1919), twenty-sixth President of the United States (1901-1909), was the youngest man ever to become President. His talents were many and varied. He was a sportsman, a naturalist, an explorer, a writer of ability, a statesman, and a soldier. Elected Vice-President in the campaign of 1900, the death of McKinley called him to the first position. He was returned to office in the election of 1904. His ability, energy, and personality, made his administration a vivid one.

In glassware, he was honored with McKinley on a plate, a tumbler, and a canteen flask. (See those items, under McKinley.)

No. 357   Theodore Roosevelt Platter

An oval platter honors Roosevelt. A profile bust portrait of Teddy against a background of faintly seen stars, forms the center. A rustic branch forms an oval frame for his portrait, and another provides the outer rim of the border. The border consists of a medley of symbols, all having some significance in the life of the President. There are teddy bears in various poses, suggesting recreations of Roosevelt: golf, tennis, hunting, music and dancing. Military effects suggest the Rough Rider. An eagle, shield, and crossed clubs refer to the Presidency. A border inscription reads "A Square Deal." Crystal glass, with portrait either frosted or clear. It is seven and three-fourths by ten and one-fourth inches in size.

352

William H. Taft

President Roosevelt selected Taft to be his Secretary of War. When he retired from office, he selected him as his successor. The Republican Party and the voters accepted the suggestion and Taft (1857-1930) became the twenty-seventh President of the United States (1909-1913). Taft's judicial temperament fitted him for the Supreme Court, and this ambition was fulfilled when President Harding appointed him Chief Justice. He was the only man who has been President and Chief Justice.

James S. Sherman

James S. Sherman (1855-1912) was long engaged in politics. He served continuously in the United States House of Representatives from 1886 to 1908, excepting the term 1891-1893. He was chairman of the Republican National Committee in 1906. In 1908, he was nominated for Vice-President on the ticket with Taft, and was elected. He was re-nominated in 1912 but died shortly before election day.

John Worth Kern

William J. Bryan again headed the Democratic ticket in 1908. John Worth Kern (1849-1917) Indiana Senator, was a prominent figure in Democratic affairs, and received the nomination for Vice-President on the ticket with the Great Commoner.

No. 358   Taft Plate

A circular plate honors President Taft. His jovial countenance is framed by a border design composed of two flags, four eagles, and forty-eight stars. It is opaque white glass, seven and one-half inches in diameter. A campaign item of 1908.

No. 357   Theodore Roosevelt Platter

No. 359   Bryan Plate

The Bryan plate is identical with the one honoring Taft, excepting the portrait. Both plates were touched with color and some of them are found with traces of paint remaining. Most have lost this feature.

No. 360   Taft-Sherman Plate

Another plate honors Taft and Vice-President Sherman. Flag draped busts of the men occupy the center. Their names are placed near their portraits. An open-work border design is composed of eagles and fleur-de-lis. The U. S. flag is at the top. Opaque white glass, with center designs in black transfer. It is seven and one-half inches in diameter. A campaign item of 1908.

No. 361   Taft-Sherman Platter

A platter honoring Taft and Sherman has portraits of the two men in the center, with the Grand Old Party elephant between them. A blanket on the elephant is lettered "G.O.P." The American eagle, with outstretched wings, is above the elephant. "Our Candidates" is placed beneath it. Names of the men, in large letters, are inscribed beneath their portraits. The border design is the most attractive part of the platter. It is a lovely arrangement featuring stars and stripes. It is crystal glass, eleven and one-fourth by eight inches in size. A campaign item of 1908.

No. 362   Bryan-Kern Platter

A platter honoring Bryan and Kern has portraits of the two men in the center, with the figure of a crowing cock between them. Above the cock is an American eagle with outstretched wings. Inscribed beneath the cock "Our Candidates." Inscribed beneath portraits "W. J. Bryan" and "J. W. Kern." The border is identical with No. 361. Size, too, is the same.

1908 was a great campaign year. The symbol of a crow-

No. 358   Taft Plate   No. 359   Bryan Plate

No. 360   Taft-Sherman Plate

ing cock was used, and the Democrats did plenty of crow-ing. Many bets were laid, with the loser furnishing a meal of "crow pie" (chicken pie) to the winner.

No. 363   Taft-Sherman Hat

A coin bank is shaped like Uncle Sam's hat. A slotted metal disc closes the opening. Paper portraits of the candidates were pasted on these discs. Names are beneath the portraits, and the words: "Republican Nominees" are above them. When distributed, these hats were filled with red peppermint candy. When empty, they were useful as children's penny banks. Opaque white glass, with red and blue decoration. Rim, at largest part is three and five-eighths inches across. A campaign item of 1908.

No. 364   Bryan-Kern Hat

This hat matches the one above, excepting the portraits are those of Bryan and Kern, with the words "Democratic Nominees" above them, and their names beneath.

No. 365   Taft-Sherman Lamp Chimney

A lamp chimney has bust portraits of Taft and Sherman, within oval medallions, placed on opposite sides. Names are beneath the portraits. Flags, stars, and an eagle surround the ovals. The figure of a raccoon, grinning and thumbing its nose at opponents, is placed between the ovals, at each side. Crystal. A campaign item of 1908.

No. 361   Taft-Sherman Platter

No. 362   Bryan-Kern Platter

Thomas R. Marshall

Thomas R. Marshall (1854-1925) had never held public office until he became Governor of Indiana in 1908. He did not achieve national prominence until he was nominated for Vice-President on the Democratic ticket with Woodrow Wilson, and elected.

No. 366 Marshall Cigar Bottle

During his term of office, someone asked him, in the "enquiring reporter" manner, what he thought was the greatest need of the country. The Vice-President did some quick thinking, saw the question was not one to be taken seriously, and replied: "A good five-cent cigar." This story soon was circulated throughout the nation. Report says that a small amber bottle, in the size and shape of a cigar, was produced as the "Marshall cigar."

Calvin Coolidge

Calvin Coolidge (1872-1933), thirtieth President of the United States (1923-1929) proved his ability, when Governor of Massachusetts. He was elected Vice-President on the Republican ticket in 1920. When President Warren Harding died, he became President. In 1924, he was nominated and elected President. In 1928 he stopped a "draft Coolidge" movement by saying "I do not choose to run for President in 1928." He advocated and emphasized economy in public affairs, efficiency of public service, abstention from the League of Nations but adherence to the World Court, and common sense in general matters.

No. 363   TAFT-SHERMAN HAT   No. 364   BRYAN-KERN HAT

METAL DISC FOR 363

METAL DISC FOR 364

No. 365   TAFT-SHERMAN LAMP CHIMNEY

No. 367   Coolidge Lamp

When President Harding died, the Presidential oath of office was administered to Calvin Coolidge by his father, John C. Coolidge, a justice of the peace, in the family home at Plymouth, Vermont, early in the morning of August 3, 1923.

The lamp, and lamp chimney pictured, are identical with the ones which lighted this dramatic scene.

Franklin Delano Roosevelt

Franklin Delano Roosevelt (1882-1945), thirty-second President of the United States (1933-1945), accepted an appointment as Assistant Secretary of the Navy in 1913. In 1920 he received the nomination for Vice-President on the Democratic ticket, but lost to Coolidge. He was elected Governor of New York in 1928 and again in 1930. In 1932 he was elected President. In 1936 he was re-elected. He was elected for the third time in 1940 and for the fourth time in 1944. He was the first President to serve more than two terms. He instituted the "New Deal" and "fireside talks" over radio networks. He died in office.

In the election of 1936, Roosevelt was opposed by the Republican candidate, Alfred M. Landon, of Kansas. In 1940, Wendell Willkie, a dark horse candidate of the Republicans, was his opponent.

No. 368   Landon Tea-Cup

Alfred Landon (1887-   ) was Republican candidate for President in 1936. A slogan used in this campaign was "Elect Landon, Save America." Landon's portrait and this slogan are etched on a crystal glass tea-cup.

No. 366   Marshall Cigar Bottle

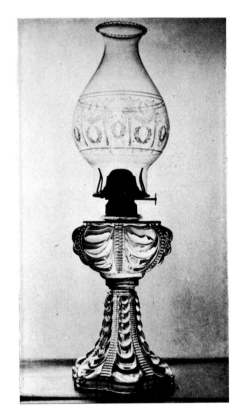

No. 367   Coolidge Lamp

No. 369   Landon Tea-Plate

The same portrait and slogan are deep-etched in the center of a tea-plate. The border is plain. Diameter is eight inches. The cups and plates were used at a reception given for the candidate during the campaign of 1936. After the reception, guests kept these glassware items as souvenirs of the occasion.

No. 370   Willkie Tumbler

Wendell Willkie (1892-1944) secured the Republican nomination in 1940. A tumbler honoring this candidate has his portrait placed within an oval, on one side. It is inscribed "The Winner." Crystal glass. Height: four and one-half inches. Top diameter: two and five-eighths inches.

No. 371   Willkie Acceptance Speech Tumbler

A portrait of Willkie is flanked by a battery of horizontal bars. Three rows of stars are placed around the top, and the same number around the base. Inscribed on reverse: "Wendell L. Willkie, Acceptance Speech, Aug. 17, Elwood, Indiana." Crystal glass. Stars at top are red, portrait and bars are white, and lower stars are blue. Height: four and one-half inches. Top diameter: two and five-eighths inches.

No. 368   Landon Tea-Cup

No. 369   Landon Tea-Plate

No. 370   Willkie Tumbler
No. 371   Willkie Acceptance Speech Tumbler

No. 120   T.V.A. Bottle

A large bottle displays the portrait of President Franklin D. Roosevelt. Beneath the portrait is the Coat-of-Arms of the United States, and the date, 1936. A dam, over which water is flowing, is pictured on the reverse. Below the dam, the date 1936 is inscribed. Above the dam, a hand is clenched around a bolt of lightning. It suggests the hand of man has the force of electricity within his control. The letters "T.V.A." are above the hand. They stand for Tennessee Valley Authority, the government-owned hydro-electric project. Capacity: forty-two ounces. Color: aqua. (Reprinted from Chapter V.)

* * *

No country in the world can present a list of leaders so renowned for talent and character as the Presidents of the United States. Records of these men point out something it is good to remember: that our nation is fortunate in not being forced to endure, as in most countries, leaders who are not competent and qualified to govern.

Presidential Nicknames

"A good name will wear out; a bad one may be turned; a nickname lasts forever."

George Washington.....................The Father of his country
Americus Fabius
The Cincinnatus of the West
Atlas of America
Deliverer of America
Savior of his country
Step-father of his country
(by his political opponents)

John Adams...............................Colossus of Independence
Duke of Braintree
Colossus of debate

Thomas Jefferson......................Sage of Monticello
Long Tom

Andrew Jackson.......................Sharp knife
Old Hickory
Hero of New Orleans

Wm. Henry Harrison.................Old Tippecanoe
Old Tip
Washington of the West
Cincinnatus of the West
Old Granny
Farmer President

Zachary Taylor.........................Rough and Ready
Old Zach
Old Buena Vista

Abraham Lincoln.......................Honest Abe
Uncle Abe
Father Abraham
Railsplitter

U. S. Grant...............................Unconditional Surrender Grant
Hero of Appomattox
American Caesar

R. B. Hayes..............................President de facto
Dark horse President
Fraud President
Granny Hayes
Old 8 to 7

James A. Garfield......................Martyr President

367

C. A. Arthur _____ Our Chet
Prince Arthur
His accidency
Arthur the gentleman
Dude President

Grover Cleveland _____ The Man of Destiny
Uncle Jumbo
Old veto

Benjamin Harrison _____ Son of his grandfather
Grandfather's hat
Little Ben

Wm. McKinley _____ Advance agent of prosperity
Napoleon of protection
Idol of Ohio
Stocking-foot orator

Theodore Roosevelt _____ Teddy
Rough Rider

Calvin Coolidge _____ Silent Cal
Watchdog of the treasury

F. D. Roosevelt _____ Father of the New Deal

It is a well established custom to provide some sort of catchy slogan for party use, in Presidential election years. An old one "Those Who Own the Country Ought to Govern It" suggested that men of refinement, education, and property owners, were better fitted to guide the nation, than were the masses.

1828

Andrew Jackson's Party used "The Democracy of Numbers Against the Monied Aristocracy of the Few."

1832

Jackson ran again, on his "Poor Against the Rich" slogan.

1840

The slogan "Tippecanoe and Tyler Too" used for Wm. H. Harrison, was one of the most highly successful slogans ever coined.

1844

James K. Polk used the slogan "Blow the Trumpet, Beat the Drum, Run Clay Coons, We Come, We Come." Henry Clay had kept the raccoon insignia used by his predecessor Harrison. "Fifty-Four-Forty or Fight" was used, too, in this campaign. This referred to the Northwest Boundary question, wherein the U. S. Government demanded territory up to the 54 degree 40 minute parallel; this demand being disputed by Britain. A compromise fixing the line at 49 degrees was finally accepted.

1848

"Old Rough and Ready" was the Whig slogan. The Democrats used "A Northern Man With Southern Principles" referring to Lewis Cass, their candidate.

1856

The slavery question now was responsible for "Free Soil, Free Speech, Free Labor, Free Men, and Fremont," the slogan for John C. Fremont. James Buchanan retaliated with the phrase "Black Republicans" and won the election.

"Vote Yourself a Farm" referred to a Republican homestead plank promising prairie farms west of the Mississippi, for the asking.

1864

The Lincoln slogan of this campaign was "Don't Swap Horses in the Middle of the Stream."

1868

"Reduce Taxes Before Taxation Reduces Us" was used against U. S. Grant, but Grant won. "The Same Money for the Bondholder and the Plowholder" was used also.

1872

"Turn The Rascals Out" was used against Grant but failed to defeat the candidate.

1884

"Rum, Romanism, and Rebellion" was a phrase used to characterize the Democratic Party. Reaction against it elected Grover Cleveland.

1888

"Public Office is a Public Trust" was used by Cleveland, but he lost to Benjamin Harrison.

1892

The Populist Party coined the humorous slogan "In God We Trusted, in Kansas We Busted."

1896

W. J. Bryan said "You Shall Not Crucify Mankind Upon a Cross of Gold." This referred to the free coinage of silver issue.

1900

"Four More Years of the Full Dinner Pail" was a slogan

that helped return McKinley to office. "Protection and Prosperity" was another Republican slogan used for McKinley.

1904

The admonition of Theodore Roosevelt to "Speak Softly But Carry a Big Stick" was popular, and he won the election.

1912

Vice-Presidential candidate Thomas R. Marshall's phrase, "What This Country Needs Is a Good Five Cent Cigar," was widely circulated.

1916

"He Kept Us Out of War" helped win the election for Woodrow Wilson, but we were not kept out of war.

1920

"Back to Normalcy" was offered by the Warren G. Harding campaign.

1924

"Keep Cool With Coolidge" was the Republican offering.

1928

Prohibition was one of the chief issues of this campaign. Republicans called it "The Noble Experiment." Other Republican slogans were "A Chicken in Every Pot" and "Hoover and Happiness or Al Smith and Soup Houses." Smith was offered as "The Happy Warrior" by the Democratic Party.

1932

"A New Deal For the Forgotten Man" was used by F. D. Roosevelt, while Hoover's Party predicted that "Prosperity is Just Around the Corner."

CHAPTER VIII

HEROES OF THE ARMY AND NAVY

The following list of names is a file of 51 army and navy men honored in glassware, whose commemoratives the author has been able to secure. Other items relating to some of these veterans have been reported, and some honoring other military men were made. Many of these were honored for service in other lines of achievement too, and this over-lapping makes full credit a complex procedure, with some inevitable dislocation and repetition.

INDIAN WARS
  Wm. H. Harrison
  Israel Putnam
  John Stark

FRENCH AND INDIAN WAR
  Benjamin Franklin
  Wm. Prescott
  Israel Putnam

REVOLUTIONARY WAR
  George Washington
  John Paul Jones
  Lafayette
  John Hancock
  Israel Putnam
  John Stark
  Joseph Warren
  Wm. Prescott
  Thomas Heyward, Jr.
  Wm. Whipple
  Arthur Middleton
  Caesar Rodney
  Noah Webster
  Edward Rutledge
  George Walton
  Oliver Wolcott

WAR OF 1812
  Wm. H. Harrison
  Andrew Jackson
  Zachary Taylor
  George Peabody
  Zebulon Pike

BLACK HAWK WAR
  Abraham Lincoln
  Zachary Taylor

MEXICAN WAR
  U. S. Grant
  Zachary Taylor
  W. S. Hancock
  John A. Logan
  Braxton Bragg
  Samuel Ringgold

THE WAR BETWEEN
THE STATES
  C. A. Arthur
  J. A. Garfield
  U. S. Grant
  Benjamin Harrison
  R. B. Hayes
  Wm. McKinley

W. S. Hancock
B. G. Brown
J. A. Logan
Michael Corcoran
Fitzhugh Lee
Philip Sheridan
R. D. Evans
Braxton Bragg
J. C. Bates
Wm. T. Sampson
W. S. Schley
George Dewey

SPANISH-AMERICAN WAR
J. C. Bates
Wm. R. Shafter
Theodore Roosevelt

W. J. Bryan
R. P. Hobson
W. S. Schley
Wm. T. Sampson
George Dewey
C. V. Gridley
R. D. Evans
C. S. Sperry
Fitzhugh Lee

WORLD WAR I
John J. Pershing
Douglas MacArthur
Wendell Willkie

WORLD WAR II
Douglas MacArthur

* * *

No. 30   BENJAMIN FRANKLIN FLASK

The attainments of Benjamin Franklin (1706-1790) in other fields were so many and brilliant that we seldom hear him mentioned as a soldier. He lived among Quakers and shared their love of peace. He often said: "There never was a good war or a bad peace." Peace at any price however, was not approved in this phrase, as is shown by his attitude towards defensive warfare. At one time he was chosen to be colonel, by organized forces for the defense of Philadelphia, but declined. He was active in securing supplies during the French and Indian War, and wrote the militia law which was passed in those days. He was in charge of a military expedition to the frontier and assisted the inhabitants in defense work by raising troops and building a line of forts. Again, he was chosen to be colonel of a regiment, and this time accepted. His military career was not of long duration since his services in other fields were of more importance to the country. During the first part of the Revolution he was engaged in pushing military affairs, but his work abroad as a diplomat was more necessary and his soldiering days were soon ended.

373

One of the most popular glassware items honoring Franklin is a pint-size flask showing his portrait, with his name placed above it. The reverse has a portrait of Dr. Dyott with his name just above. On the edges, inscriptions read "Where Liberty Dwells, There is My Country" and "Kensington Glass Works, Philadelphia." Found in aquamarine and amber.

No. 31 Benjamin Franklin Statuette

A bust of Franklin, in milk-glass, with frosted surface, closely resembles marble. It is six and one-half inches in height and shows workmanship of the highest quality. (See also Nos. 30 and 31.)

No. 42 The Signers Platter

Nine of the men who signed the Declaration of Independence have military records.

Benjamin Franklin was colonel in the French and Indian War.

John Hancock (1737-1793) was a major-general of the Massachusetts militia.

Thomas Heyward Jr. (1746-1809) commanded a battalion in the siege of Charleston, in 1780.

Caesar Rodney (1728-1784) served under General Washington in the Delaware Campaign.

George Walton (1740-1804) commanded a battalion in 1778.

William Whipple (1730-1785) commanded a brigade in 1777.

Oliver Wolcott (1726-1797) also led a brigade.

Edward Rutledge (1749-1800) commanded a company of artillery.

Arthur Middleton (1742-1787) served during the Revolutionary War.

(For other details concerning the Signers platter, see No. 42. See also Chapter VII.)

No. 31 Benjamin Franklin Statuette

The Battle of Lexington was fought in April of 1775. In the month of June following, came the Battle of Bunker Hill. The heroes of this occasion were Colonel William Prescott (1726-1795), General John Stark (1728-1822), General Joseph Warren (1741-1775), and Major-General Israel Putnam (1718-1790). Colonel Prescott was one of the commanding officers, and gave his order to fire when the Red-Coats were within a distance of ten rods. General Stark achieved further fame at the Battle of Bennington, in Vermont, when Burgoyne attempted to seize supplies which the American troops had collected there. As Stark saw the British forming for the attack, he exclaimed, "There are the Red-Coats; we must beat them today or Betty Stark is a widow." His bravery so inspired his raw troops that they did defeat the British Regulars. General Warren lost his life at Bunker Hill. As he was trying to rally his troops, a British officer who knew him, seized a musket and shot him. He was buried near the spot where he died. General Gage, the British leader, boasted that the fall of Warren was worth that of five hundred ordinary rebels. Major-General Israel Putnam was in command of the American forces. He had charged his men not to fire until they saw the whites of the enemy's eyes and to take good care to pick off the officers by aiming at their waist-bands. The troops then delivered a fire so deadly that the British line broke in disorder. A second assault met the same fate, but Gage's troops had spirit for still a third assault which was successful because the ammunition of the Americans had been exhausted. Although our American forces finally lost the Battle of Bunker Hill, the British loss was 1,054 men wounded and killed while the American casualties amounted to but 420. The moral effect of this conflict on American troops and citizens was decidedly tonic. They had proved that hastily assembled volunteers could withstand the assaults of trained British Regulars and that the odds against them in the enterprise in which they had embarked were not so overwhelming as to deny

No. 44   Bunker Hill Platter

No. 30
Benjamin Franklin Flask

No. 46
Lafayette Jar

them ultimate success. This is the story it is hoped you will think about when you look at a platter commemorating the Battle of Bunker Hill.

In the center, a picture of the Bunker Hill Monument is shown, above which is inscribed "Birthplace of Liberty." Around the border is found "Prescott 1776 Stark" "Warren 1876 Putnam" "The Heroes of Bunker Hill" "The Spirit of Seventy Six." The handles are shield shaped, showing stars and stripes. It is crystal, thirteen and one-fourth inches long by nine inches wide. (Reprint from Chapter I.)

MARQUIS DE LAFAYETTE

The Battle of Bunker Hill, and the Declaration of Independence so fired the heart of Lafayette that he determined to leave his home in France, and offer his services to the rising republic. His zeal and "love of liberty" were so sincere that he offered to serve in the American Army on two conditions: first, that he should receive no pay, and second, that he should act as a volunteer. He was at once accepted and was appointed Major-General before he had reached the age of twenty. George Washington so heartily approved of this young champion of liberty and freedom that he told him "he should be pleased if he would make the quarters of the Commander-in-Chief his home, establish himself there whenever he thought proper, and consider himself at all times as one of his family." This friendship continued and never for one moment was interrupted. It is written that "if there lived a man whom Washington loved and admired it was Lafayette" and his services through all the varying fortunes of war endeared him forever to every American, too.

After the fall of Cornwallis, Lafayette returned to France. Several items of glassware were made in commemoration of Lafayette. His portrait appears on a number of flasks, and on mugs and jars.

No. 47   Lafayette Flask

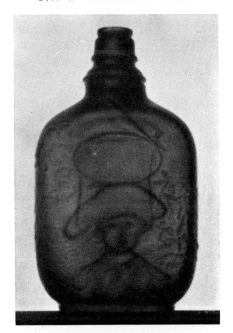

No. 48   John Paul Jones Flask

No. 46   Lafayette Jar

A jar (or container) honoring Lafayette, has a large profile portrait, facing left, on the side. Beneath this is the word "Lafayette." It is seven and one-half inches high, and three and five-eighths inches in diameter at base. Color: aqua.

No. 47   Lafayette Flask

This flask, half pint in size, presents Lafayette in profile, facing right. His name is inscribed above the portrait. Below is "Coventry C - T." (The flask was made at Coventry, Conn.) On the reverse, the French liberty cap on a pole is enclosed in an oval frame. Nine stars are above this frame. Below the frame "S & S" suggests that the flask was made by Stebbins and Stebbins. The edges are ribbed. In color it is olive amber, but was made in other colors, also.

It seems certain that Lafayette memorial items were made to honor him about the time of his visit to the United States in 1824-25. At this time he visited each state in the Union, and received such honors as have been given to few guests of the nation.

No. 48   John Paul Jones Flask

John Paul Jones, naval hero, was born in Scotland, 1747, the son of a gardener named John Paul. He became an apprentice sailor and when twelve years of age, came to Virginia. When he was twenty-six he inherited an estate from a deceased brother. For some reason he assumed the surname of Jones and was always known from that time on, as John Paul Jones.

When the Revolutionary War began he offered his services to the Colonies and was appointed Lieutenant in the American Navy. In 1776 Lieutenant Jones had the honor of displaying from his flagship the first naval American flag. It was of yellow silk, bearing the figure of a pine tree, and a rattlesnake, in a field of thirteen stripes with the legend "Don't Tread on Me." He sailed to the British coast. His boyhood days had made him familiar with things here and helped him win success in several adventures. His best known exploit was the capture of the English man-of-war Serapis. Jones was in command of the Bonhomme Richard, an old French ship that Benjamin Franklin had secured for him. It was by moonlight on the evening of November 23, 1779, that this battle commenced. During the engagement the vessels were lashed together, and hand to hand fighting ensued. The American vessel became badly damaged so that the British commander expected a surrender. He called out, "Has your ship struck her colors?" To this came Jones' surprising reply, "I have not yet begun to fight." The Serapis finally struck. But the American ship was so badly damaged that Jones transferred his crew to the Serapis, leaving his own ship to sink.

The bust of John Paul Jones, in uniform, appears on a glass pint flask. Behind him is an expanse of sea. At his right, three men seem engaged in fighting, on ship deck. Two ships, probably intended to represent the Bonhomme Richard and the Serapis, are included in the design on the reverse of the flask. Color: amber.

George Peabody (1795-1869) was a native of Danvers, now Peabody, Massachusetts. He was apprenticed to a grocer, became assistant to his brother and later to his uncle, who was a businessman in Georgetown, D. C. He served as a volunteer in the War of 1812. Later, he became a partner in a dry-goods store at Georgetown. The business prospered so that, when his partner retired, Peabody became head of one of the largest business firms in the world. In 1837 he went to London, England, and became merchant and banker there. In 1843 he withdrew from business in America. He distributed money as readily as he acquired it. The record includes fifty thousand pounds for educational purposes at Danvers; two hundred thousand pounds to found and endow a scientific institute in Baltimore, Maryland; various sums went to Harvard University; seven hundred thousand pounds to promote education in the southern states; five hundred thousand pounds for dwellings for working-class people in London. Queen Victoria offered him a baronetcy which he declined. The United States Congress gave him a special vote of thanks in 1867. He died in London and his body was returned for burial to the place of his birth, in Danvers. His memory is revered in England and in America.

No. 372   PEABODY MUG

In a mug honoring Peabody, decoration consists of ornamental letters spelling the name of this great philanthropist, placed between two rows of stars, twelve stars in each row. Letters and stars are in high relief. The background is threaded. An English registry mark is on the bottom of the mug. It may be had in amethyst, and blue. The top diameter is two and one-half inches. Height: two and three-eighths inches.

No. 373   PEABODY BOWL

The central motif of this bowl is symbolical; a crown superimposed on a heart. It seems to suggest: a crown of

No. 372   Peabody Mug

No. 373   Peabody Bowl

383

esteem for his great-heartedness as revealed by his philan-
thropies. The name "George Peabody," gives further
ornament. The letters are large and are interspersed with
stars, many stars. The background is threaded. It is
crystal glass, eight inches in diameter, and is English in
origin.

No. 374   Sheridan Plate

A circular plate honors General Philip H. Sheridan, West
Point graduate and cavalryman, who won fame during
the War between the States, and who turned Lee's flanks
at Five Forks, forcing him to retreat toward Appomattox,
where he surrendered to Grant, 1865. He was the subject
of the poem, "Sheridan's Ride."

A bust portrait of Sheridan is in the center. A laurel
wreath against a stippled background forms the border.
The name of Sheridan is placed beneath his portrait.
"Memorial" is inscribed on the border. It is crystal glass,
ten inches in diameter.

No. 375   Bates Plate

A circular plate honors John Coulter Bates. General
Bates was a native of Missouri, and a grandson of Edward
Bates, Attorney-General in President Lincoln's cabinet. He
served in the War between the States, achieving the rank
of Lieutenant-Colonel. After the war, he remained in the
regular army. During the Spanish-American War, he was
promoted to Brigadier-General, and Major-General. Was
made military Governor of the Cuban province of Santa
Clara. Later was sent to the Philippines. He negotiated a
treaty called the Bates treaty, with the Sultan of Sulu. In
1906 he was made Lieutenant-General.

A bust portrait of Bates is in the center, within a border
design composed of small dewdrops. A vine, composed of
dewdrops, is within the border design. Scalloped edge.
Integral handles. Diameter: eight inches. Crystal glass.

Some believe the plate honors Jefferson Davis, and it does
bear a strong resemblance to the President of the Confederate States of America.

384

No. 374　Sheridan Plate

No. 375
Bates Plate

No. 376
Pike's Peak Flask

Zebulon Pike (1779-1813) of the U. S. Army, explored the Mississippi River to its source in 1805. Later, he was engaged in explorations in Louisiana Territory and discovered Pike's Peak, in Colorado, which was named for him. During the War of 1812, he commanded an expedition to Canada, and was killed by the explosion of a magazine of a captured fortification. In 1858, gold was found in the Pike's Peak region. In 1859 "Pike's Peakers" were trekking to the scene of adventure, and flasks were being made relating to the subject.

A quart size flask shows the crude figure of a man representing a Pike's Peaker. He is using a staff and carries a hobo pack on a stick over one shoulder. "For Pike's Peak" is placed above the figure. A large American eagle is on the opposite side. Color: aqua.

No. 377   CORCORAN TUMBLER

Michael Corcoran (1827-1863), born in Ireland, was an American by choice. He came to this country in 1849. He became Colonel of the 69th New York Militia. He declined to order out his regiment when the militia paraded in honor of the Prince of Wales (Edward VII) in 1860. For this he was ordered to be court-martialed, but the War between the States began and he answered the first call for troops. With his regiment they erected Ft. Corcoran on Arlington Heights. He fought and distinguished himself at the first battle of Bull Run, where he was wounded and taken prisoner. After a year's confinement he was exchanged. He had previously declined to accept exchange on the condition that he would not again take up arms. He was made Brigadier-General and raised the Corcoran Legion (Irish Legion). This legion was attached to the army of the Potomac. While riding with his staff he was thrown from his horse and fatally injured in 1863.

A whiskey tumbler honors Michael Corcoran. The shield and the harp, emblematic of the United States and

No. 377   Corcoran Tumbler

No. 378
Fitzhugh Lee Plate

No. 379
Fitzhugh Lee Plate

Ireland, are framed by a wreath of laurel and oak leaves. The name "Corcoran" is inscribed beneath these emblems. On the reverse, a seated figure of Columbia holds an American and an Irish flag. On one side, between the obverse and reverse, a liberty-cap on the liberty-pole is placed. On the opposite side is a long handled battle-ax. It is crystal glass of fine quality and bell tone. Height: three and one-eighth inches. Top diameter: two and three-fourths inches. Scarce.

No. 378   FITZHUGH LEE PLATE

Fitzhugh Lee was the grandson of Light-Horse Harry Lee, and a nephew of Robert E. Lee. He was a West Point graduate. When Virginia seceded from the Union, he joined the Confederate Army and served as a Cavalry General. On April 9, 1865, he led the last charge of the Confederates. After the War he was diligent and persistent in trying to reconcile the southern people to the results of the war. He served as Governor of Virginia. President Cleveland appointed him Consul-General at Havana, Cuba, in 1896. President McKinley retained him in that office. When the Spanish-American War began, he re-entered the army and served as Major-General of U. S. Volunteers, 1896-1898. He was military Governor of Havana in 1899, and retired as a Brigadier-General, U. S. Army, in 1901.

A small plate honors General Lee. His portrait, against the U. S. flag background, is placed in the center. It is encircled by stars. His name and rank are inscribed beneath the portrait. Border design is that often known as one-o-one. Crystal glass. Diameter: five and one-half inches.

No. 380   Shafter Salt Shaker

No. 381   Schley Statuette   No. 382   Hobson Statuette

389

No. 379 Fitzhugh Lee Plate

Another plate honoring General Lee, shows him wearing a beard. His likeness again is placed against a background showing the U. S. flag. His name is inscribed beneath the portrait. It is opaque white glass, with club border. Decoration is done in red transfer, with the field of the flag in blue. Diameter: seven and one-fourth inches. Scarce.

No. 380 Shafter Salt Shaker

During the Spanish-American War, General William R. Shafter (1835-1906) commanded the first military expedition to Cuba, in 1898. On July 17, of that year, General Toral surrendered the city and the strongholds of the city of Santiago to General Shafter who received them in the name of the United States Government.

A salt shaker is made to represent a portrait bust of the General. The metal shaker top represents a cap headdress. It is opaque white glass, natural finish. Height: three and three-fourths inches.

No. 381 Schley Statuette

Rear-Admiral Winfield Scott Schley (1839-1911) is honored by a portrait bust, or statuette. Schley was a veteran of the War between the States. During the Spanish-American War he held the rank of Commodore. At the Battle of Santiago, Commodore Schley, in Sampson's absence, was the senior officer. The Brooklyn was his flagship. He received his commission as Rear-Admiral in 1899. The bust is opaque white glass, natural finish. Height: five and one-fourth inches.

No. 382 Hobson Statuette

Lieutenant Richard P. Hobson (1870-1937) was a mechanical engineer in the United States Navy during the Spanish-American War. With seven companions, he sank the "Merrimac" in the mouth of Santiago Harbor, June 3, 1898, to prevent the Spanish fleet from slipping out and escaping. These men were all volunteers for the dangerous

No. 383   Dewey Statuette

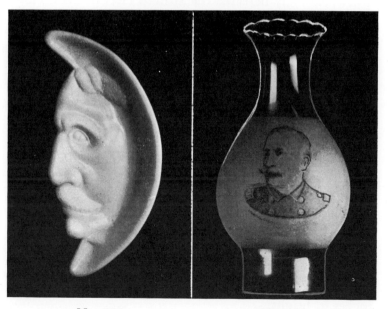

No. 384
Dewey Bone-Dish

No. 385
Dewey Lamp-Chimney

work which was successfully accomplished, but all eight were captured and confined in Morro Castle. Their exchange as prisoners of war was effected some time later. Their exploit thrilled the country, and the Senate thanked Hobson and his crew. Hobson received a transfer to the line with rank of lieutenant. He became one of the most popular heroes of the war.

Hobson is honored by a statuette of opaque white glass, satinized finish. Height: five and one-fourth inches.

No. 383 Dewey Statuette

Admiral George Dewey (1837-1917) was a native of Vermont, and a graduate of the United States Naval Academy. He served during the War between the States, on the steamsloop Mississippi. He is best known, however, as the Hero of Manila. During the Spanish-American War, Dewey was ordered to "capture or destroy the Spanish Fleet," then in Philippine waters. On May 1, 1898, he overwhelmingly defeated the Spanish Fleet in Manila Bay. He won this victory without the loss of an American man. This exploit electrified the world. Congress tendered its thanks; presented the hero with a sword, and issued bronze medals in his honor. In March, 1899, he was given the rank of Admiral, a title previously borne only by Farragut and Porter. When he returned to America, a grateful public gave him an ovation seldom equaled. Manufacturers of glassware offered numerous items to help glorify the "Nelson of America."

A statuette honoring Dewey, shows him in the uniform of a Rear-Admiral. It is clear glass with satinized finish; five and one-half inches in height.

Another statuette of Dewey may be found, which must have been made at a later date, since he wears four stars, the rank of an Admiral. In this, his hair is parted on the left side while in the preceding item the part is in the middle. It bears the inscriptions: "Dewey" "Manila 1898", and the letters PS are on the back of the bust. It is five inches in height.

No. 386   Dewey Canteen

No. 387
Dewey Covered Dish

No. 388
Dewey Ink-Well

No. 384   Dewey Bone-Dish

This item may safely be called unique. It is a bone-dish presenting Admiral Dewey as the man-in-the-moon. The effect is rather more startling than pleasing. It is opaque white glass, six and three-fourths by three and one-fourth inches in size. Scarce.

No. 385   Dewey Lamp-Chimney

The bulbous portion of a lamp-chimney is frosted. A portrait of Dewey, in black transfer, is used for ornament. Inscribed beneath the portrait "Admiral George Dewey Hero of Manila May 1, 1898." Obverse shows two crossed American flags, done in black transfer. It is crystal glass, nine inches in height.

No. 386   Dewey Canteen

A small bottle, or flask, is shaped like an army canteen of the Spanish-American War period. The obverse is much ornamented with a portrait of Dewey, an American eagle, two flags, U. S. shield, fasces, two swords, and a lone star. Inscribed "Our Hero." The reverse carries in large letters "U. S.", and the inscription "Patent Applied For." A red, white, and blue cord is attached. Clear glass, with a capacity of six ounces. Diameter: four and one-fourth inches.

No. 387   Dewey Covered Dish

A small dish has bust of Dewey, in uniform, on the lid. Shoulder insignia shows two stars, indicating the rank of Rear-Admiral. This suggests the dish was issued in 1898, since he received the rank of Admiral (insignia would show four stars) in the year 1899. Made in amber glass, in blue, and in opaque white.

No. 388   Dewey Ink-Well

An ink-well is shaped like the bust of Dewey. The head is hollow and serves as an ink-pot. The cap is removable and forms a lid. Crystal glass, three and one-eighth inches across the shoulders, and three and three-eighths inches high. Scarce.

No. 389   Dewey Covered Dish

No. 390
Dewey Covered Dish

No. 391
Dewey Covered Dish

395

No. 389   DEWEY COVERED DISH

A covered dish, round in shape, has a basketweave base. A well modeled portrait bust of Dewey features the lid. Inscribed "Dewey." It is opaque white glass. Height: five and one-half inches. Diameter: four and one-half inches. This is a rare dish, and one of the best executed items made in his honor.

No. 390   DEWEY COVERED DISH

Another covered dish commemorates Dewey. The oval base has an ornamental pressed tile effect. Two flags, on staffs, are placed on the lid, with bust of Dewey rising above them. Inscribed "Dewey" in weak lettering. Opaque white glass. Height: four and one-half inches. Length of base: six and three-fourths inches.

No. 391   DEWEY COVERED DISH

Dewey is honored by yet another covered dish. The base has some resemblance to a boat. A bust of Dewey features the lid. It is opaque white glass. Height: five inches. Length of base: five and one-half inches.

No. 392   DEWEY PLATE

A small plate shows a bust of Dewey placed against the flag. The portrait is framed by a strand of cable, tied in a bow-knot beneath the portrait. A pennant at top of flagstaff is inscribed "Victory." Inscription beneath portrait "Admiral George Dewey U. S. N." It is crystal glass, five and one-half inches in diameter.

No. 393   DEWEY PLATE

A likeness of Dewey is placed in the center. Stars are in the background. "Rear-Admiral George Dewey" is inscribed beneath the portrait. It has a club border. Opaque white glass, seven inches in diameter.

No. 392   Dewey Plate

No. 393   Dewey Plate

No. 394   Dewey Tumbler

A tumbler honoring Dewey has his bust pressed in the base. Sides are plain. It is three and five-eighths inches in height. Top diameter is three and one-sixteenth inches. Heavy glass.

No. 395   Dewey Tumbler

Another tumbler shows a different portrait of Dewey in the base. A ribbed area, having a zigzag top, is around the lower part of sides. Three bands are above this, near the center. A band at the rim is thickened. It is three and three-fourths inches in height, and two and seven-eighths inches top diameter. Heavy glass.

No. 396   Dewey Tumbler

A third tumbler has portrait of Dewey placed on the side, within a wreath. Inscribed beneath the portrait "Admiral George Dewey, U.S.N." Crystal glass, very thin; three and three-fourths inches in height.

No. 397   Dewey Tumbler

A fourth tumbler shows a similar portrait of Dewey framed by a laurel wreath. Inscribed above the portrait "Admiral Dewey, The Nelson of America." Inscribed beneath portrait "Battle of Manila Bay, May 1st, 1898." Crystal glass, thin, three and five-eighths inches in height.

Lord Nelson, to whom Dewey is here compared, was famed as an English Admiral. His signal "England expects that every man will do his duty," made as his fleet moved into action in which he lost his own life at the moment of victory, is an often quoted phrase. His dying words were: "Thank God I have done my duty."

No. 398   Dewey Tumbler

In a fifth tumbler honoring Dewey, many symbolical figures are used. Most important is a portrait of Dewey within a laurel wreath, topped by a spread eagle. Then, Dewey's flagship, the Olympia; ammunition; the U. S.

No. 394
DEWEY TUMBLER

No. 395
DEWEY TUMBLER

No. 396
DEWEY TUMBLER

No. 397
DEWEY TUMBLER

No. 398
DEWEY TUMBLER

flag; mounted cannon; rear-admiral's flag; Cuban flag; signal corps flags; and a line of cable. These designs are made more effective by a heavily stippled background. The tumbler matches a water pitcher, No. 400. It is crystal glass, two and three-fourths inches in diameter, and four inches in height.

No. 399   Dewey Pattern Footed Bowl

A footed bowl is one form in a pattern of glassware produced in honor of Admiral Dewey. It is called "Port-Hole," and is also known as "Flower Flange." The original name was "Dewey," since it was issued in his honor. It was made at Greentown, Indiana. The design is highly original, and pleasing. Three medallions, suggestive of port-holes, ornament the sides. Areas at top and bottom are threaded, to suggest ocean waves. A floral flange extends from the rim of the bowl, providing an unusual and striking effect. The dish rests on three rounded feet, with scrolling between. The one illustrated is vaseline in color, but the pattern was made in crystal, blue, amber, and caramel slag also. Diameter: eight and one-fourth inches. Width of flange: three-fourths of an inch.

No. 400   Dewey Pitcher

Most important of the many decorations used here, is a portrait of Dewey framed by a laurel wreath, with a spread eagle above. An anchor and cable, and two stars, are placed beneath. Other motifs include: cable, mounted cannon, crossed cannon, crossed rifles, crossed swords, United States flag, Cuban flag, flags of the signal corps, the flagship Olympia, four stacks of cannon balls, two of them topped with cartridge shells, and a cross moline. The cross moline is a symbol used in heraldry, and probably bears some reference to the Admiral's ancestry. Inscriptions used are "E Pluribus Unum" "In God We Trust" "Olympia." Heavy stippling provides a background for the ensemble. Crystal glass. Height: nine and one-eighth inches.

No. 399 DEWEY PATTERN FOOTED BOWL

No. 400
DEWEY PITCHER

No. 401
DEWEY PITCHER

No. 401 Dewey Pitcher

A bust portrait of Dewey is framed by a laurel wreath. At one side of this portrait, a soldier stands under the U. S. flag flying from a staff. On the other side, a sailor stands under the four-star admiral's flag flying from a staff. Beneath the pouring spout, an eagle holds a shield inscribed "Liberty." Below this is the order given by Dewey which opened the battle "Gridley You May Fire When Ready." (Gridley was Captain of the Olympia.) An anchor fills a bit of remaining space here. The reverse shows a scroll inscribed with a partial list of battleships participating in the event: "Olympia, McCulloch, Petrel, Concord, Raleigh, Boston, Baltimore, Manila, May 1st, 1898." Beside this scroll is a monument. A number of bursting shells are placed where space permits, on both sides of the pitcher. A row of beading outlines the rim, and a picket-fence-like row of shells encircles the base. Crystal glass. Height: nine and one-fourth inches. This pitcher is of better quality and design than the one previously described, and is much more difficult to secure.

No. 402 Sampson Pattern Pitcher

A pitcher in the "Sampson" pattern honors Rear-Admiral William T. Sampson (1840-1902). This pattern is better known as "Teardrop and Tassel" but it was issued as "Sampson," a name that should be kept because of its intention to honor a naval commander of that name. It was produced at Greentown, Indiana. The body of the pitcher is decorated with leafy garlands, or festoons, tassels, and drops. Since the pattern was produced primarily to honor Admiral Sampson, we may safely assume that festoons were used as a token of rejoicing, and a recognition of honor due Sampson because of the Santiago victory.

Sampson, who had seen naval service during the War between the States, was in command of the United States Fleet which destroyed the Spanish Fleet at the Battle of Santiago, July 3, 1898. He was not actually present at the

No. 402   Sampson Pattern Pitcher

No. 403   The Pacific Fleet Platter

battle, having gone to confer with General Shafter who was in command of the land forces. He reached the scene of battle as the last Spanish vessel surrendered, but the engagement was fought in accordance with his instructions. The pitcher is crystal glass, with partly stippled background. It was also made in "navy" blue, canary, and amber; and rarely encountered in green and in opaque.

No. 403   The Pacific Fleet Platter

A platter honors Admiral Robley D. Evans (1846-1912), Admiral Charles S. Sperry (1847-1911), and the Pacific Fleet.

Admiral Evans, or "Fighting Bob" as he is better known, was one of the most picturesque figures in the American Navy. He disliked his nickname, but it stuck. He was wounded and permanently lamed during the War between the States. In the Spanish-American War, he commanded the Iowa, in Sampson's Fleet, at Santiago.

In 1907, President Theodore Roosevelt started the U. S. Battleship Fleet on a round-the-world goodwill cruise. They were termed "Heralds of Peace" but also served to call attention of the great powers, and especially Japan, to the fighting strength of the United States. The voyage also dramatized the navy and its needs to the American people. It was brilliantly successful and was made without accident.

Fighting Bob became ill during the trip, and was succeeded by Rear-Admiral Sperry who had been in command of the second squadron.

In the center of this platter, bust portraits of the commanders are shown above an expanse of water, crossed by a procession of battleships. The American eagle hovers above. Inscribed "Admirals C. S. Sperry, R. D. Evans." The border is ornamented with cable and laurel branches against a stippled background; and the inscriptions "The Pacific Fleet" "Souvenir 1908." It is crystal glass, eleven and one-fourth by eight inches in size. Rare.

404

No. 404   Pershing Paperweight

No. 124   General Douglas MacArthur Bottle

A paperweight honors General John J. Pershing (1860-1948). Pershing was a native of Missouri, and one of the many famous Americans destined to rise from humble circumstances. His record is a long list of difficult military assignments carried through to brilliant and successful completion. He received the permanent rank of General, a grade held previously by only four Americans: Washington, Grant, Sherman, and Sheridan. He was Commander-in-Chief of the American Expeditionary Forces in World War I. At this time, General Pershing insisted that the integrity of the American Army be preserved and took a firm stand against the French desire to infuse the new blood of America's man-power into their own weakening military ranks. This position was justified by future developments and was of immense value to the morale of American troops. Pershing defeated the Germans at Belleau Wood, Cantigny, Chateau-Thierry, Vaux, The Marne, St. Mihiel, and The Argonne.

A portrait of Pershing in uniform, is placed in the center, with "General John J. Pershing 1917" inscribed around it. Inscribed on rim of the base, in small letters "Northwestern Glass Co. Mpls." This paperweight was distributed by the Northwestern Glass Company of Minneapolis, to customers, as a souvenir, but was not made by them. It is crystal glass, four inches in diameter. It is five-eighths of an inch in depth, and the top is flat, with rounded edges.

General Douglas MacArthur graduated from West Point in 1903, holding top honors. He held various ranks and positions, including service in the Philippines, one year in Japan as aide to his father, General Arthur MacArthur, and another year as military aide to President Theodore Roosevelt. In 1917, he became Chief-of-Staff with the Rainbow Division, and participated in most of the heavy fighting of World War I. He was twice wounded in action, received citations for heroism, and the Distinguished Service Cross. After war ended, he was with the Army of Occupation in Germany. On his return he became head of the Military Academy at West Point, being the youngest officer ever to hold that position. In 1920, he was made Brigadier-General in the Regular Army, and saw three years of service in the Philippines. In 1930 he served as Chief-of-Staff under President Herbert Hoover. He rose in rank to the highest position, General of the Armies, the youngest to receive that post since U. S. Grant. He retired from the army in 1937, but remained in the Philippines. World War II called him once more to service. In 1941, President Roosevelt placed him in charge of land and sea forces in the near East. He was made a full General for the second time, and is one of the most decorated officers of all time; having been honored by the United States, Mexico, Ecuador, Italy, France, Belgium, Poland, Hungary, Czechoslovakia, Yugo-Slavia, and Roumania. He has proved himself one of the ablest men in our history, as military strategist, as a statesman, and as an administrator.

A half-pint bottle honors General MacArthur. A portrait of him decorates the obverse. Above the portrait "General MacArthur" is inscribed. Below is a popular wartime slogan "Keep Them Flying." The reverse shows a large letter V and the date 1942. An American flag is flying on either side of this letter. Above, is the inscription: "God Bless America," and below, three dots and a dash are placed. These, in telegraphic Morse code, represent the letter V. At that time, "V for Victory" was another wartime slogan in constant use.

Presidents, Vice-Presidents, and Defeated Candidates

Many Presidents, Vice-Presidents, and defeated candidates for those offices knew military service at some time.

George Washington was Commander-in-Chief of the American Army during the Revolutionary War.

Wm. H. Harrison fought in Indian Wars in Indiana, and was Major-General in the War of 1812.

Andrew Jackson was Major-General in the War of 1812.

Zachary Taylor began soldiering in 1808. He served in the War of 1812, became a Colonel during the Black Hawk War, and Major-General in the Mexican War.

Abraham Lincoln served as Captain and private in the Black Hawk War.

U. S. Grant, a West Point graduate, saw service in the Mexican War and became the greatest General in the War between the States.

James A. Garfield served as Major-General in the War between the States.

W. S. Hancock was First Lieutenant in the Mexican War, and Major-General in the War between the States.

B. G. Brown commanded a Brigade during the War between the States.

R. B. Hayes was Major-General in the War between the States.

C. A. Arthur was Quartermaster-General in the War between the States.

John A. Logan was a Major-General in the War between the States.

Benjamin Harrison attained the rank of Brigadier-General in the War between the States.

Wm. McKinley was a Major in the War between the States.

Theodore Roosevelt was Colonel of the Rough Riders in the Spanish-American War.

Wm. J. Bryan was Colonel in the Spanish-American War but saw no active service.

Wendell Willkie, in 1917, enlisted for military service in World War I and became Captain.

(For memorial items of these men, see Chapter VII.)

CHAPTER IX

A phrase "The Pen is Mightier Than the Sword" is familiar to everyone. Glassware has something to suggest about the influence of the pen on American life. Vagaries and sublimities of humanity were learned from the works of Shakespeare and Dickens. Wit and wisdom were culled from the sayings of Benjamin Franklin. The importance of simple and common things was taught through fabler La Fontaine. "Immortal longings" were satisfied by promises found in the Bible. Music and mystery came from the rhymes of Tennyson, Scott, Byron, and Burns, and from the pen of Whittier.

In some cases the writer is honored by the memorializing of a character created by him rather than by direct attention. It has been said that: "The great characters of fiction live as truly as the memories of dead men. For the life after death it is not necessary that a man or woman should have lived."

No. 405   SHAKESPEARE STATUETTE

William Shakespeare (1564-1616), the greatest English poet and playwright, was also an actor. He began writing plays about 1589. Comedy, romance, tragedy, and drama, all were presented in such perfection that they have continued to be popular until the present time.

A bust of Shakespeare was distributed at the Centennial of 1867. It is crystal glass, with satinized finish, and comparatively small, being five inches in height. The base is round, two inches in diameter. It carries the maker's name on the reverse, "Gillinder and Sons" "Centennial Exhibition." One word is placed on the front of the base: "Shakspeare." This is a recognized spelling, although not the customary one.

410

No. 405   SHAKESPEARE STATUETTE

No. 406
LA FONTAINE TUMBLER

No. 407
WHITTIER'S BIRTHPLACE
TUMBLER

411

No. 406   La Fontaine Tumbler

The fable is essentially a short story, composed to enforce some moral idea. It introduces persons, animals, and even inanimate things as rational speakers and actors.

> "Fables in sooth are not what they appear;
> Our moralists are mice, and such small deer.
> We yawn at sermons, but we gladly turn
> To moral tales, and so amused we learn."

A French writer, La Fontaine, is reported as the greatest of all fablers. His fables have been read by most of us, joined with the work of other fablers, in a volume of Aesop's Fables.

A tumbler honors La Fontaine. His portrait, a cameo incrustation, is placed on one side and forms a heavy bull's eye in the glass. (See No. 263 for details of cameo incrustations.) The base is much like the base of the first pressed glass tumbler made at Sandwich in 1827. Sides are ornamented with ribbing, some horizontal and some vertical. The name "La Fontaine" in small letters, is placed on the shoulder. It is crystal glass of fine bell tone, and very heavy. Height: three and three-fourths inches. Top diameter: three inches.

No. 407   Whittier's Birthplace Tumbler

A tumbler honors John Greenleaf Whittier (1807-1892), America's "Quaker Poet." The homestead pictured on this tumbler was an old house when Whittier was born there. It was built by an ancestor before 1700 and sheltered several generations of Whittiers. Experiences here, inspired the verses of "Snow-Bound" which gave a simple and radiant word picture of his boyhood associations.

The poet was born in the Quaker faith, and held to its beliefs, its dress, and speech, throughout his lifetime. It was not an easy life, as a farmer boy in this New England home, with its isolation, and limited opportunities for education. Poverty, bodily exhaustion, disappointed love, and ambition, combined to make some periods very unhappy. He accepted every challenge, and step by step won his way to success. To material success, and to the greater success suggested by him in these lines:

> "Victory
> The smile of God
> To do is to succeed ... our fight
> is wag'd in Heaven's approving sight ...
> The smile of God is victory!"

It is said "the inward voice was his inspiration, and of all American poets, he was the one whose song was most like a prayer."

Whittier was a member of the Massachusetts Legislature from 1835 to 1836. He disliked slavery, and some of his most vigorous poems were aimed at that institution. When the anti-slavery movement began, he was active in its interests, as a writer, poet, and editor. When he died, he had been an active writer for more than sixty years, and left more than that number of publications bearing his name as author or editor.

The tumbler displays a picture of the homestead, beneath which is inscribed "Whittier Birthplace, Haverhill, Mass." Crystal glass, shading to blue near the top. Decorated in enamel. Height: five inches. Top diameter: two and three-eighths inches.

No. 408   WEBSTER TOOTHPICK HOLDER

A toothpick holder honors Noah Webster (1758-1843). Webster was a native of Connecticut, a descendant of the Pilgrim Governor Bradford. He was a student at Yale College, and a soldier in the Revolutionary War, serving in the militia under his father. He taught school, published books, lectured, practiced law, edited a magazine and a newspaper. In 1783-1785, he published "A Grammatical Institute of the English Language" in three parts, a spelling-book, a grammar, and a reader. This found a place in most of the schools of the United States. Sales from the

413

spelling-book were his chief source of support during the twenty years he was preparing his dictionary. The dictionary was published in 1828.

The dictionary, in glass, is a small-sized memorial, but Webster's Dictionary which it represents, has been a force in the growth of the nation. This toothpick holder is made in the shape of a book, with "boards and binding" characteristic of a dictionary. Inscribed, in large letters, on the back "Webster." It is crystal glass, two and one-half by two inches in size. One and one-eighth inches thick.

No. 409   Mr. Pickwick Bottle

Charles Dickens (1812-1870), English author, had a reputation as an actor, too. His ability in this line was best shown in public readings of selections from his own works. These readings were popular in both England and America. In 1842 Dickens visited America, after which he wrote sarcastic accounts of American manners and life. His characters are taken from actual life, and "David Copperfield" is said to be largely a story of his own life.

A bottle represents Mr. Pickwick, a character from "Pickwick Papers." He was president of the Pickwick Club, presented as stout and fatherly. He was a good-natured fellow, fond of travel, and distinguished for his blundering simplicity. He is shown wearing a great-coat, a hat, standing collar, watch-fob, and spectacles. He carries a cane in his left hand. Inscribed "Mr. Pickwick." Crystal glass, eight and three-fourths inches in height.

No. 408   Webster Toothpick Holder

No. 409
Mr. Pickwick Bottle

No. 410
Byron-Scott Flask

No. 410 Byron-Scott Flask

Sir Walter Scott (1771-1832), Scottish writer, won fame as a novelist and poet. His works became very popular and also profitable. His generosity and liberality used up large sums, and when his publishing firms failed, Scott found himself heavily in debt. At the age of 55, he undertook to pay off a debt of $700,000 by his pen. He worked fourteen hours a day until failing health finally forced him to rest. When he died, at the age of 61, over $500,000 of his debt had been paid; and soon after, copyrights of his work brought sufficient funds to pay all. Among his best liked works are "The Lady of the Lake," "Ivanhoe," and "Marmion."

Lord Byron (1788-1824) was an English poet especially famed for his power of description. He showed great ability as a writer while young, and won fame, but did not find personal favor with the public. He is considered one of the greatest of English poets. Perhaps his best known work is "Childe Harold."

A half-pint flask is said to honor these writers. Two portraits, one on either side, are believed to represent them. There are no inscriptions or other decoration. Color: amber.

No. 411 Elaine Plate

A plate honors Elaine, a character of fiction created by Lord Tennyson (1809-1892), English poet laureate. She was the "lily maid of Astolat" who pines and dies of love of Lancelot, bravest of the Knights of the Round Table. Well known works of Tennyson are "Idylls of The King," "Charge of The Light Brigade," "Ulysses," "The Holy Grail," "Maud." Perhaps the most widely known lines from his pen are:

No. 411 ELAINE PLATE

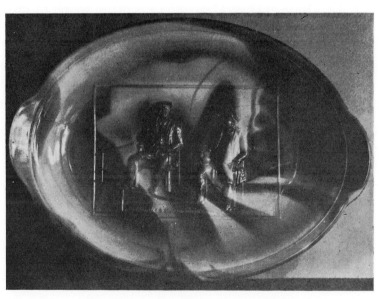

No. 412 TAM-O'-SHANTER PLATTER

417

"Sunset and evening star
   And one clear call for me!
And may there be no moaning of the bar,
   When I put out to sea.

*   *   *

"For tho' from out our bourne of time and place
   The flood may bear me far,
I hope to see my Pilot face to face
   When I have crossed the bar."

In the center of this plate commemorating Tennyson's character, Elaine, his flower girl is shown full length, carrying a basket of blossoms. In her right hand she holds, as though for inspection, a bunch of lilies. A garland of flowers and foliage frames the figure. Crystal glass, frosted center. Diameter: nine inches.

No. 412   Tam-o'-Shanter Platter

Robert Burns (1759-1796) was a Scottish writer of distinction. His poems are the most musical in the language. Many are simple and touching, others sparkle with life and wit, and his humor is very fine. His life was short, yet long enough to win lasting fame. He died at the age of thirty-seven.

In Burns' poem, "Tam-o'-Shanter," the hero is a drunken good-natured farmer who fancies himself pursued by witches. A platter presents this character of fiction created by Burns.

A centrally placed rectangle shows full length figures of Tam-o'-Shanter and his companion Soutar Johnny. Both are seated and both are smiling. Tam-o'-Shanter holds a glass as though drinking a toast while Soutar Johnny balances a pitcher of grog on one knee. The names of the characters are inscribed beneath them. It is opaque glass (purple slag) twelve by eight and one-half inches. Rare.

418

No. 413   Little Boy Blue Plate

No. 415
Hey Diddle Diddle Plate

No. 414
Little Bo-Peep Plate

ELIZABETH (MOTHER) GOOSE

Identity of the immortal Mother Goose seems none too positive. There is some variation in statements concerning the origin of Mother Goose Rhymes. It seems likely that the verses so familiar to every American home, should be attributed to a lady who lived in Boston, Massachusetts. She was Elizabeth, daughter of William and Ann Foster who became the wife of Isaac Vergoose (or Goose) in 1692. In the course of time, Elizabeth Goose became a grandmother, and being widowed, spent most of her time in taking care of the grandchild. She crooned the ditties she had learned in her younger days until her son-in-law was all but distracted. Since he could do no less than submit to the situation, he decided to write down the songs to which he was forced to listen, collect others, and publish them. The book which he brought forth bore the title: "Songs for the Nursery, or Mother Goose's Melodies for Children."

For generations, a "Mother Goose Book," anthology of nursery rhymes, often differing slightly in wording, has been a source of joy to childhood and a boon to parents. To adults, these rhymes seem largely nonsense, but in the child's world, nonsense is fun. And when the germs of truth are largely sprinkled through the fun and nonsense, nothing else can take its place. A number of pictures illustrating Mother Goose rhymes have been used to ornament glassware, usually forms intended for children's use.

No. 413   Little Boy Blue Plate

Little Boy Blue is a favorite of everyone:

"Little Boy Blue, go blow your horn,
 The sheep's in the meadow, the cow's in the corn.
 Where's the little boy, that tends the sheep?
 He's under the haycock fast asleep."

In the background, beyond a rail fence, a cow is seen in a cornfield. Boy Blue lies asleep under the edge of a haystack, his horn loosely held in one hand. Two rabbits and a frog suspiciously watch the sleeping child. It is crystal glass, five and one-half inches in diameter.

No. 414   Little Bo-Peep Plate

Little Bo-Peep is another favorite:

> "Little Bo-Peep has lost her sheep,
> And can't tell where to find them;
> Leave them alone, and they'll come home
> Wagging their tails behind them."

Little Bo-Peep, carrying a shepherd's crook and wearing a large sun hat, stands crying. The first line of the rhyme is inscribed at her right. The second line is placed at her left. A border composed of sixteen dancing bears is an added attraction. The plate is crystal glass, six and one-fourth inches in diameter.

No. 415   Hey Diddle Diddle Plate

A companion plate to the preceding, illustrates another popular verse:

> "Hey, diddle diddle!
> The cat and the fiddle;
> The cow jumped over the moon.
> The little dog laughed
> To see such craft;
> And the dish ran away with the spoon."

In this plate, the cat is seen playing the fiddle, the cow is jumping over the moon, the dish and the spoon are making away together, and a small dog sits laughing at the strange antics. "Hey! diddle diddle" is inscribed beneath the picture. A border design composed of sixteen dancing boys and girls wearing Dutch costumes, is an interesting feature. The size is identical with the preceding plate.

Benjamin Franklin

As a writer, Benjamin Franklin rated among the best. He wrote books and pamphlets, he was a journalist of distinction, his "Poor Richard's Almanack" carried his shrewd wit and wisdom to every home; and the publication he founded, even now is published as the Saturday Evening Post. He was an associate of Jefferson and Adams in drafting the Declaration of Independence, and at the age of 81 his work in the Convention which drafted the Constitution was indispensable. (For further detail concerning Franklin, see Chapter VIII, and Nos. 30 and 31.)

John Mitchell

John Mitchell was best known as an American labor leader, but he was a writer also. (For details concerning him, see Chapter XII.)

Samuel Francis Smith

Samuel Francis Smith was a clergyman but he was also a talented writer. (See Chapter XII for details concerning him.)

The Bible

Although shrouded in antiquity, perhaps those who gave us the books of The Bible, should be included in the group of writers commemorated in glassware. In such a connection, all of Chapter VI, especially numbers 199, 200, and 201 would be a tribute to those responsible for our sacred literature.

CHAPTER X

THE STAGE

THE ACTRESS PATTERN

Portrait glass in complete sets seems not to have been thought of until about 1879. Perhaps the success of political portrait-ware gave someone an idea for placing pictures of stage favorites on glass, and the idea was extended to cover all forms of tableware. It is the only full line of portrait glass reported. The writer has examined many specimens: pitchers and goblets, sugar-bowls and butter-dishes, spoon-holders and creamers, celery holders and jam-jars, bread-trays and pickle-dishes, relish dishes and bowls, compotes and sauce-dishes. On all these, actress favorites are pictured. One lone form, the cheese-dish, was yielded to the men. The women honored are Kate Claxton, Maggie Mitchell, Lotta Crabtree, Adelaide Neilson, Fanny Davenport, Annie Pixley, Maud Granger, and Mary Anderson. Men favored are William H. Crane, Sanderson Moffatt, and Stuart Robson. Many, but not all of the pieces, are inscribed with the names of the stars.

A distinguishing design is found on all Actress portrait glass. It consists of a stippled shell, and a pendant of conventionalized laurel leaves, flowers, and figures. Two of these, crossed, are placed opposite each other on some forms. For convenience we shall call them "Actress Shells." A report concerning the inspiration for this design is interesting, if true.

In olden times, crusaders brought back with them, a scallop shell from the Mediterranean as evidence that they had been to the Holy Land. It was the "badge" of the wayfarer. Stage folks were wayfarers (travelers), too. Each star expected to be a trouper, making one-night stands across the continent, probably for a number of seasons. So the shell was chosen as a fitting emblem to identify glassware honoring celebrities of the stage.

423

The pattern was produced in two ways: all clear items, and in clear with frosted portions.

No. 416   Actress Pattern Pickle-Dish

The Actress pattern pickle-dish honors Kate Claxton (1848-1924). Her fame as an actress rests chiefly upon her creation of the role of Louise, the blind girl, in "The Two Orphans," produced in 1874. She played this role more than 4,000 times. During one performance at the Brooklyn Theatre in 1876, the theatre burned down around her. Two actors met death and 300 of the audience were killed in this fire. Because of her composure in the emergency, she became known as "The Fire Actress."

A portrait of Kate Claxton is in the center. Border inscription reads "Love's Request is Pickles." Ends are ornamented with the distinguishing design of the Actress pattern. Notched rim. Crystal glass, some frosting. Length: nine and one-fourth inches. Width: five and one-fourth inches. Kate Claxton appears again on the sugar-bowl, and on the goblet of this pattern.

No. 417   Actress Pattern Compote

The compote, open or covered, honors Fanny Davenport (1852-1898) and Maggie Mitchell (1837-1918). The former made her first appearance on any stage, in Boston, July 4, 1858, when her father (a prominent actor and manager) and the whole theatrical company sang "The Star-Spangled Banner." Fanny waved an American flag, but being so small, her father had to help. She began playing roles when thirteen. She appeared in dramas, farces, and operas, and her repertory was of appalling length and scope. A wealth of artistic temperament made her without a rival in emotional powers of the first order. She is especially remembered for the title roles in "Oliver Twist," "Fedora," "La Tosca," and "Cleopatra." In glassware she is honored also, on the standard sauce-dish, the butter-dish, and the cream-pitcher.

No. 416   Actress Pattern Pickle-Dish

No. 417   Actress Pattern Compote

425

Miss Mitchell was an actress who profited greatly by her work. She began at the age of fourteen and rose quickly. Her first distinct success was in "Oliver Twist." She made a very great hit as Fanchon, the elfin child, slightly "touched by the moon" in an adaptation of George Sands' novel "La Petite Fadette." She retired in 1893. She is honored again on the water pitcher, on standard sauce-dishes, and on relish dishes.

Bust portraits of these stars are placed on opposite sides of the compote bowl. Midway between them, on each side, Actress shells are placed. The base is rayed. Portraits of Annie Pixley and Maud Granger are opposite each other on the lid, and between them, as on the bowl, are Actress shells. This cover is domed, and eight stars are molded in relief on the inside, forming a circle beneath the finial. Four small shells are on the lower half of the globe-shaped finial. Base and stem of the dish are frosted. A band of frosting is on the rim of the lid, and the upper half of the dome is frosted. Portraits and shells are stippled. Diameter: ten inches. Height: fourteen and one-half inches.

No. 418   Actress Pattern Cheese-Dish

A covered cheese-dish honors William H. Crane, Stuart Robson, and Sanderson Moffatt. William H. Crane (1845-1928) made his stage debut in 1863. His fame rests on comedy, although he played Shakespearean roles and other classics. Perhaps his greatest hit was David Harum, a dramatization of Edward Noyes Westcott's popular novel.

Stuart Robson (1836-1903) was a comedian with an odd voice and a quaint personality. His real name was Henry Robson Stuart. He ventured on the stage at the age of sixteen years and was there continuously for fifty-one years. He acted over 700 characters. Robson and Crane first came together in 1877, a partnership that lasted for twelve years, until 1889, and a friendship that endured until death. They were an outstanding success in Shakespeare's "Comedy of Errors," and this is the play in which they are honored in glassware. The two Dromios represent

No. 418   Actress Pattern Cheese-Dish

twin brothers who are servants of the twins Antipholus, constantly mistaken for each other.

They are represented on the base of the cheese-dish, as two full-length figures wearing Shakespearean costumes, posed in front of a gateway. Inscribed beneath the figures "The Two Dromios."

The domed lid shows two fishing scenes, placed on opposite sides, with Actress shells between them. These represent Sanderson Moffatt in a curtain raiser, "The Lone Fisherman." The dish is crystal glass. The base, which is found frosted or clear, is eight and one-half inches in diameter. The lid has a frosted band at the rim, and a frosted area is beneath the finial. The extreme height is seven inches. Rather scarce.

No. 419   Pinafore Platter

An oval platter, or tray, commemorates the operetta, "H.M.S. Pinafore," written by Gilbert and Sullivan, English composers. "Pinafore" was the first genuine success of the American musical stage, and swept the country like a prairie fire. Within a few short months after its premiere in 1878, the whole New World was whistling its tunes. Because of the lack of international copyright laws at this time, the work was pirated by practically every manager who could raise enough money to put it on. At the height of its success, there were more than ninety companies playing it in the United States.

In the center of the tray, a character from this operetta stands on ship-deck, presumably the H.M.S. Pinafore. The cap-band is inscribed with the last five letters of the word "Pinafore." This figure may represent some individual; if so the identity seems to have become lost. A wreath, composed of what appears to be conventionalized laurel leaves and blossoms, surrounds the oval center. The border is scalloped. Ends are ornamented with shells. Whether this item belongs to the Actress pattern, or should be called a variant, is a subject for discussion. The shells are identical

428

No. 419   Pinafore Platter

No. 420   Actress Pattern Bread-Tray

429

with those of the Actress pattern, but the pendant is missing.

"Pinafore" is honored again on the celery holder. It is decorated with scenes from the operetta, and the word "Pinafore." The tray is crystal glass, twelve by seven inches in size.

No. 420   Actress Pattern Bread-Tray

A platter, or bread-tray in the Actress pattern, honors Lillian Adelaide Neilson, pseudonym of Elizabeth Ann Brown, English born Shakespearean actress whose most famous role was that of Juliet.

An oval portrait of Miss Neilson is in the center. That name is inscribed beneath the portrait. The daily bread motto appears on the border. Ends are ornamented with the Actress shells. Miss Neilson is also portrayed on the butter-dish, the cream-pitcher, water pitcher, bowl, flat sauce-dish, and relish dish of this pattern. The bread-tray is twelve and three-fourths by nine and one-fourth inches in size. Crystal glass.

No. 421   Actress Pattern Spoon-Holder

The spooner honors Mary Anderson and Maud Granger (see jam-jar). Miss Anderson was an American actress, born in California, 1859. She was brought up in Louisville, Kentucky, where her step-father practiced medicine. Here she made her stage debut in "Romeo and Juliet." She appeared in varying parts, here and abroad. Was said to have been the most beautiful Shakespearean actress of her time and was popularly known as "Our Mary." In 1890, she married a wealthy Mexican and retired to England to live.

Bust portraits of the stars are placed opposite each other on the bowl of the spooner. Names are inscribed beneath the portraits. Actress shells are placed opposite each other between the portraits. Crystal glass, with base and stem frosted. Five and one-half inches in height.

Miss Anderson is honored again, on a bowl.

No. 421   Actress Pattern Spoon-Holder

No. 422   Actress Pattern
Jam-Jar

No. 423   Actress Pattern
Goblet

431

No. 422   Actress Pattern Jam-Jar

The jam-jar honors Maud Granger and Annie Pixley. Miss Granger is honored also, on the spoon-holder, cake-stand, and relish dish. She had her debut in 1873 and enjoyed a long career that covered fifty years.

Miss Pixley grew up in Nevada, and is said to have been "discovered" by Joe Jefferson. She made her New York debut March 22, 1880, in M'liss.

As in other forms, portraits of the stars are placed opposite each other, with Actress shells between. Their names are beneath their portraits. The bottom of the jar is rayed. The lid boasts eight shells, four on the cover and four very small ones on the finial. The lower inch of the jar is frosted and two rings of frosting are on the lid. Portraits and shells are stippled. Height: six and one-half inches. Diameter: three and three-eighths inches.

No. 423   Actress Pattern Goblet

The goblet honors Lotta Crabtree, and Kate Claxton (see pickle-dish). Lotta Mignon Crabtree (1847-1924) was one of the brightest soubrettes that ever entertained a public. She was born in New York but her parents went to California during gold rush days. Her first appearance, in singing and dancing, was made at the age of eight. Her active career began in 1864 and extended to 1891. She gave black-face impersonations, and did intricate step-dancing as well as her more celebrated work. Her manner was sprightly and saucy, and her comic faculty seemed boundless. She became very popular in "Little Nell and the Marchioness," (the Old Curiosity Shop) written for her by John Brougham. Her popularity was well deserved, and she thoroughly earned the competence which allowed her to retire and live comfortably for many years.

Portraits of the stars are placed opposite each other on the goblet, with Actress shells between them. "Lotta" and "Kate Claxton" are lettered beneath the portraits. Crystal glass, with lower part of bowl frosted. Found also in all clear. Diameter: three and one-half inches. Height: six and one-half inches. Lotta appears also on the sugar-bowl, and a low, round bowl.

No. 424   Jenny Lind Compote

An open compote honors Jenny Lind (1820-1887), "The Swedish Nightingale," who was proclaimed the most popular woman in the world. She has always stood somewhat in a world apart, the idol of all classes. She was presented to the American public by P. T. Barnum, and her first American concert was given at Castle Garden, New York City, September 1, 1850. Her last appearance here also was at New York, May 24, 1852. During her stay, she married, in Boston, the young German pianist, Otto Goldschmidt, whom she had known before coming to America.

Commercial houses named articles for her: there were Jenny Lind gloves, bonnets, riding-hats, shawls, mantillas, robes, chairs, sofas, pianos, stoves, beds, cakes, cigars, glassware, and even a teakettle "which, being filled with water and placed on the fire, commences to SING in a few minutes." In this way, she became a part of American life and tradition. Her name and fame have lived, and will continue to endure. Barnum used all the devices known to the show-man, to awaken interest in Jenny Lind and fan it to fever heat, but she was a great artist, a serious artist, and an impressive personality, though physical beauty was a thing she never possessed.

Mendelssohn said of her, "She is as great an artist as has ever lived, and the greatest I have known." After returning from America, she and her husband lived in Dresden for three years. Then they removed to England where she was more interested in teaching than in singing. Her last public concert was in 1880, but teaching was continued to 1886.

Many glassware items give tribute to the charms of Jenny Lind. Bottles and flasks, in numbers, were made. In the dish which has proved so popular, the frosted compote stem is made to represent Jenny Lind. The base is

433

No. 424   Jenny Lind Compote

No. 425   Jenny Lind Lamp

ornamented with flowers and leaves against a frosted background. The bowl is fluted, and shows a small conventional pattern. It is crystal glass, eight inches in height. Diameter: eight and one-fourth inches.

No. 425   Jenny Lind Lamp

The stem of a lamp is fashioned to represent Jenny Lind. She wears a wreath of laurel leaves on her flowing hair. Classical drapery clothes the bust. The step-back base is hexagonal in shape. Opaque white glass. The detachable, crystal bowl is ornamented with a leaf and flower design. This design in clear glass is effectively placed against a frosted background. The lamp is well balanced in design, the materials are good, and the workmanship is excellent. Made by Atterbury and Company about 1875. Height: eleven inches. Diameter of base: five inches.

No. 426   Jenny Lind Match-Safe

A wall match-safe is fashioned as the head of Jenny Lind wearing a coronet and swathed in flowing drapery. The lower portion is corrugated for the striking of matches. Inscribed on the back "Pat'd. June 13, 1876." All-frosted, crystal glass, pierced for hanging. Length: four and one-half inches.

No. 427
Charlie Chaplin
Candy Container

No. 426
Jenny Lind
Match-Safe

No. 428   Jenny Lind Bread Tray

No. 427 Charlie Chaplin Candy Container

A candy container, that might well double for toothpicks or matches, honors Charles Spencer Chaplin, English-born cinema star.

At the age of 21 he came to the United States where he soon engaged the attention of Hollywood producers. In his first picture made in 1913, he adopted the strange costume which has ever since been associated with the name of Chaplin. His success as a screen comedian was immediate and continuous.

Chaplin stands beside a container for small candy. He wears the typical costume: baggy breeches, outsize shoes, tight jacket, or coat, derby hat, and carries a cane. Inscribed beneath the figure "Charlie Chaplin." Inscribed on under side of base "Patent applied for. Geo. Borgfeldt and Co. New York Sole Licensees." "Serial No. 2862." Crystal glass, four inches in height.

No. 428 Jenny Lind Bread-Tray

A bread-tray, highly original in conception, may or may not glorify Jenny Lind. The portrait of someone selected for honor is placed on each corner. The elaborate hair-dress suggests royalty, the stage, or some character of mythology. Since the lady wears large, pendant ear-rings in the shape of a cross, the latter theory is given considerable discredit. Of the other two, the second seems more likely. The profile strongly resembles Lind, and so subject to welcome correction, we present the tray. The center is rayed, a form of design popular in the 1870's, and this was a period when celebrities of the stage were immortalized in glass. Border decorations are molded on the back of the tray. Sprays of laurel are placed on the sides and on the ends. Areas receiving these motifs are slightly concave. Integral handles show rosettes, and cord streamers, having knotted ends. This ornamentation is molded on the top surface. The item is so unlike others, that it suggests the originator made considerable effort to produce something original and worthy, to exalt the individual represented. It is crystal glass, twelve by seven and one-fourth inches in size.

No. 429   Lillian Russell Plate

A small plate honors Lillian Russell (1861-1922). Her true name was Helen Louise Leonard. She often was called "Nellie." Also known as the "Queen of Light Opera," "Queen of American Beauty," and "Airy-Fairy Lillian," although there was nothing wraith-like about her. She was a very substantially built person. She possessed a lyric soprano voice of true pitch and impressive quality which enabled her, for four decades, to dominate the American stage. She played a minor part in the premiere of "Pinafore" in 1878. Played the title role of "Pocahontas" in 1885. Sang for sixteen weeks at the Chicago World's Fair. "The Grand Duchess" was one of her outstanding roles.

Bust portrait of Lillian Russell, within a decorative medallion, forms the center. Border design called egg-and-dart, or one-o-one. It is crystal glass, five and one-half inches in diameter.

No. 430   Emmy Destin Plate

The portrait on a plate matching the one above resembles pictures of Emmy Destin (1878-1930). She was a native of Prague, Bohemia. Her real name was Kittel, but for stage purposes she assumed the last name of her teacher, Mme. Loewe-Destinn. She made her debut in Dresden, 1897. Her beautiful voice and rare dramatic genius won the Berlin public, and she also became a favorite in London. She came to the Metropolitan in New York City, in 1908. The opinions of London and Berlin critics were echoed here. Her wonderful voice was preserved for posterity through the medium of victrola records, of which she made many.

The identity of this person is not positive, and is subject to correction.

438

No. 429　Lillian Russell Plate

No. 430　　　　　　　No. 431
Emmy Destin Plate　　Frieda Hempel Plate

No. 431   Frieda Hempel Plate

A third plate is identical with the two preceding, excepting the portrait, which is believed to be that of Frieda Hempel (1885-   ). This singer is a native of Leipsic, who made her debut in Berlin in 1907. Her success was immediate and she rapidly became the chief coloratura singer of the opera. Following her American appearance, victrola records of her voice became popular. In these, brilliant opera airs and waltz songs, the quality and flexibility of her voice are well displayed.

This series of plates may include celebrities other than the three reported here. An intensive search might well be undertaken, to establish beyond question, the identity of the portraits presented here, as well as the discovery of others.

No. 432   Sothern Match-Safe

Edward Hugh Sothern (1859-1933), American actor, was the son of a noted English comedian. He began playing small parts with his father's company, and gradually rose to prominence. He married Virginia Harned in 1896, and in 1899 formed his own company with her as his leading lady. In 1900 he appeared in the title role of "Hamlet," in 1901 that of "Richard Lovelace," and in 1902-3 in "If I Were King," three of his greatest roles. In 1904 he entered into combination with Julia Marlowe, the two first appearing together in "Romeo and Juliet," at Chicago. Except for two years, 1907-09, they played together almost continuously until their retirement from the stage. They were married in 1911. Besides "Romeo and Juliet," they presented "Much Ado about Nothing," "Taming of the Shrew," "Merchant of Venice," "Twelfth Night," "Macbeth," "Jeanne D'Arc," "John the Baptist," "When Knighthood was in Flower," and "The Sunken Bell." Although his fame rests on Shakespearean parts, he had a repertory of more than 125 diverse parts.

A match-safe is shaped to represent E. H. Sothern. It is all-frosted glass, pierced for hanging. Length: four and one-half inches.

No. 433   Marlowe Match-Safe

Julia Marlowe (1870-   ) was the stage name of Sarah
Frances Frost, American actress born in England, who with
her family, came to America in 1875.   Her first stage appearance was in New York in 1887.   She rapidly gained
popularity, and position as a star.   Her greatest success was
with E. H. Sothern in a notable series of Shakespearean
plays, and modern drama.

The match-safe is shaped to represent Julia Marlowe.   It
is all-frosted glass, matching the one representing E. H.
Sothern.   The patent date 1876 is on the back.   While this
type of portrait match-safe must have been patented in
that year, the Sothern-Marlowe items could have hardly
been produced before 1904.

No. 434   Elssler Flask

In 1840, a German danseuse, Fanny Elssler (1810-1884),
took this country by storm.   No one seemed immune to
her charms.   "Perfect," "Fascinating," "Airy," and "Goss-
amer," were some of the adjectives used in her praise.   When
she visited Congress, the House of Representatives directed
her to sit in the Speaker's chair.   When she entered the
Senate chamber, the Senate stood while she entered.   Her
tour lasted about two years.

An unusual pint flask is said to have been made in her
honor.   One side shows the figure of a dancer in ballerina
costume.   The word "Chapman" is placed beneath, and
suggests the name of the producer of the flask.   On the
reverse, a soldier is shown.   He carries a gun, with fixed
bayonet; and wears a large helmet, with a very long spike.
A drum is at his side.   "Balt. Md." is placed beneath the
figure, and suggests the location of the bottle-works.
Color: aqua.

No. 432
SOTHERN MATCH-SAFE

No. 433
MARLOWE MATCH-SAFE

No. 434   ELSSLER FLASK

CHAPTER XI

This nation is often referred to as a Melting Pot, because the characteristics of many nationalities are blended in most American individuals. Names that have come from most, if not all European countries are found here, on lists of pupils in our schools, the workers in our shops, and of voting citizens. A justifiable pride is felt by these in the land of family origin, and objects that refer to persons, places, or events there, are cherished along with those relating to American subjects. This inclination probably is responsible for the fact that glassware honoring many persons of foreign birth may be found here. English subjects are more often encountered than others; but Scotland, Ireland, France, Italy, Germany, Hungary, Sweden, and Denmark are represented. Some of these items are of foreign make, while others no doubt were produced here.

No. 435   Queen Victoria Plate

A profusely decorated plate honors Victoria (1819-1901) who came to the British throne in 1837. The Queen celebrated her long reign with a Golden Jubilee in 1887 and a Diamond Jubilee in 1897. The plate probably was issued in one or both of these years. It appears in slightly varying forms.

One shows a profile bust portrait of the mature Queen superimposed on a similar portrait of the youthful Queen, framed by a sunburst. The border carries the Arms of Great Britain, the cross of St. George, the cross of St. Andrew, the thistle of Scotland, and the rose of England. Integral handles show laurel branches and crowns. It is crystal glass, ten inches in diameter. Extreme width is eleven and three-fourths inches.

No. 435   Queen Victoria Plate

No. 436   Queen Victoria Plate

No. 436   Queen Victoria Plate

Another plate is much like the preceding one. A laurel wreath has replaced the sunburst, and the date "1837" is placed beneath the wreath. Handles have been removed from top and bottom, and placed at the sides. Dimensions have not been changed.

No. 437   Rule Britannia Plate

A very handsome plate seems to be to Great Britain, what the "Rally round the flag" plate meant to this nation; a rallying-cry in time of danger. (See No. 53.)

In 1900, the Boer War in South Africa was a source of grief to Queen Victoria and the British Empire. The Boxer trouble in China, in this year, complicated other difficulties.

The winds of war always make the flag of a nation stand out stronger than before, and patriotism reaches a new high.

"Rule Britannia" is a patriotic song that first appeared in the drama "The Masque of Alfred" produced in 1740.

> "When Britain first, at Heaven's command,
> Arose from out the azure main,
> This was the charter of her land,
> And guardian angels sung the strain:
> Rule, Britannia! Britannia rules the waves!
> Britons never shall be slaves."

A crown, resembling the coronation crown of Queen Victoria, and no doubt intended to represent it, fills the center of this plate. The date "1900" is beneath it. On the border "V. R." (Victoria Regina) is placed between crossed military flags, on opposite sides of the plate. "Rule Britannia" in large letters, is inscribed on the border above and beneath the crown. The plate is crystal glass. Diameter: ten inches.

A paperweight honors King Edward VII (1841-1910), known as King Edward the Peacemaker. He was the eldest son of Queen Victoria and succeeded his mother on the throne. In 1860, while Prince of Wales, he visited the United States, traveling under the name of Lord Renfrew, as was his custom when away from the Dominion. Edward was the great grandson of George III, the King against whom we waged a war. His visit therefore, assumed more than ordinary importance. Everywhere, he was received with the spirit of Good Will. He was received at the boundary line between Canada and the United States with great ceremony. He visited Chicago, St. Louis, Cincinnati, Richmond, Baltimore, Philadelphia, Albany, Boston, Washington, and other cities. He visited Mt. Vernon and the tomb of Washington. Grand balls were held in his honor. A military reception was given at West Point. And Albert Edward made an agreeable impression wherever he went.

In 1877, when President Grant had finished sixteen years of strenuous life as soldier and President, he had need to relax and recruit his strength. He visited Europe, and an account of his reception there includes reference to Edward. Much discussion had arisen in England as to whether Grant should be received as a private citizen or as a sovereign ruler. At length, Lord Beaconsfield (better known as Disraeli) announced that he should be received as a sovereign. Consequently, the Prince of Wales (the future King Edward) received him at Marlborough House as an honored guest. Queen Victoria waived the usual ceremonies of presentation to Court, and extended to him and Mrs. Grant, invitations to all Court entertainments. An account of this visit is much too lengthy to be recorded here, but pictures of Edward published in connection with these events, identify him as the subject of an interesting paperweight.

It is rectangular in shape, flat, and thin. A likeness of Edward is pressed in the base. He wears civilian clothing,

No. 437   Rule Britannia Plate

No. 438
King Edward VII
Paperweight

No. 439
Silver Wedding Dish

with a flower in the button-hole. The background is frosted. Edges are beveled. It is three and one-fourth inches by four and three-eighths inches in size. Probably issued in honor of his visit to the United States.

No. 439   Silver Wedding Dish

In 1863, the Prince married Princess Alexandria, daughter of the King of Denmark; and twenty-five years from that date, the royal couple celebrated their silver wedding anniversary. Commemorative glassware was issued at that time. On one item, a central design features "Prince of Wales Feathers," the device of the Prince of Wales, three ostrich feathers, with the motto: "Ich Dien" (I serve). The border design, executed in small dewdrops, is inscribed: "The Silver Wedding of the Prince and Princess of Wales 10th March, 1888." "1863-1888." Integral handles. Crystal glass, six and five-eighths by four and seven-eighths inches in size.

No. 440   Disraeli Compote

An open compote honors Benjamin Disraeli (1804-1881), Prime Minister of England.

Disraeli was of Jewish parentage, but his father severed his connection with that religion in 1813. Benjamin was christened in 1817, and it was this act that made possible the political career from which, as a Jew, he would have been debarred, because of existing laws of that time.

One of the great triumphs of his career was the outcome of the Congress of Berlin, in which the principal European powers established the borders of the southeastern states and dependencies of Europe, after much trouble had been experienced by several nations.

The obverse shows a laurel wreath framing an oval portrait of the Earl of Beaconsfield, commonly called Disraeli. The reverse shows the following inscription, framed by a laurel wreath: "Earl Beaconsfield the Hero of the Congress of Berlin July 1878." The remainder of the bowl is ornamented by a design in high relief, composed of the rose of

448

No. 440   Disraeli Compote

England, the thistle of Scotland, and the shamrock of Ireland. Opaque white glass, of English origin. Diameter: five and one-half inches. Height: five and one-half inches.

No. 441 GLADSTONE MUG

A mug honoring the English statesman, displays his name in large letters around the bowl. "For the Million" is placed beneath it. Below this, three units of a design made up of the English rose, Scotch thistle, and Irish shamrock are shown. Background area is studded with tiny dewdrops. A row of larger dewdrops is on the handle, and two rows of larger ones encircle the rim. Color: amethyst. Height: two and one-half inches. Diameter: the same.

No. 442 GLADSTONE PLATE

A small plate honors William Ewart Gladstone (1809-1898), four times Prime Minister of England, popularly known as "The Grand Old Man."

A profile portrait of Gladstone is in the center. The border is inscribed: "In Memory of England's Greatest Statesman W. E. Gladstone, The Grand Old Man" "Born Dec. 29, 1809 Died May 19, 1898." Color: aqua. Diameter: five and one-eighth inches.

No. 443 JOHN BRIGHT PLATE

A small plate honors John Bright (1811-1889), English statesman, Quaker, and eloquent orator, who served in Gladstone's cabinet, elected to Parliament in 1843.

Bust portrait is in the center. Inscribed above the portrait: "John Bright." Inscribed beneath the portrait: "Peace and Plenty." The border is ornamented with a wreath of grain. The inscription and wreath of grain refer to his activities in Parliament in the interests of peace, and in bringing about repeal of the notorious Corn Laws. Corn Laws were statutes occupying much time and attention in Parliament, over a period of many years. They were efforts to hold the price of grain at a high point when

No. 441   Gladstone Mug

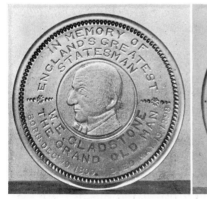

No. 442
Gladstone Plate

No. 443
John Bright Plate

all the natural economic causes in operation, were opposed to it. The story of these Corn Laws is lengthy and forms a record of the inability of legislation to do this. John Bright often spoke against the Corn Laws until they were repealed.

In June, 1883, a great demonstration was held at Birmingham to celebrate his twenty-five years of service in Parliament. He died in 1889, so this plate might have been issued in either year, or in both years. It is crystal glass, five inches in diameter.

No. 444   Bismarck Plate

A small plate honors Prince Otto von Bismarck, the great Chancellor of Germany. Bismarck's efforts to keep peace in Germany earned the title of "Peace-Maker" and "Peace-Keeper" of Europe. He also was called the "Iron Chancellor" and the "Man of Blood and Iron."

In 1870, during the Franco-Prussian War, he often was with King Wilhelm I on many battlefields, and he negotiated the treaty of peace. Since our own General Philip Sheridan accompanied the headquarters of the German Army, as guest of Wilhelm I, it appears likely that these three men often were together and on friendly terms. Wilhelm I died in 1888. His son and successor died about three months later. Frederick's son Wilhelm II (Kaiser Wilhelm of World War I) became ruler. His policies differed greatly from those of Bismarck, and Bismarck resigned his office in 1890. He and the Kaiser parted as personal enemies. Bismarck died in 1898, and expressed his devotion to Kaiser Wilhelm I, as well as his dislike of Kaiser Wilhelm II, by choosing the following inscription for his tomb: "A True German Servant of the Emperor William I."

A portrait of Bismarck is framed by a wreath of laurel and oak leaves against a stippled background. The border is inscribed in German, which translated means "We Germans Fear God but Nothing in this World." Inscribed also "1815-1895." The year 1895 was the 80th anniversary

No. 444 Bismarck Plate

No. 446
Napoleon III
Statuette

No. 445
Kaiser Wilhelm I Plate

of his birth, and perhaps the reason why the plate was issued at this time. It is crystal glass, five and one-half inches in diameter.

No. 445   Kaiser Wilhelm I Plate

A square plate honors Kaiser Wilhelm I (1797-1888), Emperor of Germany. During his reign our relations with Germany were cordial. During the Franco-Prussian War, 1870, our General Philip Sheridan accompanied the headquarters of the German Army, as guest of the Emperor. Wilhelm died March 9, 1888, and Sheridan died a few months later, August 5th; so it could be that this plate is American in origin and was issued about this time.

Wilhelm's portrait is in the center, with his name inscribed beneath it. The border is decorated with a wreath of laurel and oak leaves. Kaiser Wilhelm I was the grandfather of Kaiser Wilhelm II, German ruler during World War I. The plate is crystal glass, nine and three-fourths inches square.

No. 446   Napoleon III Statuette

Napoleon III (1808-1873), French Emperor, was a nephew of Napoleon I (Napoleon Bonaparte). During his lifetime, his influence sometimes reached this country. When Prof. S. F. B. Morse was struggling for recognition of his telegraphic invention, he was denied recognition here. He applied for patents in England, France, and Russia. England and Russia refused. France granted the patent but it was appropriated by the Government without compensation to him. In later years, when he had won success, his system was adopted throughout Europe; and finally, through the influence of Napoleon III he was presented, as an international gift, in honor of his work, $20,000.

While this nation was absorbed in the War between the States, Napoleon III took advantage of our situation and attempted to establish a foothold in America, in violation of the Monroe Doctrine. Through help of the French

454

Army, Maximilian was established as Emperor of Mexico, in 1864. Financially and politically, he was wholly dependent upon Napoleon. The U. S. Government protested this action but was unable (because engaged in war) to enforce the Monroe Doctrine. When peace was established in the Union, the American people demanded of Napoleon the recall of French troops. Deprived of foreign aid, Maximilian was defeated and shot, in 1867. Three years later, by the Franco-Prussian, or Franco-German War, Napoleon was deposed and the dream of French domination on this continent was ended.

Perhaps this act of aggression had something to do with the fact that our Sheridan, a seasoned and successful General, accompanied the German troops (as a guest of the German Ruler, it was said) in their war against Napoleon.

After his defeat, Napoleon retired, with his wife (the Empress Eugenie) and his son, to Chislehurst, in England. Here he died, in 1873.

A statuette fashioned to represent Napoleon III honors his memory. It is identified as a memorial piece through inscriptions "Napoleon III" "Chislehurst 1873." It is a bust of remarkable artistry. It was produced in France, as shown by the inscription "S Louis de pose." Its height is seven and three-fourths inches. The base is three and one-fourth inches square, and is all-frosted excepting background for the inscription. The figure is all-frosted and the finish is unusually soft and smooth. The weight is remarkable, too, being four and one-fourth pounds.

Previous mention has been made of other individuals native to other countries. Items honoring Christopher Columbus, Americus Vespucius, Louis Kossuth, Lafayette, Pope Leo XIII, Sir Moses Montefiore, and Napoleon Bonaparte are considered in the earlier chapters of this book.

In this volume, Lord Nelson is reported in Chapter VII. Michael Corcoran is mentioned in Chapter VIII. Wm. Shakespeare, Lord Byron, Sir Walter Scott, Charles Dickens, Alfred Tennyson, Robert Burns, and La Fontaine are given in Chapter IX; and Jenny Lind is presented in Chapter X.

A summary shows twenty-six individuals native to other lands, as here reported by and memorialized through glassware. Further search, no doubt, could add others to this list.

ENGLISH
Wm. Shakespeare
Lord Byron
Sir Walter Scott
Lord Nelson
Disraeli
Victoria
Edward VII
Gladstone
John Bright
Charles Dickens
Alfred Tennyson

FRENCH
Lafayette
La Fontaine.
Napoleon I (Bonaparte)
Napoleon III

HUNGARIAN
Louis Kossuth

SWEDISH
Jenny Lind

GERMAN
Bismarck
Wilhelm I

ITALIAN
Christopher Columbus
Americus Vespucius
Pope Leo XIII
Sir Moses Montefiore

DANISH
Princess Alexandria
(wife of Edward VII)

SCOTTISH
Robert Burns

IRISH
Michael Corcoran

CHAPTER XII

Some glassware honoring individuals cannot be placed in any group arrangement that has been formed. Each one must be considered singly.

No. 447   Jumbo Sugar-Bowl

Phineas Taylor Barnum (1810-1891), American showman and circus proprietor, shares honors with the elephant which he made famous. Jumbo was the tallest elephant ever in captivity, and was brought to America by Barnum, in 1882. The purchase price was ten thousand dollars. The monster was captured in Ethiopia, as a baby three and one-half feet high, and sent to Paris. Then he was purchased by the London Zoo, where he grew to his tremendous size, and carried children on his back. After only three years with the Barnum circus, he was killed in a railway accident, in Canada, in 1885. According to taxidermists who mounted him, Jumbo measured ten feet, seven inches, at the shoulders, and weighed about six tons; but was advertised as being much larger. His prestige was due more to Barnum's clever advertising than to his colossal size. Advertising posters proclaimed his height to be eleven feet, and his weight twelve and one-half tons.

The sugar-bowl is quite plain, the figure of a man's head beneath the handles, forming the major decoration. This is said to represent Barnum. Since this bearded figure is quite unlike pictures of the smooth shaven Barnum, further research concerning this identity should be made. Jumbo stands in solitary grandeur atop the lid, his figure emphasized by an all-frosted finish. In some cases, etching is found on the bowl. It is crystal glass, nine inches in height. Diameter: four inches.

(Since this chapter is devoted to persons, other items concerning Jumbo will be found in Chapter XIV.)

457

No. 447
JUMBO SUGAR-BOWL

No. 448
MITCHELL PLATTER

No. 448   Mitchell Platter

A bread-tray, or platter, honors John Mitchell, American labor leader, organizer, and author. He was president of United Mine Workers of America 1899-1908, and vice-president of the American Federation of Labor, 1898-1914.

Bust portrait of Mitchell is in the center. Inscribed above is "Leader Counsellor Friend." Inscribed beneath the portrait "John Mitchell President United Mine Workers of America." Conventional border. Crystal glass, ten and three-fourths inches by six and three-fourths inches in size.

No. 449   Goshorn Paperweight

A paperweight honors Alfred T. Goshorn, Director-General of the Centennial Exhibition at Philadelphia in 1876. Goshorn was an attorney and business man of Cincinnati, Ohio, appointed by President Grant to the Centennial Commission and elected Director-General of the Exhibition. This post called for executive ability of the highest order. He had general charge of supervision, correspondence, and negotiation. He led an army of contractors, superintendents, clerks, exhibitors, artists, transportation companies, and commissioners, to an objective of harmonious work and success. He managed daily details of the enterprise before and during the exhibition period. His activities were crowned with brilliant success.

The paperweight is oval in shape, and has turned sides. A bust of Goshorn is pressed in the base. Inscribed "Director-General A. T. Goshorn." Sides and base are all-frosted. This item is identical with the oval Lincoln paperweight, excepting the portrait. It is crystal glass, four and seven-eighths inches by three and three-eighths inches in size. One and one-eighth inches in depth. Clearly a centennial item.

No. 449 GOSHORN PAPERWEIGHT

No. 450
OWENS STATUETTE

No. 451
SUMNER STATUETTE

No. 450   Owens Statuette

A statuette honors Michael J. Owens (1859-1923). The name "Owens" is a familiar one in recent times, to those familiar with glassware lore. In connection with the glassware industry, intricate machinery has been constantly invented or improved upon, since 1895. M. J. Owens, inventor, is given credit for the first conception, in 1899, of a fully automatic bottle machine.

The Owens statuette is somewhat different from the ones usually found. It is simply the bust of the individual, with no supporting base. It has been executed with care, details being worked out in great perfection. Inscribed "1859 M. J. Owens 1923." It is crystal glass, all-frosted, five inches across the shoulders, and five inches in height.

No. 451   Sumner Statuette

Charles Sumner (1811-1874), American statesman, graduated from Harvard and made an extensive European tour. On his return, he became interested in the slavery question and became noted as an orator. He was elected to the United States Senate and there became the chief advocate of anti-slavery sentiment. He delivered a speech most provocative to the South. Two days later, Preston S. Brooks, congressman from South Carolina, attacked Sumner in the Senate chamber and struck him till he fell unconscious to the floor. Sumner spent the next three years in a struggle to regain his health. During this time he was returned to office and his vacant chair in the Senate was regarded as a silent but eloquent pleader for the resistance to slavery. During the War between the States, he was an advocate of emancipation, and the—credit or blame—for imposing equal suffrage rights for negroes upon the southern states, as a condition for reconstruction, belongs to him. At times, Sumner was highly popular; at other times he drew bitter resentment.

The Sumner statuette stands five and one-half inches

461

No. 452
CARRIE NATION BOTTLE

No. 453
UNIDENTIFIED LADY
PLATTER

high, and the base measures two inches in diameter. Sumner died in 1874. Since this type of glassware bust was popular in 1876, this one may have been issued about that time. It was distributed in crystal glass with satinized finish, and also in opaque white. It is inscribed "Copyright secured."

No. 452 Carrie Nation Bottle

A bottle made in the shape of an old-fashioned lady carrying an umbrella and a handbag, represents Carrie A. Nation, a noted character of Kansas.

Mrs. Nation's first husband was a "drinking man" so her life was one of hard work, misery, and bitterness. She became a temperance agitator and crusader for prohibition, hoping to save other women from the grief she had known. After her husband's death, she later married David Nation. She came to believe that her name, Carrie A. Nation, was symbolic, and that she was destined to CARRY A NATION to prohibition. Her weapons were a hatchet, an umbrella, and a large handbag which often carried rocks. In the early 1900's she waged single-handed warfare against the liquor industry. She smashed saloon fixtures, and windows, and stocks, over a large territory. For this, she paid heavy fines and served innumerable jail sentences. In 1909, she acquired a home in Eureka Springs, Arkansas; operated a boarding house, and gave temperance lectures. About three years later, she suffered a stroke while speaking for temperance from the back end of a wagon. This illness ended in her death. The bottle is crystal glass, nine inches in height. It has been reproduced.

No. 454
STANTON PAPERWEIGHT

No. 455
UNIDENTIFIED LADY
DISH

No. 453   Unidentified Lady Platter

This platter honors an unidentified subject.   It has been reported as Jenny Lind, as Mrs. Benjamin Harrison, and as the Gibson girl, but positive identity has not been established.

The portrait center is framed by a floral border done in high relief.   Opaque white glass, seven and one-half by eleven inches in size.

No. 454   Stanton Paperweight

A large door-knob type paperweight has the translucent portrait of a man within.   It bears strong resemblance to Edwin M. Stanton, Secretary of War in Lincoln's cabinet, and probably represents him.   The diameter is three and one-half inches, and the depth is two inches.

No. 455   Unidentified Lady Dish

An unusual shallow dish features the portrait of an unidentified lady.   Two bands cross the dish in diagonal lines, forming a large X.   A diamond shaped area is formed at the crossing.   In this, a portrait is placed.   Remaining parts have an all-over stippled and crackled effect similar to the tree of life pattern.   Handles are large and decorated. A very desirable item made in crystal glass.   Overall length is fifteen inches.   Width: seven and three-fourths inches. Depth: one and three-fourths inches.

No. 456   Kewpie Doll Candy Container

A candy container that doubles for toothpicks, presents Kewpie, the baby-doll invention of Rose O'Neill, wife of Harry Leon Wilson.

It is said the kewpie doll with a cherubic expression that resembled a million babies, created a fortune of more than a million dollars for the humorist-author responsible for her advent in 1909.   Other dolls came, flourished for a time, and went their way; but Kewpie came for good.   She

No. 456   Kewpie Doll Candy Container

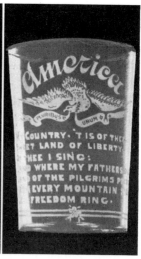

No. 457
Gibson Girl Spoon-Holder

No. 458
"America" Tumbler

was the darling of all children and of grown-ups who loved children, as well. If a census of kewpie dolls that never wore out but were merely outgrown and tucked safely away in treasure chests were taken, the count would be surprising. An orchid to the memory of Rose O'Neill who added so much pleasure to the lives of so many people.

Kewpie stands beside a paneled container. Inscribed on under side of base: "Kewpie" "Geo. Borgfeldt and Co. N. Y." "Reg. U. S. Pat. Off. Des. Pat. 43680 Serial No. 2862 Net Wt. ¾ oz." It is crystal glass, three and one-eighth inches in height, and two and three-fourths inches in width.

No. 457   Gibson Girl Spoon-Holder

A spoon-holder, one item of a four-piece table set, features the work of Charles Dana Gibson, American artist and illustrator who became famous as the originator of the Gibson Girl.

Before and after the turn of the century, Gibson became the delineator of the typical American girl in various occupations, particularly those out-of-doors.

Four oval medallions pressed in unusually high relief, present the familiar features of the Gibson Girl. Body and base of the spooner are paneled in twelve sections, and the stem is ribbed. The top is finished by a narrow flange. Crystal glass. Height: five inches. Top diameter: three and three-fourths inches.

The Gibson Girl oval medallions may be found on tumblers also. Scarce.

No. 458   The Tumbler "America"

A tumbler commemorates the hymn, "America," written by Samuel Francis Smith (1808-1895).

The author of "America" was an American clergyman, born in Boston. He was a graduate of the Eliot School and of the Boston Latin School. He attended Harvard and was a graduate of the Andover Theological Seminary. He

467

served as pastor of various Baptist churches, edited Baptist periodicals, was a professor of languages and a talented writer of verse. A Baptist hymn book contains twenty-seven of his hymns. While he was a theological student, a composer brought some old German songs and asked Smith to translate the words "or write new ones to go with the music." One tune started his mind to work, and in half an hour on a gloomy day in February, 1832, he had set down on paper, the words to "America." The hymn was first sung July 4, 1832, at a children's celebration in Boston. It became popular at once and for many years was accepted as the national anthem of the United States, although without official sanction. When a time came for official action "The Star Spangled Banner" was chosen because it is more exclusively American. The music of "America" without the words may belong to any one of many countries. France, England, Bavaria, Switzerland, Brunswick, Hanover, Wurtemberg, Prussia, Saxony, Weimar, and Norway have all used it. The beauty of Smith's verses have never failed in their appeal and the hymn has remained a general favorite of the American people. Oliver Wendell Holmes offered a tribute that is whimsical as well as complimentary. He wrote a poem which included these lines:

> "And there's a nice youngster of excellent pith,—
> Fate tried to conceal him by naming him Smith;
> But he shouted a song for the brave and the free,—
> Just read on his medal, 'My country, 'tis of thee'."

The tumbler is etched with the title and first stanza of the hymn. An American eagle lends decorative effect. With wings outstretched as if in flight he carries a banner inscribed "E Pluribus Unum." It is crystal glass, three and three-fourths inches in height, and two and three-fourths inches in diameter.

No. 459 Spark Plug Candy Container

A candy container presents the immortal "Spark-Plug," a squint-eyed race horse whose cash earnings outran most famous turf stars, created by cartoonist William Morgan "Billy" de Beck (1890-1942).

De Beck's famous comic strip was begun in 1919 when he joined King Features in New York. He added many other characters, and was credited with introducing and making popular such slang phrases as "heebie-jeebies," "jeepers-creepers," "horse feathers," and "sweet mama."

A creature bearing some resemblance to a horse wears a large blanket inscribed "Spark Plug." The hollow interior held candy. A metal strip covers the base. Inscribed on base "Copyright 1923" "King Features Syndicate Inc." Inscribed on back "U. S. A."

No. 460 Charley Ross Bottle

Charlie Ross was a kidnapping victim. The story as published in Frank Leslie's Illustrated Newspaper, August 15, 1874, reads: "On the evening of the 1st of July, Germantown, a suburb of Philadelphia, was thrown into a state of great excitement, owing to the abduction of one of the children of Mr. Christian K. Ross, who resides in Washington Lane, about two hundred yards from the railway station, in a handsome dwelling which will be found illustrated on another page. It appears that about four o'clock on the evening mentioned, while the two sons of the unfortunate gentleman, Walter and Charlie, the former six years and the latter four years old, were playing a short distance from the house, they were, as seen in our engraving, accosted by a man who asked them to take a ride in a buggy, in which another man was seated. On three or four occasions previously the children had been accosted by these persons and been given sweetmeats by them, until the little fellows at last looked for their coming, and as may be supposed, readily consented to take a drive when asked to do so. When once in the buggy the two men drove

No. 459   Spark Plug Candy Container

No. 460
Charley Ross Bottle

No. 461
Charley Ross Bottle

470

away rapidly, nor even pulled rein until the children were ten miles from home when one of them requested Walter to go into a store to buy some packages of fire crackers, it being near the Fourth. The lad complied with the request; but no sooner had he entered the store than the kidnappers drove off at a furious rate, with his little brother, and were soon out of sight.

"Here he was found crying, in the midst of a number of people, by a railroad official who recognized him and took him home to relate the sad story to his family. Notice of the abduction was given to the police, and a reward of $300 offered by Mr. Ross for the return of the boy, whose mother was away from home at the time. The amount however, did not meet the views of the ruffians; for soon Mr. Ross received letters demanding $20,000 and asserted that in default of the payment of that sum the boy should be made away with. This was terrible, and the more so as the villians, who still set the detectives at defiance, had proposed a mode of payment calculated to secure them from detection. While Mr. Ross was endeavoring to raise the money, the Mayor of Philadelphia offered a reward amounting to that sum for the return of the boy and the capture of his abductors; but this, so far, has been of no avail, so that the family are still in a state of the greatest distress. Portraits of the boy have been published in the press. They are said to be far from reliable, having led to the misapprehension and the detention of a child, erroneously supposed to be little Charlie, among a band of gypsies some distance from the city. The portrait which we give elsewhere is from a painting by Austin Street, admitted, in our presence by the uncle of the abducted boy, to be the only true likeness of the child extant. Mr. Street kindly placed the canvas at our disposal before it was framed, and just as he had given the last touches to it, so that the reader may now rest assured he has before him a true likeness of little Charlie Brewster Ross, the stolen boy." The child was not recovered.

It is said this was the first child kidnapping in the nation,

471

and the public feelings were raised to the peak of the emotional thermometer.

A cologne bottle was produced having the bust of the child, with his name lettered above, placed within a medallion. A depression on the reverse carries a round detachable mirror. Crystal glass, six and five-eighths inches in height. Capacity: three ounces.

No. 461   Charley Ross Bottle

Another bottle presents the same picture of the boy in a different way. The depression for a mirror is on the reverse, as in the other. Crystal glass, six inches in height. Capacity: three ounces.

CHAPTER XIII

MISCELLANEOUS SUBJECTS ASSOCIATED WITH WAR

The Spanish-American War

When vital questions arise in the world, men may scramble for personal safety or they can sacrifice themselves to save, or try to save, what is right. Not being beasts, but men, we choose the sacrifice in order to redeem mankind from the forces that make for destruction. In war, our country has sought no territory and no rewards. We give. We do not take. We have sought for a victory of our ideas. Arms was not an aim, but only the means. America follows no such delusion as a place in the sun for the strong, by the destruction of the weak. America has sought rather, by giving of her strength for the service of the weak, a place in Eternity.

At the time of the Spanish-American War, the question of "what is right" was in the air. The rights of man against tyranny were upheld. Men were willing to sacrifice themselves, to resist evil and redeem the rights and liberties of a wronged people. The praise bestowed on them, and memorial items created to honor them were not given merely to glorify success, but as recognition to a righteousness that opposed wrong-doing.

No. 462   Battleship Maine Plate

A circular plate commemorates the sinking of the battleship Maine. The Maine was one of the second-class battleships of the United States Navy. This vessel was sent to Havana, Cuba, in January, 1898, on a peaceful mission. She was received by the Spanish fort and naval vessels in the harbor with the courtesies usually extended to visiting war-ships of a friendly power. Her anchorage was selected by the Spanish authorities. On the night of February 15, 1898, the Maine was destroyed by a submarine mine. It was believed that the Spaniards, who at the time were

473

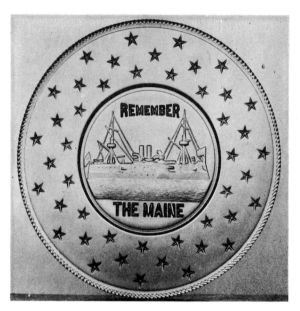

No. 462   Battleship Maine Plate

No. 463   No. 464
Battleship Maine Plate   Battleship Maine Plate

474

very much incensed at the interest Americans were taking in the Cuban insurrection, had maliciously destroyed the vessel and crew. Two officers and 264 sailors and marines lost their lives by the explosion. An investigation failed to place the responsibility for the catastrophe, and Spain hastened to send a message of regret at what she called "an incident." The blowing up of the Maine was among the causes of the war with Spain, begun soon afterwards. The rallying-cry of the war became: "Remember the Maine."

A battleship representing the Maine fills the center of the plate. Inscribed, above and below the ship "Remember the Maine." A star-spangled border has a cable edge. (Note: this border is identical with that of a plate honoring Wm. McKinley who was President at that time.) Crystal glass, nine and one-fourth inches in diameter.

No. 463   Battleship Maine Plate

In this plate, a picture of the famous warship ornaments the center. It is inscribed "U. S. Battleship Maine." Opaque white glass. Design in red and grey transfer. Diameter: seven and one-fourth inches.

No. 464   Battleship Maine Plate

Another plate commemorating the Maine has a likeness of the ship, under way. The same inscription "U. S. Battleship Maine" is used. It is green glass, five and one-half inches in diameter. Made also in crystal.

No. 465   Battleship Maine Covered Dish

A covered dish commemorates the sinking of the Maine. It is not a likeness of the Maine but is suggestive of the Spanish-American period battleship. Inscribed on each side of the base "Remember the Maine." Crystal glass, seven and one-fourth inches in length, two and three-fourths inches in width, and three and one-half inches in height.

No. 466   Battleship Maine Covered Dish

Another dish commemorates the Maine, and is intended to represent the ship as it was before being sunk. It is opaque white glass, seven and one-fourth inches in length. A well executed item.

No. 467   Battleship Covered Dishes

Another covered dish represents a battleship of the period. It is opaque white glass, seven and three-eighths inches in length, three and seven-eighths inches in width, and four and one-half inches in height.

Nos. 468-469-470   Battleship Covered Dishes

These three dishes are identical in form and size. Identification is made possible by name-plates inscribed "Olympia," "Oregon," and "Wheeling," respectively. These saw service in the Spanish-American War and won fame by their accomplishments.

The Olympia, battleship first class, was the flagship of Admiral Dewey, commanded by Captain Charles V. Gridley. At Manila, when Dewey thought the time had come to open the engagement, he said: "When you are ready, Gridley, commence firing." (These words are reported in slightly varying forms.) The captain did not wait and by his orders the first shot of the Battle of Manila Bay was then fired.

The Oregon, battleship first class, was famed for her fast run from San Francisco around South Africa, through the Straits of Magellan, and upward along the east coast to Key West, a distance of 14,133 nautical miles, accomplished in 68 days. The trip was made to join Admiral Sampson's fleet. Her commander was Captain Charles E. Clark. After filling her coal bunkers at Key West she proceeded to join the fleet.

The Wheeling, battleship third class, was smaller than either the Oregon or Olympia, and it was not so heavily armed. Its fame was less, also.

No. 465   Battleship Maine Covered Dish

No. 466   Battleship Maine Covered Dish

477

In 1925, the Oregon was loaned to the State of Oregon and preserved as an exhibit, at Portland. In 1942, during the second World War, urgent need for metal led to the decision to scrap the famous old relic whose stormy race was an epic of naval service.

In 1921, the Olympia was chosen to bring home the body of the unknown soldier; and in 1942, consent for scrapping the Oregon was regretfully given with the stipulation that the Olympia be permanently preserved as the nation's last naval relic of the Spanish-American War. The Philadelphia navy yard was chosen to hold the honored flagship.

Each dish is opaque white glass, six and three-eighths inches long, three and five-eighths inches wide, and four inches high.

No. 471 Battleship Maine Tumbler

Tumblers were made, too, to honor the Maine. On this one, a large scale likeness of the ship is shown, under way in a heavy sea, with smoke streaming from her funnels. "Remember the Maine" is above the ship. Crystal glass, three and seven-eighths inches in height.

No. 472 Battleship Maine Tumbler

Another tumbler commemorating the Maine shows a small picture of the ship between two crossed U. S. flags. The same slogan is inscribed above it. It is crystal, three and three-fourths inches in height.

No. 473 Battleship Maine Tumbler

Another tumbler pictures an American eagle holding the U. S. flag in his right talon, and a Cuban flag in his left. The familiar slogan is placed beneath the eagle. It is crystal glass, four inches in height.

478

No. 467   Battleship Covered Dish

Nos. 468–469–470   Battleship Covered Dishes
Olympia–Oregon–Wheeling

479

No. 474   Morro Castle Tumbler

A tumbler commemorates the sinking of the Maine. Within a round medallion Morro Castle and fortress at Havana, Cuba, are shown. In this Havana harbor the Maine was destroyed by an explosion. A Cuban flag flies above the medallion. A laurel wreath frames the whole, and suggests the tumbler honors the 266 American men who lost their lives at this place. It is crystal glass, three and three-fourths inches high.

No. 475   Colorado Covered Dish

A covered dish, of which the base only is shown, honors Admiral Dewey. The Colorado was a steam frigate, 44 guns, built 1855, on which Dewey served in 1867. Pictures of the Colorado show her as having large sails and one funnel. It would be of interest to know how the designer represented this feature on the dish lid. The writer has never been able to find one. It is inscribed on each side, in large letters "Colorado." Crystal, six and three-eighths inches in length.

No. 476   American Hen Covered Dish

A covered dish suggests a welcome to Porto Rico, Cuba, and the Philippines. This unusual item is suggestive of a cartoon in glass. The national bird is hatching out some more liberty and freedom loving countries, and lifts protecting wings above them. All this, of course, as a result of the Spanish-American War. An inscription "The American Hen" is used on each side of the oval base. The lid shows an American eagle hovering three eggs inscribed: "Porto Rico," "Cuba," and "Philippines," respectively.

Opaque white glass, six and one-fourth by three and five-eighths inches in size. Height: four inches.

No. 471
BATTLESHIP MAINE TUMBLER

No. 472
BATTLESHIP MAINE TUMBLER

No. 473
BATTLESHIP MAINE TUMBLER

No. 474
MORRO CASTLE TUMBLER

A quart-size flask celebrates the erection of the Baltimore Monument in 1815. Its purpose was to commemorate the defense of the city during the War of 1812. The same force that had taken the city of Washington, attacked Baltimore by land and by water, but defense of the place was so vigorous that the British were forced to retire. It was during this conflict that the "Star-Spangled Banner" was written.

The obverse of this flask is notable for its simplicity. Beneath the tall shaft of the monument is one word "Baltimore." The reverse holds a more profound suggestion. A large ear of corn is placed in the center, with an inscription "Corn for the world" in a semi-circle above it. This seems to refer to the English Corn Laws (see No. 443, John Bright). Corn exports from America were one factor in the subject of England's corn laws in general, and since Baltimore was a shipping port of importance, it was more or less affected by England's policy concerning the Corn Laws. The repeal of English Corn Laws in 1846 may have inspired makers of this flask. It was produced in many colors. The one pictured is olive green.

No. 478   Old Abe Covered Compote

A covered dish honors Old Abe, the battle-eagle. He was christened Old Abe, in honor of President Abraham Lincoln.

In the Chippewa country of Wisconsin, an Indian Chief named Chief Sky chopped down a tree containing an eagle's nest and two young birds. One died. The other grew up and became quite tame. During the War between the States, many soldiers chose good luck mascots. This eagle was secured by Company C., 8th Wisconsin Regiment, which became known as "The Eagle Regiment." He rode on a special perch fixed on top of the flagstaff. For three years, he remained with the regiment, during which time they never lost a battle. Old Abe came safely through

No. 475 COLORADO COVERED DISH

No. 476 AMERICAN HEN COVERED DISH

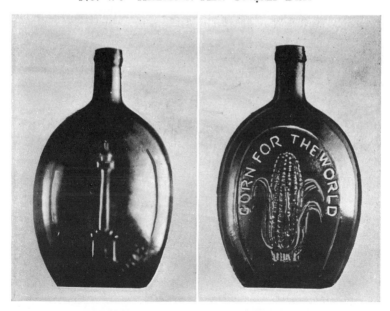

No. 477 BALTIMORE MONUMENT FLASK

some thirty-six battles and many skirmishes, although he was once wounded, in the wing.

After the war, he was presented to the State of Wisconsin and was kept in the Capitol Building. He often was called into action in raising funds for sick and wounded veterans. He made personal appearances. Tickets of admission and pictures of the bird were sold. His dropped feathers sold for five dollars apiece. Ten thousand dollars was once offered for him. It is said that P. T. Barnum raised that offer. He rode in parades. He was present when Grant was nominated for President. He attended G.A.R. encampments. He was the inspiration for a poemsong "Old Abe the Battle-Eagle" written by L. J. Bates and T. Martin Towne; and a poem "The Eagle of Freedom." He visited the Centennial Exhibition at Philadelphia in 1876. His last parade was in Chicago, 1880, for death came to the famous bird early the next year. His body was placed in the War Museum of the Wisconsin Capitol Building, near the famous old battle flags. In 1904 the building, including the body of Old Abe, was destroyed by fire. The bird became but a memory, and the story almost forgotten.

It is brought vividly to mind by glassware made to commemorate the bird and his exploits. A four-piece table set consisting of sugar-bowl, butter-dish, cream-pitcher, and spoon-holder was made. A compote and matching saucedishes are found, too; and a salt-dish is found "once in a blue moon." Possibly other items may yet come to light.

The compote illustrated has a plain bowl, with Old Abe featured on the dome-shaped lid. The frosted eagle rests on a frosted convex surface decorated with foliage, fruits, and flowers. A conventional pattern frames this area. The same pattern is repeated on the stem. The base is highly original in design. Bordered with a pattern resembling a cord, it rests on three small integral feet. This unusual base is the only identification for spoon-holder, creampitcher, sauce-dishes, and salt; for Old Abe appears only on covers.

Abe wore a leather ring on one leg. A long cord was

484

No. 478   Old Abe Covered Compote

No. 479
Civil War Mug

No. 480
Civil War Liquor Glass

485

fastened to this ring. The cord could be lengthened or shortened by winding it around the flag staff. Because the decorative feature of the base is so unusual and bears marked resemblance to a wrapped cord, the design could have been inspired by this cord used to safeguard the famous bird.

The dish is crystal glass (bowls sometimes etched). Diameter: seven inches, but was made in other sizes. The eagle is two inches in height.

The salt-dish is two and seven-eighths inches in diameter, and one and seven-eighths inches in height. It is barely possible that this item should be named a honey-dish, but that idea seems improbable.

No. 479   Civil War Mug

This mug suggests a toast to "The Union." On one side, two hands, representing the North and the South, are clasped above a scroll inscribed "Constitution." "Union Forever" is inscribed above the hands. This design is framed by a victor's wreath, one half made of laurel and the other half of oak leaves. Since ancient times, a crown or wreath or spray of laurel has been used to indicate honor or distinction. The oak also, is an emblem of strength, constancy and long life; and a crown of oak leaves was given by the Romans to a hero who had saved the life of another. Both oak and laurel are used separately, and combined, in many items of commemorative glassware. The opposite side of this mug is inscribed "A Bumper to the Flag." A flag, with thirty-five stars, U. S. shield, and crossed sabres, add to the decorative effect. Between these ornamental devices, on each side, is a liberty cap on a liberty pole, extending from top to bottom of the mug.

It is crystal glass of good bell tone. Probably issued during or soon after the close of the War between the States. It matches the Corcoran tumbler, presented in Chapter VIII, and the Civil War tumbler, presented in Chapter V. It is four and one-eighth inches in height. Diameter at base is three and one-fourth inches.

No. 481   PREPAREDNESS PLATE

No. 482
PATRIOTIC MOTTO
TUMBLER

No. 483
PREPAREDNESS
TOOTHPICK HOLDER

No. 484
PATRIOTIC MOTTO
TUMBLER

487

No. 480   Civil War Liquor Glass

The decorative features are the same as on the preceding number, with few exceptions. There are thirty-four stars on the flag, and the flag floats in the opposite direction from that on the mug. Its height is three and one-fourth inches. Diameter at top is two and three-fourths inches.

No. 481   Preparedness Plate

A large circular plate was issued in the interest of military preparedness. For some time before 1917, many far-sighted persons believed that we should be better prepared for war. In some places, meetings and parades were held to advocate this idea. There was considerable agitation to further the cause.

On July 22, 1916, in San Francisco, California, an incident occurred that drew national attention. During a parade there, a bomb exploded and caused the death of six persons. A labor leader, Thomas Mooney, was suspected. He was tried, convicted, and sentenced to death for the crime. The sentence was never carried out, and Mooney eventually was pardoned and freed.

In the center of this plate, crossed flags are placed above the word "Preparedness." The wide border is divided into six shallow panels. Each panel holds the figure of a soldier or sailor, three of each, placed alternately. It is crystal glass, ten and three-fourths inches in diameter.

No. 482   Patriotic Motto Tumbler

A tumbler shows a patriotic quotation. It is inscribed, "The Love of Country is More Powerful than Reason Itself." At the left of this quotation, the U. S. flag is shown. The flag has 48 stars. The 48th state was admitted in 1912, so the tumbler probably was issued during the period prior to World War I, when measures were instituted to advance the idea of military preparedness. It is crystal glass, three and three-fourths inches in height.

No. 483   Preparedness Toothpick Holder

A toothpick holder offers the preparedness theme.   The obverse shows crossed U. S. flags, with crossed cannon beneath them.   Inscribed above flags: "Preparedness."   A soldier and a sailor stand at opposite sides of the holder. Inscribed on base "Patent Applied for."   Crystal glass. Two and one-fourth inches in height.

No. 484   Patriotic Motto Tumbler

A tumbler similar to one above is inscribed "My Country, Right or Wrong, if Wrong, to set her Right and Defend Her; if Right, to Conquer or Die with Her."   At the left of this quotation, the U. S. flag is shown.   It has 48 stars.   Evidently another item issued in the interest of military preparedness.   Crystal glass.   Height: three and three-fourths inches.

CHAPTER XIV

Some items commemorating places, events, memorials, organizations, nautical subjects, and other topics, are associated with peacetime procedures. The American people always have been peacefully inclined, believing with Emerson that "the real and lasting victories are those of peace, and not of war" and with Milton "Peace hath her victories, no less renown'd than war." Major peacetime exploits have been considered in the earlier chapter of this book but some miscellaneous subjects remain for attention here.

No. 485   New Orleans Tumbler

An engraved panel on this footed tumbler, covers half the glass and shows the water-front at New Orleans. Sailing ships, a house boat, and various types of smaller craft are seen on the river. The city sky line, and buildings, form the background. The name "New Orleans" is placed beneath this river scene. The reverse half is covered with twenty-two thumbprints, and each one of these reflects the scene on the panel. The lower portion of the tumbler is hexagonal in shape, each unit corresponding with one of the six pseudo feet of the base. Under side of the base is rayed, forming a design. It is crystal glass of good bell tone, with much red staining. Height: five and one-half inches. Top diameter: three inches.

In 1884, a great celebration, the World's Industrial and Cotton Centennial Exposition, was held in New Orleans. This time was chosen because a bale of cotton, the first known, was shipped to England from this country in 1784. (See "Eli Whitney," Chapter V, for further details.) This tumbler may or may not have been distributed at that time, but it would have been a fitting commemorative item.

No. 485   New Orleans Tumbler

No. 486   Polar Bear Pattern Tray

491

An oval tray is one form in the Polar Bear pattern. It commemorates the purchase of Alaska.

During the administration of President Johnson, the Secretary of State, William H. Seward, proved himself an able statesman. Largely because of his recommendation, Alaska was purchased, for $7,200,000. This territory had been owned by Russia and was called Russian America. Russia found it too far away to govern conveniently, and feared losing it. Fishing and trading interests there, were in favor of a change. Since 1859, communications were passed between the United States and Russia concerning the purchase, which was completed in 1867. The general public was skeptical of the bargain. The territory was not large, but its value was not then realized. The fur trade was good, and the fishing industry of considerable value; but it was regarded as a cold, dismal, waste land of fogs and storms, containing many icebergs, polar bears, seals, and Eskimos. Since its purchase, the fur industry and fisheries have expanded greatly. Gold discoveries brought a mining boom which was followed by expansion of other phases of the mining industry. Timber production developed, too. The value of all Alaskan exports are now enormous, measured in terms of many millions of dollars annually. Secretary Seward's faith in Alaska was well-founded.

An Arctic scene fills the center of the tray. Seals and a polar bear rest on an iceberg. One seal has entered the water. Gulls circle above, and a ship approaches. Its stern is inscribed "C.G.Co." (Crystal Glass Company.) It is crystal glass, all-frosted. Comes in all clear, and in varying combinations of clear and frosted. Fifteen and one-half by eleven inches in size.

No. 487
POLAR BEAR PATTERN
WASTE BOWL

No. 488   KLONDIKE FLASK

No. 487   Polar Bear Pattern Waste-Bowl

The waste-bowl design is in three units. One shows a polar bear on an ice floe. Another shows a seal similarly placed. The third pictures two seals, one resting on the ice while the other is emerging from the water. A design at the rim resembles hanging icicles. The glass is crystal, with all designs frosted. Tips of the many icicles are left clear, giving the feeling that they are dripping wet. This skilful touch makes the item a general favorite.

No. 488   Klondike Flask

A small flask commemorates the Klondike gold rush. Rich deposits of gold were discovered in the Klondike region of Western Canada, in 1896. This discovery was followed by the most sensational gold rush in all history and lasted for several years. Perhaps 1898 was the peak. More than 30,000 men from all parts of the United States rushed to the almost inaccessible diggings and joined in a frenzied search for the precious metal. It requires a vivid imagination to realize the historic events that transpired; the ambitions, hopes, hates, despair, cruelties, haste, confusion, disorder, and lawlessness of a gold-crazed mob. Thousands of men and pack animals perished on the way. Nothing but desperation could have goaded the survivors on through Dead Horse Gulch and other barriers along the "Trail of Heartache" in Alaska.

The output from this field reached its climax in 1900 when $22,000,000 worth of gold was mined. After that date, production steadily declined.

The flask is made to represent a large gold nugget. The opaque white glass was almost concealed beneath paint (both oil and metallic) shading from light tan to medium and dark tones of brown. The word "Klondike" is impressed in the metal screw cap. A smooth round area on the obverse, two inches in diameter, might have carried a label. Capacity: four ounces. Height: six inches. It is extremely thin, in depth.

494

No. 489 Niagara Falls Tray

No. 490
Niagara Falls Plate

No. 491
Prospect Point Plate

495

A large, rectangular tray pictures Niagara Falls. Between Lakes Erie and Ontario, over a precipice bisected by the United States-Canadian boundary line, falls Niagara, the world's most famous cataract. The name comes from an Iroquois Indian name meaning the "thunder of waters." The falls were first visited and described by a French missionary, Father Hennepin, in 1687. Literature concerning Niagara would fill a library. Artists, poets, and prose writers, have pictured its wonders, but no medium can convey its grandeur. Its beauty and power must be seen to be known. Its fame as a mecca for honey-mooners is almost as great as that of its scenic attractions. More than 2,000,000 visitors every year view Niagara's majesty. In this way, and through widely distributed pictures, such names as Horseshoe Falls, American Falls, Goat Island, Three Sisters Island, Whirlpool Rapids, Prospect Point, Cave of the Winds, Table Rock, Suspension Bridge, Cantilever Bridge, Maid of the Mist steamboat, and Bridal Veil have become familiar household phrases, known to most Americans and many foreign visitors.

The Falls have been the scene of many daring feats. In 1829, Sam Patch twice leaped into the river, and lived. A number of men and women have plunged over the falls or through the whirlpool, in barrels. And Charles Blondin (real name, Jean Francois Gravelet, 1824-1897), a French acrobat, crossed above Niagara Falls, on a tight rope, in 1855, in 1859, and again in 1860 on the occasion of the visit of Edward VII, then Prince of Wales.

The tray commemorating this wonder of the world, shows a view of Niagara Falls from the American side. The irregular curve of the cataract and the deep column of descending water are shown. Spray clouds are rising, and foam is shown at the foot of the fall. Spanning this background of cataract, fall and spray, the delicate tracery of a rainbow forms an arch from one side of the falls to the other. Two men in a rowboat are seen in the foreground.

The tray is crystal glass. Scenic effect is all-frosted, and

No. 492   PAN-AMERICAN FRYING-PAN

No. 493
MEMORIAL HALL INKWELL

No. 494
MEMORIAL HALL PAPERWEIGHT

497

remaining parts are clear. It is eleven and one-half by sixteen inches in size.

No. 490   Niagara Falls Plate

A plate presents some of the popular features of Niagara Falls. The center is plain. An American eagle, with outstretched wings, stands at the top of a broad border. The United States flag is at the eagle's right, and Great Britain's merchant flag is at the eagle's left. Remaining border space shows several scenic features of Niagara Falls, molded in the glass. Molding is very shallow. It is opaque white glass, blue-white in color. Details are accented with red, blue, and bronze paint. Probably a Pan-American item of 1901.

No. 491   Prospect Point Plate

Prospect Point, as pictured in old-time albums of Niagara Falls, is shown in the center of a plate. Details are molded in relief and accented with paint. The leaf border also, shows brown paint. It is opaque white glass, seven inches in diameter.

No. 492   Pan-American Frying-Pan

A novelty commemorates the Pan-American Exposition, held at Buffalo, New York, from May 1 to November 2, 1901. Its purpose was to celebrate the progress of the entire western hemisphere during the 19th century which had just come to a close. The Buffalo citizens who organized the venture hoped that it might promote trade between the United States and other countries in this hemisphere.

Pan-American exhibits were not comparable in number with those of previous international expositions. They numbered but 3,500 but attendance records were good, more than 8,000,000 guests being reported.

The closing days were saddened by tragedy, for President McKinley was assassinated by an anarchist who had come

No. 495   MEMORIAL HALL PAPERWEIGHT

No. 496   WOMEN'S PAVILION PAPERWEIGHT

499

to Buffalo for the purpose. Vice-President Theodore Roosevelt then took the oath of office as President, in Buffalo.

This novelty offers a bit of humor. The designer accented the word "Pan" by presenting a frying-pan in which North America and South America are represented as two fried, or frying, eggs. A thermometer on the handle registers heat and cold. Inscribed "Pan-American Exposition 1901 Buffalo, N. Y. U.S.A." Opaque white glass, with design molded in bottom of pan. Grey paint and bronze paint are used for decoration. Diameter: four inches. Length: six and seven-eighths inches.

No. 493   Memorial Hall Inkwell

An inkwell represents Memorial Hall, most substantial of all the Exhibition buildings erected for the Philadelphia Centennial of 1876. Its cost of $1,500,000 was shared by the State of Pennsylvania and the City of Philadelphia. It was designed as a permanent memorial of the Centennial year of American Independence, and was to be used as a museum after the Exposition closed.

The structure was 365 feet long, 210 wide, and 59 feet high. It was built of granite, with an iron and glass roof. The shape was rectangular, with a square tower at each of the four corners. Projecting vestibules and steps were placed in the center of each of the long sides. It was crowned by a central four-sided dome, rising 150 feet above ground. This famous memorial, in Fairmount Park, Philadelphia, is now a treasure house of industrial arts, paintings, antiques, and curios.

The inkwell is shaped like Memorial Hall. The dome forms a lid for an ink-pot under it. An inscription on under side of base reads "Charles Yockel Estab. 1855, 235 Broad St. Phila. Pa. U.S.A. Glass Mould Maker 1876." It is crystal glass, six and five-eighths by four and one-eighth inches in size.

No. 497   Columbus Perfume Bottle

No. 498	No. 499
Columbian Exposition Tumbler	The Oldest Bell

501

No. 494 Memorial Hall Paperweight

A very handsome and unusual paperweight represents Memorial Hall. The building is well modeled. It is all-frosted with mirror glass beneath. This gives an effect of the building being lighted within. It rests on a base of what appears to be black opaque glass until a strong light is placed beneath. Then it is seen as a very dark red. An eight-pointed star is pressed on under side of base. The base is four and three-eighths by six and one-eighth inches in size. Extreme height is two and one-half inches. Rare.

No. 495 Memorial Hall Paperweight

Another paperweight has a likeness of Memorial Hall molded in the base. It is inscribed "1776 1876 Memorial Hall." It is oval in shape and has turned sides. The finish is all-frosted, excepting the top surface which is clear. Size: three and seven-eighths by five and one-fourth inches.

No. 496 Women's Pavilion Paperweight

This matches the preceding number, excepting the building represented. The Woman's Building was devoted exclusively to the exhibition of the results of woman's labor. Inventions of women were displayed. A machine for washing blankets, self-fitting dress patterns, a barrel cover which could be locked, for sugar and flour barrels, frames for stretching and drying curtains, dishwashing machines, and other household appliances were shown. Pictures worked in human hair, flowers and toilet articles made of fish scales, wax flowers, feather flowers, and other decorative articles were displayed. Hand embroideries, wood carvings, decorated porcelains, and needlework were prominent in the displays. Women of many foreign countries sent contributions to be shown here. The elegant and much admired items were said to reflect great credit upon the good taste and administrative ability of the ladies having it in charge.

No. 500   Electricity Building Paperweight

No. 501
Columbian Exposition
Bottle

No. 502
Century of Progress
Bottle

503

No. 497   Columbus Perfume Bottle

A novel perfume bottle honors Columbus. The bowl is
supported by a terrestrial globe which rests on a decorative
base. "Chicago 1892" is placed diagonally on one side of
the globe. "1492" is placed on the opposite side. A ribbon
inscribed "1492" is on one side of the bowl, and a corresponding ribbon inscribed "1892" is on the opposite side.
A bust of Columbus, in frosted finish, is hollow and fits
over the dome-shaped top of the bowl. It is inscribed
"Columbus." Crystal glass. Height: six and one-half
inches. Capacity: one ounce.

No. 498   Columbian Exposition Tumbler

Two overlapping medallions are shown. One frames the
landing scene of the discovery of America. The date 1492
is placed beneath it. The other frames a likeness of the
Administration Building of the Columbian Exposition held
in Chicago. The date 1892 is placed beneath it. Decorations around these medallions consist of flowers, foliage,
cat-tails, and a large bee. Crystal glass, three and three-
fourths inches in height.

No. 499   The Oldest Bell

A novelty in the shape of a bell is inscribed: "Fac Simile
of the First Bell Rung in America." "1493-1893." An
inscription around the edge of the base reads: "World's
Columbian Exposition Libbey Glass Co. Toledo, Ohio."
A large letter E is on one side of the bell opposite a small
rectangle with pressed-in figure of some person. Height:
four and one-half inches. Diameter: three and one-sixteenth inches.

No. 500 Electricity Building Paperweight

The electricity building was called the seat of the most novel and brilliant exhibit of the Exposition (1892). It covered three and one-half acres of floor space. Galleries furnished another two and seven-tenths acres.

Names of forty-one men, famous for their contributions to electrical knowledge were placed over different entrances. Over the south entrance, was an inscription referring to Benjamin Franklin, "Eripuit coelo fulmen, sceptrum que tyrannis" (he snatched the lightning from heaven, and the sceptre from the tyrant). Franklin was honored inside the building too, as a pioneer in the field of electrical discoveries. A huge statue showed him in Colonial garb, posed in an attitude of thought which has caught sight of the solution of his problem. In his hands are the key, silk kite-cord, and umbrella with which he conducted his experiments. The building held displays of the work of leading inventors and dealers in electrical equipment. Thousands of visitors were amused, instructed, and awed by the things they saw, and were especially impressed by Mr. Edison's phonograph, and his kinetograph, fore-runner of the motion picture. The paperweight is crystal glass, four and one-fourth by two and seven-eighths inches in size.

No. 501 Columbian Exposition Bottle

A bottle is ornamented with what appears to be the obverse and reverse sides of a medal. Obverse shows Columbus setting foot on the New World. It carries the inscription "Christopher Columbus Oct. XII MDCCCXCII" (1892). The reverse reads "World's Columbian Exposition in commemoration of the four hundredth anniversary of the landing of Columbus. MDCCCXCII MDCCCXCIII (1892 1893). A medallion monogram "M.F. & Co." centered above, probably refers to the distributor. Crystal glass, with medallions in gold. Capacity: twenty-four ounces.

No. 502   Century of Progress Bottle

A crystal water bottle commemorates the International Exposition held at Chicago, Illinois, in 1933. The pattern of "A Century of Progress International Exposition" was unlike any former fair. It was the first World's Fair unsupported by taxes. Until this time, it had been the custom both here and abroad to support such enterprises by subsidies from the public treasury.

The purpose was to dramatize the rise of mankind during the last one hundred years, 1833-1933, the greatest era of the world's scientific and industrial history. Chicago was incorporated as a village in 1833, so the advancement of this city during its first century was demonstrated; but in every sense the larger theme of world progress was presented. The venture was highly successful in every way.

A modern sky-scraper is pictured on the obverse. On opposite sides, in a much smaller scale, an Indian teepee and a primitive log cabin are shown. These were the fore-runners of the cloud-touching structure between them. Inscribed "A Century of Progress 1833-1933." Capacity: one quart.

No. 503   Trylon and Perisphere Bottle

In 1939, an International Exposition was held in New York City. An architectural wonder was produced, as a feature of this event. To the average visitor, the trylon and perisphere seemed an architectural miracle.

The perisphere was a white, hollow globe two hundred feet in diameter. It rested on eight columns which were placed in a circular form eighty-one feet in diameter, located in the center of a large pool of water. Each column was encased in a larger glass column. Jets of water pumped up from the bottom, between the structural columns and their glass jackets, screened the structural columns so that the great ball seemed to be poised on fountain-like streams of water.

Inside the huge ball, visitors looked down from a moving platform, on a panorama presenting the role of co-opera-

No. 503
TRYLON AND PERISPHERE BOTTLE

No. 504   EGYPTIAN PATTERN BREAD-TRAY

tion in modern civilization, and suggesting a greater co-ordination in the better "World of Tomorrow." This was the Theme Center of the Exposition.

The Trylon was a seven hundred foot triangular obelisk, towering beside the perisphere. A new word was coined for this structure. It was derived from "tri" for its three sides, and "pylon" for its position as gateway to the Theme Center. It was useful as a Fair beacon and broadcasting tower.

These dominant symbols became the trademark of the Exposition, and the designs became familiar to everyone through the countless reproductions of them in manu-factured articles.

A bottle was produced, suggestive of this theme. Its globular body, the perisphere, is modeled to represent the world. The neck is designed to suggest the trylon. It is opaque white glass, inscribed "1939 World's Fair 1939." The greatest diameter is five inches. Height: nine inches.

No. 504   Egyptian Pattern Bread-Tray

It is said the Egyptian pattern of glassware was inspired by the gift of Cleopatra's Needle, to this country in 1877.

The obelisk is an Egyptian form of commemorative pil-lar. Cleopatra's Needles were obelisks built for sepulchral use. They were large ones which stood at Heliopolis and were carried away by Rameses II, one of the Egyptian Kings, to Alexandria where they were placed at the tomb of Cleopatra. In 1877, one was presented to England and the other given to the United States, by the Khedive of Egypt, Ismail Pasha. The American gift was presented to the City of New York, through the Department of State, and erected in Central Park in 1881. The entire expense was borne by the late William K. Vanderbilt.

This bread-tray has an oval center showing the full length figure of a woman believed to represent Cleopatra, Egyptian Queen who lived from 69 to 30 B.C. She was noted for her beauty and fascination, and no less for evil tendencies which earned for her the title of "Serpent of the

No. 505   G.A.R. Platter

No. 506 G.A.R. Goblet   No. 507 G.A.R. Canteen

509

Nile." A landscape background includes the figure of the Sphinx. In the beginning, the Great Sphinx of Gizeh is thought to have been an enormous rock shaped somewhat like a lion. Workmen improved the similarity, carving the face to resemble their King, implying the union of physical and intellectual forces. Its measurements vary with the drift of sand around it, but are approximately 189 feet long, 30 feet from forehead to chin, with a total height of 70 feet. The tray is inscribed with the daily bread motto, and has a highly decorative border. It is crystal glass, thirteen and one-fourth by eight and one-half inches in size.

No. 505   G.A.R. Platter

A rectangular platter honors the Grand Army of the Republic. The G.A.R. was organized at Decatur, Illinois, April 6, 1866. It was, and is, composed of men who enlisted in the service of the Federal Government, in the War of 1861-1865, honorably discharged. Its objects were the cultivation of fraternal spirit, cherishing of loyalty, and provision for soldiers' widows and dependents. It possesses a political as well as social importance. John A. Logan was one of its founders, and first National Commander.

G.A.R. insignia ornaments the rectangular center. Inscribed on medal, in small letters and figures "Grand Army of the Republic, Veteran 1861-1866." A decorative border is inscribed "Grand Army of the Republic." U. S. shields decorate the corners. It is crystal glass, eleven and one-eighth by seven and five-eighths inches in size.

No. 506   G.A.R. Goblet

A goblet honoring the G.A.R. shows its insignia on the obverse. Reverse is inscribed "21 Encampment September 27, 28, St. Louis, Mo." Top diameter is three inches. Height: six and three-fourths inches. Evidently issued in 1887, at the 21st encampment.

510

No. 508   Elk's Tooth Flask

No. 117   The Frigate Franklin Flask

No. 507   G.A.R. Canteen

A bottle shaped like an outmoded army canteen honors the G.A.R. Insignia of the organization ornaments the obverse. Crossed U. S. flags and laurel provide an attractive background. Reverse is plain. It is crystal glass, four inches in diameter. Capacity: six ounces.

No. 508   Elk's Tooth Flask

A small flask refers to the Benevolent and Protective Order of Elks. This is a fraternal order founded in 1868. The order does not include a department for life insurance, but is eminently a charitable organization, disbursing large sums for relief of members in need of assistance. Many lodges hold real estate, total holdings amounting to several million dollars.

The flask is made in the shape of an elk's tooth. A plain medallion has the initials B.P.O.E. at the sides. An elk's head is pictured beneath. The reverse is plain. It has a metal screw cap. Capacity: three ounces.

No. 117   The Frigate Franklin Flask

Freemasonry is an order both ancient and extensive. There is record of a Lodge in our country as early as 1730, of which Benjamin Franklin was a member. The institution has held greater prosperity in this than in any other country. But it never could be told, in a few short paragraphs, what the Masonic Order is or does. Masonic emblems have been freely used on glassware in many countries. Most of this antedates the era of pressed glassware, so is not easily found at this time. Some blown bottles and flasks are to be had, since many were made prior to 1830.

A pint-size flask shows the Masonic arch, with pillars and pavement. Inside the arch "Farmer's Arms" are pictured: the sickle, and sheaf of rye, pitchfork and shovel, the axe, the rake, and the scythe. Reverse shows the Frigate Franklin. (See Chapter IV for details of the Franklin, and edge inscription on the flask.)

512

No. 509   Masonic Hat

No. 510
Masonic Loving Cup

No. 511
I.O.O.F. Goblet

513

A blue hat honors the Masonic Lodge at Cambridge, Ohio. An inscription on the rim reads "Cambridge No. 66 F. and A. M. 1822 1922." This shows it to be an item commemorating the centennial of the Lodge named. In connection with the identity of this piece, it is interesting to note that there are fifteen states having towns named Cambridge. There are nine towns named Cambridge that have Masonic Lodges. Six of these have Lodges named "Cambridge Lodge." One of these is No. 66 A. F. and A. M. The one at Cambridge, Ohio, is No. 66 F. and A. M. The difference between A. F. and A. M. and F. and A. M. is that those with "A" get their charter from the Old Country or from a state that is older in point of charter, Masonically speaking, than another.

The hat is blue semi-opaque glass, with ribbed crown. The rim measures three and one-fourth by two and seven-eighths inches. Height: two and one-eighth inches.

No. 510   Masonic Loving Cup

One of the few pressed glass items showing Masonic symbols, is a small loving-cup. It seems to have been issued by a Lodge at Pittsburgh, Pennsylvania, for an assembly at St. Paul, Minnesota, in 1908. The stem is in the form of a sheaf of rye, tied with a wisp of grain. Two simitars form handles. Another is placed horizontally on the obverse, near the rim. It is inscribed "Syria." Beneath it, hangs the quarter-moon and star. Beneath these, "Pittsburgh, Pa." is inscribed. The reverse is inscribed "St. Paul, Minnesota, 1908." Simitar blades are in silver. Hilts, grain, star, and inscriptions are in gold. Crescent is in white enamel, and the rope edge of the base is black. A band at the rim is stained red. The height is five and one-fourth inches. Diameter: two and three-fourths inches.

No. 512 Knights of Labor Platter

No. 513
Knights of Labor Mug

No. 514
Knights of Labor Mug

515

No. 511 I.O.O.F. Goblet

A goblet honors the Independent Order of Odd-Fellows, a secret society having benevolent and social aims, and patriotic flavor. The order has mystic signs of recognition, initiation rites and ceremonies, and varying degrees of dignity and honor. Its services to members has been of inestimable value, especially so among pioneers, and in rural communities.

A goblet made in the Horseshoe pattern, has I.O.O.F. insignia, three links, superimposed on a stippled panel. This decoration is repeated three times on the sides of the bowl. Crystal glass, six and one-fourth inches in height.

No. 512 Knights of Labor Platter

A platter, or bread-tray, honors the Knights of Labor, an organization dating from 1869. It symbolizes the unity of labor. In the center, in an oval panel, a laborer clasps the hand of a knight, wearing armor and a plumed helmet. Surrounding this panel is the inscription "United We Stand, Divided We Fall." The border shows four symbols: early railway train, ocean-going vessel, agricultural worker, and a horse. Made in crystal glass and in several colors. The one illustrated is vaseline. Eleven and three-fourths by eight and three-fourths inches in size.

No. 513 Knights of Labor Mug

A mug also honors the Knights of Labor. The obverse shows a laborer clasping the hand of a knight wearing armor and a plumed helmet. Inscribed "Knights of Labor." Reverse is plain. It is crystal glass, six inches in height. Diameter: two and three-fourths inches.

No. 514 Knights of Labor Mug

Another mug suggests the idea of arbitration. It shows a laborer clasping the hand of a bearded man wearing a high hat and frock coat, probably intended to represent the employer. Inscribed beneath the figure "Arbitration."

The handle is distinguished by a thumb-rest. Crystal glass, seven inches in height. Diameter: three inches.

No. 515   The British Lion Covered Dish

Not all actions worth recounting are of human origin. The animal kingdom has something to honor. An eagle, the national bird, symbolic of strength and authority, is a favorite motif used by designers of glassware. It has been reported here as decoration on the Washington-Adams-Jefferson flask, Pike's Peak flask, the American Hen, and other items. A long list of eagle items could be given.

What the eagle is to the United States, the British Lion is to Great Britain: a symbol of national strength. It should be remembered that the British Lion was the symbol of "our" country until we won independence through the Revolutionary War.

A covered dish represents the British Lion. An inscription "The British Lion" is used on each side of the oval base. A recumbent lion, well-modeled, is shown on the lid. Opaque white glass, six and one-fourth by three and five-eighths inches in size. Height: four and one-half inches.

No. 516   British Lion Paperweight

A paperweight representing the British Lion is said to have been issued in commemoration of the laying of the second Atlantic cable. It was sold at the Centennial at Philadelphia in 1876, and an inscription on under side of the base reads: "Gillinder and Sons Centennial Exhibition." It is crystal glass, with all-frosted finish, five and five-eighths by two and three-fourths inches in size. Height: two and three-fourths inches.

No. 517   Lion Pattern Sugar-Bowl

Popular report says the Lion pattern of glassware is associated with the laying of the Atlantic Cable. While there seems to be no documentary proof the idea is reasonable. A lion *is* the national symbol of Great Britain. The

No. 515
BRITISH LION COVERED DISH

No. 516
BRITISH LION PAPERWEIGHT

No. 517
LION PATTERN SUGAR-BOWL

No. 518
HORN OF PLENTY PATTERN
SUGAR-BOWL

518

rope-like design found on this pattern *does* resemble a cable, and such association would furnish nostalgic appeal in great measure to the many citizens of English parentage. Although we fought and won a war to establish our independence, ties of blood, and love of the mother country were strong; so that the suggestion of a bond holding together the might and glory of Britain with the hopes of a developing young America would be an acceptable and welcome idea.

The sugar-bowl pictured is crystal glass, eight and one-half inches high. Top diameter of the bowl is four and one-fourth inches. It is the belief of some that this type of the Lion pattern commemorates the first laying of the Atlantic Cable, and those items showing frosted and collared bases, the second.

No. 518 Horn of Plenty Pattern Sugar-Bowl

Comet was the original name of the pattern now known as Horn of Plenty. It was so called in honor of Halley's Comet which made history in 1835 by a sensational appearance in the sky. It appears approximately every seventy-six years, and creates considerable excitement, being a once-in-a-lifetime experience.

Horn of Plenty is one of the most distinctive and desirable patterns of pressed glass. It is heavy and brilliant, has a fine bell tone, and was made in a large variety of forms.

From the historical point of view, a butter-dish having the knob molded to represent the head of George Washington, is the most important item in the pattern group.

The sugar-bowl pictured is crystal glass, seven and one-half inches in height. Top diameter of the bowl is four inches.

Commemorative Patterns

No less than sixteen patterns of glassware are reported as having association with significant historical events. They are collectible in sets, although in some patterns, the forms are limited.

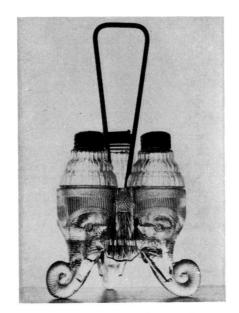

No. 519   Jumbo Castor Set

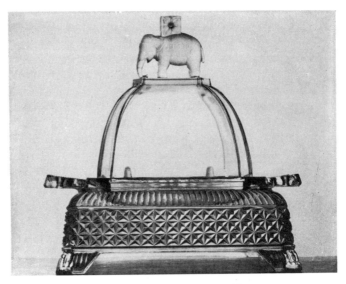

No. 520   Jumbo Butter-Dish

Mention of the Cable, Liberty Bell, Westward-Ho, Log Cabin, and the U. S. Coin pattern is made in Volume I; and the Horn of Plenty (or Comet), Lincoln Drape, Lincoln Drape with Tassel, Garfield Drape, Dewey, Sampson, Polar Bear, Jumbo, Lion, Egyptian, and the Actress pattern are considered elsewhere in this Volume. These are given primarily in connection with the events which they commemorate. Details concerning most of these have been effectively reported in the books by Ruth Webb Lee, so repetition of such particulars by this writer seems unnecessary.

No. 519   Jumbo Castor Set

A triangular castor set features the much publicized Jumbo. Three elephant heads form the base. A large tassel is placed on each side between the heads. Bottles are blown. Two have shaker tops. The third has a wider mouth and is fitted with a slotted top, evidently intended for mustard or horseradish. The metal handle is removable. Crystal glass. Height to top of handle is nine and one-fourth inches.

Another set is identical with this one, in form and size, excepting the tops. All have narrow mouths and are supplied with shaker tops. The color is a cobalt blue. Both are scarce.

No. 520   Jumbo Butter-Dish

The story of Jumbo has been given in connection with Phineas T. Barnum, in Chapter XII. A butter-dish was made, too, in honor of the circus elephant whose name has become a synonym for something extremely large.

The base is highly ornate. A dome-shaped lid is plain, with finial made in the shape of an elephant. Jumbo wears a blanket with his name inscribed thereon. This is believed to be the only form in the pattern inscribed with the word Jumbo. Glass pegs at one side of the base provide a rest for the butter knife. The dish is highly original in design, and is scarce. In some cases the bowls of

521

the butter-dish, sugar-bowl, cream-pitcher, and spoon-holder are etched with an attractive pattern. Compotes in various sizes are to be had; and a spoon-rack of unique design offers a challenge to collectors seeking all forms made in commemoration of Jumbo. Even more scarce are goblets decorated with three panels, with an elephant shown within each.

Novelties, too, were made, honoring the huge animal.

No. 521   Jumbo Match-Safe

A match-safe is shaped like the head of Jumbo, dressed in circus trappings. It is well executed and the glass is particularly brilliant. Extreme width is four and five-eighths inches. Height: five and one-eighth inches. It is a hanging type with the receptacle large and roomy.

No. 522   Baseball Salt-Dish

A standing, covered, salt-dish presents the subject of baseball, called the National Game, and the National Pastime. Baseball has been played in this country for more than one hundred years and has given rise to many figures of speech that are in common usage. "Can't get to first base" means inability to succeed. "Play ball" means to get busy. "Ninth inning finish" rallying strength near the end of an effort. "Right over the plate" perfection. "A shut-out" means complete victory. "He's got something on the ball" means he has real ability. Understanding of the game is so common that no further comment is needed.

Three baseball bats, crossed, provide the standard. Bowl and lid are spherical in shape and suggest a baseball. Finial is a smaller sphere. Bowl and base are stippled. Bats and finial are clear. Four panels of drapery with tassels, ornament the lid. It is crystal glass. Bowl is two and one-half inches in diameter.

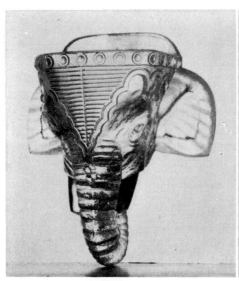

No. 521   No. 522
JUMBO MATCH-SAFE   BASEBALL SALT-DISH

No. 523   BARRY PLATE

No. 523   Barry Plate

A circular plate honors the work of St. Bernard dogs. The St. Bernard won his name and his fame in the Swiss Alps. The Great St. Bernard Pass is a road across the main chain of the Alps. At the highest point of the Pass, nearly 8,000 feet above sea level, near the line of perpetual snow, is the monastery or hospice, of St. Bernard, the highest dwelling in Europe. This hospice was founded by St. Bernard of Menthon, in 982, for the relief of travelers crossing the mountains. The monks of this hospice use the celebrated St. Bernard dogs to assist them in saving the lives of travelers lost in the snow. For more than 900 years, the dogs have daily patroled paths and trails. Usually they have worked in pairs, one with a cloak and the other with a two-quart cask of brandy fastened around the neck. More recently they operate alone. Their keen scent makes it possible for them to find those lost even when covered with snow.

One of these dogs, named Barry, saved the lives of forty people and was killed by the forty-first who mistook him for a wolf. Probably this plate was intended to honor Barry, the famous St. Bernard dog.

A scene in the center of the plate shows mountain crags, the highway of the Pass, and the St. Bernard hospice. In the foreground, a St. Bernard dog has a coat strapped around its body and a cask fastened about its neck. Two eagles circle the crags. It is framed in a plain border having a scalloped edge. Crystal glass, frosted center. Ten inches in diameter.

No. 524   Cadmus Cup-Plate

A cup-plate, identified as a Sandwich product, is said to represent the Cadmus, sailing ship chosen to bring Lafayette to this country in 1824. The voyage required about one month. Lafayette's popularity reflected distinction on anything connected with the illustrious general whose services during the Revolution had been of such

No. 524   Cadmus Cup-Plate

No. 525   Coronet Pickle-Dish

value to our country. The renown of the Cadmus rested on the prestige of her famous passenger. The cup-plate pictured is crystal glass, three and one-half inches in diameter.

No. 525   Coronet Pickle-Dish

In 1887, an ocean race was run, between the schooners Dauntless and Coronet. The course lay between Sandy Hook, in New Jersey, and Ireland.

A pickle-dish commemorates the Coronet. It is flat and shallow. Inscribed "Coronet." Crystal glass, eight by five and one-half inches in size.

No. 526   Yacht Plate

The yacht plate represents a great American sport. The America cup is a silver prize cup offered by the Royal Yacht Squadron of England, first won by the schooner-yacht America, in 1851. In 1857, the cup was presented by the owner of America to the New York Yacht Club, to be held as a trophy of international yachting supremacy, open to challenge by yachts of all nations. Its possession has been contested no less than thirty-seven times, and American yachts have won thirty-four of these thirty-seven races.

A sailing yacht almost fills the center of this plate, which has chain and anchor border. Probably the yacht represents a winner in one of the America cup races. Opaque white glass, and accented with light gray, blue, green, and bronze paints. Diameter: seven and one-half inches.

No. 527   Lusitania Plate

A plate commemorates the Lusitania, British mail and passenger ship of the Cunard line, sunk without warning, by a German submarine off the Irish Coast, May 7, 1915, with a death toll of 1,154. There were 188 American citizens aboard and 114 of them were lost. This inhumane offense was one of the causes of the first World War. In the book, "My Experiences in the World War," General

No. 526   Yacht Plate

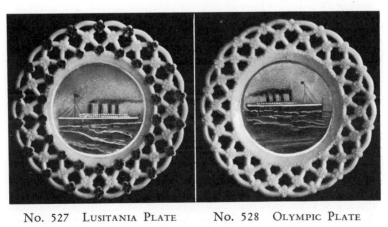

No. 527   Lusitania Plate   No. 528   Olympic Plate

John J. Pershing says: "Here was provocation enough for very positive action by any government alive to its obligations to protect its citizens. The fact is that the world knew only too well that we had for years neglected to make adequate preparation for defense, and Germany therefore dared to go considerably further than she would have gone if we had been even partially ready to support our demands by force."

The Lusitania was 785 feet long, 88 feet wide, and was built at a cost of nine million dollars. She sank in twenty minutes after being struck.

In the center of the opaque white plate, a likeness of the ocean liner is seen, under way. It is presented in colors. The hull and the smoke are in black, the funnels are in red and black, the sky in light blue, and the water in blue-green. An open-work border is in forget-me-not design. It is inscribed "R.M.S. Lusitania." Diameter: seven and one-fourth inches. The letters R.M.S. stand for Royal Mail Service.

No. 528   Olympic Plate

A similar plate honors the Olympic, British steamship for passenger and mail service. The Olympic entered service in 1911, as property of the White Star line. With the advent of steam, the funnels of steamships offered a splendid means of identification and have come to possess a lore readily understood by those who are informed. Various steamship lines have colors and markings all their own. Funnels on the White Star Line are painted in a shade of tan, with a black band at the top.

Cunard Line funnels are painted red, with black band at the top; and three black lines on the red. Such details have been carefully shown in these pictures of the Olympic and Lusitania.

A picture of the Olympic fills the center of this plate. It is presented in colors. Black hull and smoke, tan funnels, light blue sky, and blue-green waves. Forget-me-not border. Forget-me-nots in the first and third rows are

No. 529
STATUE OF LIBERTY
TOOTHPICK HOLDER

No. 530
STATUE OF LIBERTY
JAR

529

touched with bronze paint. Inscribed "R.M.S. Olympic." Diameter of plate: seven and one-fourth inches. R.M.S. means Royal Mail Service.

As the covered wagon was a symbol of migration in our nation, carrying people overland from place to place, in their efforts to "get ahead," the passenger ship was a symbol of immigration, carrying people overseas from other lands to America, in a quest for peace and prosperity. What a happy circumstance it is that this movement has been an invasion-for-work, and not an invasion-for-war; for immigrants have come and come until they and their children make up more than one third of our whole population. Many thousands have become loyal and praiseworthy American citizens. Many have rendered valuable services to the land of their adoption.

No. 529 Statue of Liberty Toothpick Holder

A toothpick holder represents the hand and torch of the Statue of Liberty. It is blue glass, four and one-fourth inches in height.

No. 530 Statue of Liberty Jar

A tall jar honors America's most famous woman: "The Lady of Liberty." The correct full name of Bartholdi's statue is "Liberty Enlightening the World." She is only a statue, yet she stands for more than any woman living, or having lived. Since 1886 she has stood enthroned on Bedloe Island in New York Harbor, facing the sea and giving mute welcome to all who enter there. In her welcome is the meaning of everything for which America stands: freedom of thought, freedom of worship, freedom of action, freedom from tyranny. In her right hand she holds a torch that burns with a never-dying light, symbolizing the fire of freedom that never can be cooled.

The Statue of Liberty is 305 feet 6 inches from foundation to torch. The forefinger is more than 8 feet long; the finger-nail more than a foot; and the head about fourteen and one-half feet high. Forty persons can stand together in the head, and twelve within the hollow torch.

The statue was a gift from the people of France, made in commemoration of the one hundredth anniversary of the Declaration of Independence. It was not completed in time for the Philadelphia Centennial, but the arm holding the torch was finished, was brought over and exhibited. The work was finished in France, in 1883, delivered to this country in 1885, and unveiled October 28, 1886. President Cleveland received the gift for the American people.

The jar is divided into three panels, separated by tall columns. The Statue of Liberty is placed within one, the others being plain. In her right hand she holds the torch of freedom and in her left is a tablet on which is carved the words "July 4, 1776" although this inscription is not seen in the glass. Stars encircle the rim. An American eagle, bird of freedom, is placed on the base, beneath the Lady of Liberty. It is crystal glass, twelve and one-half inches in height. Diameter: five inches.

*　*　*

The Statue of Liberty enlightening the world, at the main gateway of our country, has been symbolic of our national attitude. We have believed, and still believe, that liberty, WITHIN THE MORAL LAW, contains a magic healing power for most of the miseries of men. We know the rays from freedom's torch have lighted the pathway of our people in their quest for better things in a better world.

We have believed, and still believe, that if the magic of those rays can be turned upon the troubles which have caused bitterness and strife between peoples, the world will become safer, saner, and better.

For Liberty's benison is the right, the light, and the might, not only of our Land, but of the world.

INDEX

537

538

539